Karen and Dave's Excellent Camino

Leon to Santiago de Compostela

by Karen Olwell

Monterey, CA
2015

This is, from our perspective, a mostly true story. Karen wrote it, and Dave edited it. The publisher apologizes to anyone who may be offended by this version of reality.

A short trailer for the book may be viewed on YouTube at `http://youtu.be/zETaq2cA4aQ`

Disclaimer: The author and publisher make no representation of warranties with respect to the accuracy or completeness of the contents of this work, and specifically disclaim all warranties, including without limitation warranties of fitness for a particular use. The advice and strategies contained herein may not be suitable for every situation. Neither the author nor publisher shall be liable for damages arising herefrom. Readers should be aware that internet website addresses may change.

Additional copies may be ordered for $15 plus shipping. Send orders via email to:

Dave.Olwell@me.com.

Trust me, it's a steal.

Aguajito Oaks Press
Monterey, CA 93940

©2015 by Karen Olwell. All rights reserved.
ISBN: 978-1505441710 Paperback

Foreword and author's disclaimer

Please don't read this book if you are a relative of a guidebook author.

Or know one. Or are one.

Or don't have a sense of humor.

    That's right. Put this down. Go pick up "Walk in a Relaxed Manner," by Joyce Rupp, or "The Pilgrimage" by Paul Coelho, or one of the other thousands of books out there that paint a nice, spiritual picture of walking 500 miles across rural Spain. Turns out I'm not a fan of the pilgrimage guidebooks that most everyone else reveres as their "Bible."

    This is not a guidebook. At all. This is my attempt to make sense of the diary I kept, my journal and notes, while we were in Spain. I've written the truth – as I see it. This pilgrimage was a struggle for me and it didn't fit what I had read in dozens of books that mostly differed in my experience. I don't write about centering prayer and how wonderful this walk is. I don't believe a lot of the hype. I am not well-versed in the history of the region or in religion. I try hard to fit in and believe. I am open and friendly. But, my tone is not very reverent at times. Most times. I complain. I hurt. I hate it. I'm not happy most of the time, well, until we reach our destination each evening and have settled down with a glass of wine. Or two. I keep going. I persevere. I want to be a pilgrim. I want to reach Santiago. I want to "get it." But. I'm honest.

    I've written this mainly for me, to help process and comprehend what I went through, and for my close family members – to remember, to let people know what we went through, what it's like, really. I haven't changed any names. I haven't embellished any events. I've thrown in relevant pictures, though I have left out about 3,000 others. It was hard to decide. They are better in color, but it's cheaper to print in black and white. Sorry. I included my Fitbit readings, although mine differed from Dave's, whose were much higher. Blame Fitbit. I do. I'm pretty sure I walked much farther than

Fitbit said I did. And from Dave. Shorter stride, you know. I don't mean to deter anyone from walking the Camino. Do it. I really mean it. It's an experience you will never forget. You will not regret it. I do not regret it. I may be somewhat negative, but it was a positive experience. I say that now that I am sitting here comfortably typing this up. At home. It's sort of like childbirth, actually. You forget. Sure, let's have another baby... and let's walk another pilgrimage while we're at it – longer this time...

Everyone's "Camino" is their own. You hear that over and over. This is my own personal journey and one I do want to share. But. It's my experience and, again, not a guide, and perhaps not even typical of what all those other pilgrims throughout the ages experienced.

Since we've been back, I've been asked many times, "was it fun?" or "did you have a good time" or "was it a transformative experience?" No, it was not "fun" by any means. No, I really did not have a good time. I spend the rest of this book trying to answer the other question and the best I can come up with is, how could it not have been a transformative experience?

So, that's my big explanation for this book. Take it or leave it. And, my apologies to some authors, whose guidebooks don't come off so well here[1]. Hey, I was tired and cranky. "Gentle slope" be damned.

That's all. You have been warned.

Much love,

Karen and Dave

---

[1] They were usually pretty helpful, but the few times they weren't really stick in one's mind. –Ed.

About the Author

Our Author!

　　I was born in Minneapolis, Minnesota in December 1958. I remember having great "Pearl Harbor Day" parties to celebrate – my birthday, not the war. Luckily, my mom changed her mind about naming me Holly (for the Christmas season), as "Holly Hosler" would have been unbearable and I may have ended up in the San Fernando Valley making bad movies, instead of living my life as it should be, here in Monterey, California with Dave and our three sons, David, Jim, and Matt, and various dog members of the family. I love St. Bernards and grew up with one, Spice, but we now have a golden retriever, a chocolate lab, and a poodle/terrier mix instead. Misty, Cleo, and Buddy. At the moment. We also have one four-and-a-half-year-old adorable grandson, Isaac, who brightens the world. My world especially.

　　I prefer sitting, while sipping on a glass of red wine, laughing and telling stories, to any heavy cleaning in the house. I graduated from Cottey College in Nevada, Missouri with an AA degree and transferred to St. Cloud State University in St. Cloud, Minnesota where I received a Business degree. I had two interesting jobs in my 20s – I was the second person hired and helped open the Hyatt Regency Minneapolis downtown on Nicollet Mall in 1980-1981. I was actually there to assist in booking groups into the hotel for future dates, but this is where I learned to love fresh cold crab legs and other F & B delicacies, including wines and champagne – it wasn't my job but I was always willing to help out with any tastings going on or setting up for group functions. Moving on, I later worked at Martin/Williams, a fun, award-winning advertising agency downtown and there I continued with my love of champagne – and that company was always celebrating new ad campaigns or awards or new clients by drinking in the afternoon. What a great group. I have since moved on to Prosecco. And other jobs.

In fact, fate intervened and I met Dave while on a trip to Europe. I found him in the Vicenza Officer's Club but, despite my college roommate's protestations, after a whirlwind romance, we married, and I became indoctrinated into the military lifestyle, learned a lot of abbreviations, signed "hold harmless" agreements about the lead paint in military housing, and we moved about for the next 26 years or so. Now settled, and retired in Monterey, for the past 17 years I've worked for an insurance company, mostly remotely from home, with a quick two-year detour when we moved to Tucson and then back to Monterey. But, I love words, and writing long stories – the truth of course. I do have a lot of material to work with. I like to pretend I'm a writer and that I'm pretty good at editing, too. For even more fun, I enjoy knitting scarves, the only thing I know how, and quilting, too, as I love fabric. I like to cook and to entertain, studying ambitious recipes and planning menus. I read a lot, I like music, and I take a lot of photographs. Flowers especially.

Me, in a nutshell. Or not.

Also by this author:

Making Memories – Karen's Greatest Recipes
(Volumes 1, 2, and 3, from 2007. Also known as her magnum opus.)

Huevos Dias!
(Dave and Karen, and Matthew, go to Barcelona and on a Mediterranean Cruise)

The Coven of Money-Grubbing Lesbians
(Dave and Karen spend a year in Hawaii)

Karen and Dave Go To Rio
(Karen and Dave to to Rio de Janeiro)

Death on the Hop-On, Hop-Off Bus
(Dave and Karen, and Mimi, go to Rome)

Who's Jimmy Kimmel?
(Karen and Mimi, and their mother, go to Ojai)

Looking for Vacation Mode
(Dave and Karen, and Mimi, go to France)

I Don't Get It – An American in London
(Dave and Karen, and Mimi, go to London)

What I Did on My Summer Vacation
(Dave and Karen, and Mimi, go to Washington, DC, in the summer. It's hot.)

The Last Good Time
(Dave and Karen, and Mimi, go to NYC. The government can no longer afford our trips.)

Pack Your Muumuu, Mimi!
(Dave and Karen go to Hawaii, via Los Angeles. Mimi visits later)

London Bridge is Calling, also known as *Spectacular, Spectacular.*
(Karen and Mimi, and their mother, go to Yosemite)

The Old Man and His Stick
(Dave and Karen go to Montreal)

Where's My Chocolate Bunny?
(Mimi and Erin visit Dave and Karen in Monterey visit for Easter)

You Have Been Summoned to Look Up!
(Dave and Karen Go To Vegas. Karen is traumatized by the *Lord of the Rings* machine. It still owes her money.)

This Is It
(The Kids are Fine but Dave Gets Boating out of his Blood)

It's Not all Paradise – I Think My Swine Flu Is Acting Up
(Karen and Dave go to Hawaii. Again)

My Dog, Butterscotch
(A short story by Karen Hosler, age 8, about her pretend dog)

Our editor, celebrating the end of the day in Rabanal.

About the Editor (by the author)

Dave was born in Seattle, Washington, in 1955 and he grew up on Capitol Hill, part of a large Catholic family. He frequently laments that if he had only gone to Lakeside High School, he (and I) would be ensconced in an estate on Lake Washington right now, as he would have been best buds with Bill Gates and Paul Allen – they were there and in the same class. They could have been all together in his garage, too, playing and inventing and starting up all sorts of businesses there. But, alas, he did not, though he aptly managed to scrape together a fine life with the help of the Army. He graduated from West Point in 1980 and spent the next 20 years PCSing from one post to another. He spent plenty of time jumping out of airplanes, visiting great spots like Panama, Spain, Germany, Austria, Alaska, Korea, Turkey, Yakima, and my favorite, Italy, going through military schools, getting his PhD, and finding his special niche as a teacher and advisor to students. Helping others, service, dedication, sacrifice – just some of his values.

He moved on to parenting, parenting, parenting, getting the kids out of trouble, and more parenting. Now settled and retired from the Army, he is a tenured full professor in the Systems Engineering Department at the Naval Postgraduate School here in Monterey. Still teaching, still parenting. Full-time jobs. For the past few years, he has been great at working on the kind of assignments that involve frequent travel, lots of European destinations, and was accepted as an ACE Fellow where we spent a year living in Hawaii. Well,

The author and editor, on Day 1. Poor, naive fools.

less than a year – eight months maybe. But that's another story.

Dave is a great sailor[2] and taught local sailing courses. It helped if one knew what "fend off" meant. He knows how to tie knots. So your boat won't float away. He is also very active in the Knights of Columbus and is now a "Mission Walker" which is explained in the Epilogue and hopefully describes what he is doing as a west-coast pilgrim these days. He is a member of the Board at Catholic Charities here in Monterey. They do important work.

Dave is good in a crisis and he is the one I would want to be stranded on a desert island with. He's computer-savvy, knows how to prepare and cook a squash, loves to hold babies, can recite old poems from heart, and knows how to lead a productive meeting. He's also the best I know at making up dialogue and providing new, meaningful lyrics to old familiar tunes. He can sing. He loves "Survivor" as much as I do, still, and, best of all, always seems to know when it is 5 o'clock somewhere.

What a great editor!

---

[2]This is a debatable assertion. –Ed.

Cast of Characters

Karen	Me! aka "I"
Dave	Hubby/soulmate
David	Oldest son who needs a job
Jim	Middle son, sometimes gloomy, aka Eeyore/newly hired Cisco Kid
Matthew	Youngest son, loves math/music – computer gamer – still in college
Misty, Cleo, Buddy	Slobbering menagerie, likely sleeping on furniture at home
Mimi	Karen's sister in Minnesota/aka Mary Ellen
Mom	Karen's mother in Minnesota
Isaac	Beloved grandson, a joy
Erin	Isaac's mom, David's friend and on-again, off-again girlfriend
Lisa	Karen's cousin in Texas
John Brierley	Noted author of famed Camino Guides with allegedly inaccurate mileage and lodging listings
Father Tom Hall	Priest who neglected to mention a few things, and two-time peregrino
Martin Sheen	Actor who does not break a sweat; in cult hit, "The Way"
Beautiful Niece	Dave's youngest sister Allison's husband's niece from Washington looking for temporary housing in Monterey area
Mark and Susan	Karen's cousin, Mark, and his red-haired wife, Susan, who live in Texas
Older bartender	Saint in Castrillo de Polvares
Dianne	Dave's younger sister, gravely ill
Allison	Dave's youngest sister in Washington
Connie and Mary Jo	Dave's mom and aunt, both in Hawaii at the time of our pilgrimage
Becky	Niece who lives in Poland at the moment but had her pistachio liqueur stolen from her luggage in France
Eddie Miller	Sort of uncle/aunt who died while we were on the Camino
Andrew	Karen's agreeable boss
Meg, Teresa, Sara	Childhood friends
Prunedale	Local rural community near Monterey – many residents keep chickens.

Other Pilgrims

Joe
Helena
Sue
Beth
Mark
Roz
Teri
Japanese girl — The limper, never returned Dave's pole

Snoring Korean — Pariah of the Camino – "POTC"
Paul and Stephanie — From Napa
Lynne and David — From Australia
Lynne and Ray — From Australia
Chris — Perplexed Briton
Don Simon — Maker of Spanish boxed wine
Don Alvaro — "¡No existe!"
English snob — Authority on all things Camino, where to stay, and women barkeepers

Three Korean girls
12 French traveling pilgrims
Five golden rings... — (Just kidding)
Carlos and Luis/Luis and Carlos — "Enter from rear" albergue
Bruce — Possible medic from maybe London (truth is an optional quality)

Couple from Lethbridge — Man with numb leg and wife who uses woods as bathroom stop

Couple who met and hooked up on Camino — From Colorado and maybe NE America
Liverpool soccer hooligans — Havoc-mongers
Lunatic jogger from London — Substitute Halloween table host

Prologue

If all I have to do is walk, how hard can it be?

Ha ha ha. That's a good one. Ah, you poor naive fool. Let me just stop laughing and gather my thoughts here.

Well. That's long enough. What follows is the "play by play" and then I'll give some analysis, thoughts, and, hey, suggestions for next time...

Click.
And with that, Dave had forwarded the confirmation email from United to me so that I could print out the details of our now looming air travel to Madrid. What the hell did we just do?
We've got to stop drinking. And making plans while drinking. That just leads to trouble. I will make a note of that for the future.
So, non-refundable tickets to Spain, leaving in two months, to walk for three weeks on "The Camino." $1200 for each ticket. The anxiousness started immediately. Like in the next two minutes. But then, – sip – sip –, we weren't leaving for two months – that's a long time away. We'll think about it in Vegas.
Surely we'll be fine by then. Two months is plenty of time to train, prepare, get my mind wrapped around it all. October is a long way away. And, we did also buy the travel insurance for $160. It is possible one of us could break his leg, hit his head and come down with amnesia, get Ebola and die, or something like that where we'd have to cancel our trip. Those options sounded kinda good right then. I did feel a little twinge of guilt, hoping all those mishaps happened to Dave and not me. I'd have to cancel my trip, too, to care for him/attend funeral. Hey – I'm kidding.
"We're going to walk the 500-mile pilgrimage route known as Camino Frances across Northern Spain in October." "The Camino," for short. To Santiago de Compostela. "Field of stars." Sounds romantic, doesn't it? I could say my "fluent" Spanish kicked in, but the truth is I read that's what "Compostela" means. We started to tell people about our intentions. Well,

Poor naive fool.

actually, we were limited in our time and funds and could only budget for 200 miles.

"We're going to walk 200 miles of the pilgrimage route known as Camino Frances across Northern Spain in October." The last 200. Doesn't sound quite so impressive, but it still shocked our friends and family. The ones who knew me. We did the math calculations, well, Dave did the math. We had approximately three weeks to walk, plus a day or two getting there and then getting back home. We figured we could walk about 12 miles a day. On average. That equals roughly 200 miles back from Santiago. Give or take. I'm not good with fractions.

However, if you translate miles into kilometers, it's a much bigger number and it does sound more impressive. Spain's on the metric system. I added it to my list to learn the metric system. They're also on the Euro system as opposed to dollars but in this case, when you translated the euros, it added up to a lot more dollars. I added that to my list, too, to learn their money system. Tomorrow. While I was making a list, I added "brush up on my Spanish, too." Might come in handy.

We did, of course, want to finish walking in Santiago and I wanted the proof in my hot, sweaty hands – the Compostela certificate they hand out at the end (to those who survive) by the Cathedral. So, approximately 200 miles out from there meant we would start in Leon, Spain, which is a fairly big city and one that shouldn't be too difficult to get to from Madrid. We had considered other routes but decided on the most well-known route, which had

Do not drink and plan.

Planning in Vegas.

better infrastructure in place and, besides, it looked very nice in the movie, "The Way." The usual beginning point for the 500-mile trek is in St. Jean Pied de Port, France. But, then one had to hike <u>over</u> the Pyrenees ("over" being the key word here) into Spain and then on to Pamplona (think bulls), Burgos (big Cathedral), etc., etc. We could have started there, done the hardest part of the mountain scaling, then taken a bus here and there to skip some parts and walked just the last 100 miles. Or, we could have walked the first 200 miles, finished up around Burgos, and planned to come back and finish it all up another year. Come back? Hah. Immediate gratification kicked in and ta dum/wha-la/ay caramba! We were going to Leon.

The following is a sample of responses we got when we started to inform people what we were planning.

Statement: "We're going to fly to Spain in October and walk over 200 miles on The Camino."

Response:

"Over my dead body"	Mom
"Um, and what's the point of that?"	Jim (cynical son)
"I want to do that!"	Isaac (age 4)
"Do you think Karen's up to that?"	Most of our friends
"What's The Camino?"	Everyone else
"Oh."	Matthew
"How long will you be gone?"	David (the schemer)
"You'll need to buy this"	All the salespeople at REI
"But when are we going back to Paris?"	Mimi
"I think I've made a huge mistake"	Me
"Maybe you'll run into Mark and Susan"	Lisa, my cousin

As for the last response, Lisa had sent me a short, vague Facebook message to let me know that her brother (my cousin), Mark, and his wife, Susan, were going to be in Europe about the same time as us and she thought they were maybe walking the Camino, so we'll "probably run into each other." I hadn't seen my cousin Mark in about 50 years but it was amazing he might be in Spain at the same time. However, 500 miles was a long way and I thought it was a pretty remote chance that we would connect over there. But, we'll see. I'll be watching for Mark – I suppose he's taller now and grown up since he was ten. And Lisa passed on that Susan has red hair. So, I'm on the lookout for an adult man with a possible family resemblance, and his red-haired wife.

My mother, who possibly knows me too well, thought all that walking might be awfully difficult and I might get hurt, I might get lost and lose the trail as "there are a lot of roads over there," or something bad might happen, or my plane might crash, or something might happen to the kids while I was gone, or to her, etc., etc. She tends to worry a bit. Truthfully, I was worried about all those things, too, but I was hoping a pilgrimage involving God and praying and religious contemplation would help me stop worrying and, if anything did happen, well I would just blame God for letting it happen after all I was doing for Him. I'd be mad.

The Spark

So, several years ago I picked up a book to read at a book store, when they still had book stores where I live. It's hard to find a good book store. Ah, I miss those days. It was "What the Psychic Told the Pilgrim" by Jane Christmas and I don't know what made me pick it up and buy it but from the first sentence, I couldn't put it down. It was well-written, very amusing, and how I first heard about the Camino. Wow – what a great idea! Here was a woman from Canada who wanted to do something memorable for her 50th birthday. She heard about the Camino (while drinking on an airplane) and decided that would be it. It was a great book. I handed it to Dave. "Let's do this!" It's true I was drinking at the time, too. Dave looked at me like I was insane but he did read the book. His response – "Wow! When shall we go?"

I've read that "your" Camino starts when you first hear about it. Well, now we'd both heard about it. The clock was ticking. And the desire to walk the Camino wouldn't let go – we dreamed about it for years. I began researching and collecting book after book written about the Camino. And there are a lot out there. I wondered if everyone who ever walked the Camino wrote a book about it. Hmmmmmm. Now that's an interesting idea, too. I kind of like to write.

I spent a small fortune on "research." Every book I read was enthralling, compelling, stoking my desire to do what millions of others had done throughout the ages. I joined the Camino Forum online, run by Ivar Revke who lives in Santiago. I studied all the nitty-gritty and read hundreds of threads, from different routes, to the Spanish healthcare system, to bedbugs. And more. We spent about five years planning in our heads what we would do, and when we would go. And then the movie came out. "The Way" starring Martin Sheen. I saw it in the theater. Loved it. Bought the DVD when it came out. Downloaded it on the TV, too. We watched it pretty much weekly.

Next, we got a new priest up at Fort Ord. Father Tom Hall. He used to be a Navy Chaplain with the Marines down at Twenty-nine Palms in the desert. He also used to be the chaplain at the Betty Ford Clinic down that way. We liked him. He was great at giving homilies. We liked that he introduced the readings at Mass by giving five minutes of background about what you were going to hear. I learned something. Every Sunday. Well, every Sunday that I went to Mass. And then we learned that he himself had walked the Camino. Twice. And loved it. The most transformative experience of his life. He gave several homilies on his experiences. It was so moving. He had over the past years unfortunately had to bury over 200 young Marines stationed down in the desert. How tremendous. What a tragedy. I don't know how you could do that. Later in the summer we had dinner with him one night at the Loose Noodle. We pumped him for info. He was excited that we wanted to do it. He encouraged us. He needled us. He twisted our arms. He made us. He was very insistent that we do it and do it now. Every time we saw him he asked when we were going. No excuses. Well, everyone knows you have to keep your priest happy with you. We really, really thought harder about going.

I thought I should at least make an effort to show I was trying very hard to go. I decided to ask my boss, Andrew, if it would be okay if I missed work for, say, six weeks. Surely I was indispensable – no, I couldn't go! Well, the answer was "yes, that sounds like a great idea. You should do it." Hmmmmm. I said I'd think it over some more.

And then, finally, something happened that shaped the course of history. Dave turned 59. All those years and he'd been pulling me up there with him – I was 55 now. Still a spring chicken, true, but not quite as youthful as one would like. And in July, one of his cousins died. Unexpectedly, though he did have cancer. The cousin, Joe Mead, was only a year older than him. The next day Dave made a "bucket" list. He was determined to check off each item by the time he was 60. While he still could. Well, "walk the Camino" was on his list! Looking back, going to the Paul McCartney concert at Candlestick Park in San Francisco was a lot more fun. Check. Camping in Yosemite for a few days was also quite fun. Even in a tent. Even with a four-year-old. Check. Hiking across Spain sounded like a good adventure and fun while at the same time fine-tuning our spirituality. I want to check that off, too! I make this comment now because even though it started as my idea, the walk ended up on Dave's bucket list.

My boss piped up again. He wanted to know if and when I was going to be away from work so that he could adjust work schedules, mark the files, etc. He brought it up. Hmmmmm. I'm still thinking about it I told Andrew but I'd let him know as soon as we made any concrete plans.

Dave argued we had to do it now before we got older, while we still could. His calendar was filling up at work for the fall. He wanted to block out the time. Tonight! So, one night late in August, while drinking, we checked for airfare rates and picked a date and time, clicked a few buttons, typed in all the numbers on our Visa and it was done. We were locked in. And now I had printed off the reservations and started a folder. "Camino 2014" I scrawled in permanent ink across the top. We stumbled off to bed. I said I'd think about it tomorrow. I did a lot of thinking about stuff "tomorrow."

The nerves kicked in. I started to devise "Plan A," which involved a plausible, understandable reason for having to cancel our pilgrimage. Perhaps my employer would not let me go. I emailed Andrew to tell him that, yes, we were going and we had bought our tickets to Spain. Sorry about the late notice but I'd only need four weeks for a leave of absence instead of six. Maybe he'd say it was too late now to plan around me and I wouldn't be able to go. "Approved!" Hmmmmmm.

Plan B of my escape from "The Way" came by way of the media news. Ebola! That Ebola was certainly everywhere. You'd think. In fact, the biggest hot spot, most likely place to get it in the US was – ha ha – in Brooklyn Park, Minnesota! My hometown! I guess there are a lot of settlers from Liberia there. And, my mom was still there. Hmmmm. Maybe I should plan to go visit mom. Hmmmmm. The way Brian Williams was talking, you'd just have to go stand on a street corner in a potential spot to be exposed to it. Maybe he even had it! (LOL) All those contaminated body fluids were everywhere. I thought some more. A visit with mom and Ebola versus A Long Walk. I settled back down. There's nothing to worry about. It's just walking. I mean, really, how hard can just walking be?

Pre-Camino Thoughts

So, my first plan of action when I'm facing uncertainty is to make a list. I wanted to be very honest and sort out my fears, hopefully coming to a realization that there wasn't anything to fear. I made a list of everything crowding my mind I was worried about. The list was rather long. Briefly:

1. **Bathrooms** As I'm being very honest here, bathroom issues would be my Number 1 (and 2 ha ha) biggest concern. What's a pilgrim to do? Fortunately, this topic is addressed in the Camino Forum and I learned that while you are out there walking and "nature calls," you just do what you gotta do. Discreetly. I've never actually been out in the big outdoors and done this, so I may need to practice this skill here at home. On a training hike. Yep. But, hopefully, you are able to wait until you reach a café or bar but sometimes they aren't a convenient distance away. I will just have to hope for the best and for good tummy days. I am glad to hear that it is quite acceptable to wander off the path a ways and, besides, I plan to pack a lot of Imodium. And Pepto Bismol tablets. Just in case.

2. **Feeling sick** I don't like feeling nauseous and sick to my stomach. But, who does? I have read a lot about food poisoning out there and people being sick. My stomach does not do well with Spanish food to begin with. I will take extra Pepto Bismol tablets to be on the safe side.

3. **Spanish food** I remember not liking it. In 1976. And in 2008 when we were in Barcelona. I remember many local delicacies that I couldn't eat. I will plan to survive on Diet Coke and sangria. And bread. I will avoid the pulpo – octopus. And the seafood that comes to your table with all its limbs. And head. And eyes. I will carry Pepto Bismol in my pockets.

4. **I hear this experience "changes" people** I don't want to change. I like me. Like I am. Well, I'm open to change. Really.

5. **Walking in the rain and mud. Weather.** If all I have to do is walk, this will be a vacation. I'm sure my rain gear will be fine.

6. **Hot flashes** At the moment, spring chicken or not, I am still having those horrible hot flashes. When will they ever end? This is five years at least and they're getting worse. I will make an appointment with my doctor to see what I can do. I don't want to be miserable while I'm over there.

7. **Can I actually do it?** Good question. Of course I can. It can't be that hard. Martin Sheen did it in the movie. It didn't look that bad. I've read tons of books about people in their 70s and even 80s that did it. They made it. Of course I can do it, too. This is not really a big concern. I wonder about Dave, though. He might just trip and fall over something and break a bone. Then what would I do? What if we're off the path and he falls and I have to go get somebody or do something? How would I move him? That's more a concern. Besides, there are buses and taxis all over – we can catch one of those if we need to.

8. **Getting lost** Maybe. Maybe not. I've read it's easy to stay on the trail. There are arrows everywhere.

9. **It won't be like our favorite movie** I will play the soundtrack to "The Way," which I downloaded, while I am walking. Maybe it will be the same thing. I think it will be fun trying to recognize the same scenes in the movie.

10. **Can I get up that early every morning?** I'll be tired. I guess I'll just drink a lot of café au lait. Oh – no, that's French. What do they call the Spanish kind? I remember it's very tasty. But then again, coffee = bathroom troubles. Coca Cola, por favor? Maybe.

11. **Blisters. Really?** Now I'm not sure about the shoes to take. I concede – it will most probably rain. I resisted the possibility lately but after checking weather reports, I admit, it will likely rain with 80 percent chances coming up. So, Gortex or not? Just waterproof shoes? They feel a tad tight on my right foot. Should I take the low profile hiking tennis shoes that aren't waterproof but feel pretty good? Or the sandals that I had planned on but now are giving me trouble with the ball of my right foot? My foot really hurts. I wonder if I have a bruise under the skin or a bone problem or a blister under there? I hope I don't get any blisters but I've read that everyone gets blisters. Can't avoid them. I will take the lotion stuff I bought in Carmel for our feet. At least Dave shouldn't get blisters because his feet are so abnormally soft and nice – like a baby's butt. Will have to find needles and thread. I don't know exactly what you use the thread for but everyone says to bring needle and thread.

12. **Getting annoyed with Dave** Likely.

13. **Really get hurt** I hear the care over there in Spain is really great. Well, not if you have ebola, but other stuff I'm sure they do well with – especially when you translate it into Spanish...

14. **Training** Yeah. Right. It can't be that hard if you are just walking. And you have all day. And you aren't in a rush. You take your time and rest if you get tired. You can always take a taxi. Or send your

backpack on ahead. Or just stop and check into an albergue. It's not a race. You walk your own Camino. I read that.

15. **Bedbugs** Just read this morning about a pilgrim over there who unluckily got bitten by 85 bed bugs and her whole body was a mess (not sure how they/she knew it was 85 exactly, but that's what the blog said). What to take – treated bed sheet? Spray you can buy over there? There are hundreds of things printed about the subject. Most say they never saw a bed bug. The ones that did, suffered. If you get bitten, you have a big procedure to do to treat your backpack and stuff and try to rid yourself of them. Since I'm so tender and juicy and spiders love me, mosquitoes, poison oak dogs, etc., I'm sure if there are bed bugs to be found, they will find me. Some people on the blog are so indignant about the subject and say of course there aren't any and those other people are just lying. I think I tend to agree with the bedbugs. They are probably there. I also read that Fall is when they are the worst. I am worried about this issue.

16. **Break a tooth, break glasses, break a bone, an ankle, etc.** Did I mention cousin Mark will be on the trail – he's a dentist... I don't think anything will happen, truthfully. I'll be careful where I am stepping. And I am bringing two walking sticks. Dave just wants to take his one wooden stick.

17. **Something happens at home while we're gone** I can't Heeeaaarrrrr you... Well, I am kind of worried about the kids. Maybe they will rise to the occasion and everything will be fine. I hope Matt gets up in time for his early classes. He has to graduate this winter.

18. **Being over-prepared/under-prepared/disappointed** Striking a balance. Like Madonna strikes a pose..... I would like to lean toward being underprepared. I'd like to be surprised and pleasantly surprised over there. I don't want to think everything out and plan stuff. I want to be more spontaneous.

19. **What to pack** Um. I guess I'm ready. As of last count, I'm at 14 pounds, which I think is tremendous. Of course, I haven't packed a few things – my shoes, toiletries, camera, notebook, iPod, etc.

20. **What not to pack** Probably a lot of what I have.

21. **What is your reason for walking The Camino?** This appears to be a frequent topic of conversation as a pilgrim walks along toward Santiago. And when they arrive in Santiago, I understand they are asked why they chose to walk. There are lots of main reasons – spiritual/religious, health, touristy reasons. Out for a nature walk. Looking for a miracle. To say you did it. Yes, I like that last one. I am anxious to be able to tell people that I did it. I made it. I had an adventure that was difficult

and meaningful. I want to write about the experience. I want to try something completely different from my usual grandma/caretaker role. Find the stamina. Improve my health. See northern Spain from the ground up.

22. How much is this going to cost? Yes, a biggie.

So, we'll pay it off over a few years. One of these days I'll retire and get that ESOP, right? Building Value Together! Well, that was last year's slogan that pays... didn't win this year and can't remember the winning entry except it really sucked. I'll just try again next year. I can't believe they didn't like "Sharing Our Success!"

I Think I've Made A Huge Mistake

So, I may have made a huge mistake already. I let people know what we were doing. In fact, I posted something about it on Facebook and actually asked everyone to let me know their favorite song and I would add it to my "Play & Pray List." Some of the responses I was getting back were just a touch worrisome. As an example, someone's favorite song is "It's A Small World After All" ??? From the ride at Disneyland? I'm going to have to listen to that? I have a friend who likes that song the most of all of all the songs there are in the world?

Next up, "White Christmas"– really? I might have to lie right off the bat and say I played their songs and prayed for them. Actually, it sounds like they may really need praying for. How 'bout some current songs like "Happy" or "Everything is Awesome?" I think if not everyone responds, I will just assign a song to them and pray for them anyway. A song I pick. I already added Isaac to the list and assigned him the "Awesome" song. I don't think he'll mind. I do have a bunch of friends who are probably offended I asked because they don't like prayers, or religion, or spiritual stuff, or God, or pilgrimages, etc. I'll give them the songs I like, too.

But – at least I'm not weighed down carrying a bag full of rocks. Dave, not to be outdone by my outreach to all my friends and family put out his own message: "I'll carry a rock for you and place it at the Cruz de Ferro,"... where we will pray and drop your worries and troubles at the foot of the telephone pole, er, cross. Boy, did he get a lot of responses! Pounds and pounds of rocks poured in. My mom sent him a package of little rocks that had been at the bottom of a planter she had where the plant died. Chuck brought him a baggie full of 15 rocks, representing most everyone in the family. Church friends handed over rocks. I gave him a rock. He gave it back.

Nevertheless, he labeled all his rocks and put them in a large ziplock baggie. We were glad the Cruz de Ferro was fairly near the beginning of our walk.

Some of the rocks we collected for the trip.

I went back to organizing my own music for the trip. I decided to make my own play list. Of songs I actually wanted to listen to. With a zippy beat. Something that would make me walk faster. Not put me to sleep. I ended up with about 650 of my library of 8,000 songs or so on my Camino Play List. I listened to my other Pray List several times to make sure it played correctly. It did. I then typed up the names of the songs and the people who requested them. I folded it neatly in my journal to take with me.

Next up I started planning for the book I was sure to write about my excellent experience. I needed some topic sentences. Maybe titles for different chapters. Dave helped me come up with some of these and I compiled them as follows:

- The Soul of a Pilgrim (a la Diane Chambers – soul of a dancer speech)[3]
- The Camino They Didn't Walk
- There's No Nordstrom on The Camino de Santiago
- I'm Gonna Need a Lighter Rosary
- Do You Know the Way to San...tiago?
- Are We There Yet?
- Are You Kidding Me?
- I Think I Made a Huge Mistake
- Why Are There No Benches Along Here?
- Is Anyone Else Hot?
- My Hip Hurts
- I Don't Feel Like Walking Today
- Where's The Bus?
- Just Kill Me Now
- How Do You Say "Taxi" in Spanish?

---

[3] From an early *Cheers* episode.

- What the Hell Are We Doing?
- There's No Licorice in the Albergue
- Murder on The Camino

The Week Before

So, my training period was about over. I was out of time. I had done a lot of walking after dinner– we live across the street from the Del Monte Golf Course and at dusk each night I would go out and do the loop, or half the loop to be accurate. Took me about 40 minutes– maybe two to three miles, on blacktop, nice level ground, except for the yard markers that the golf course people set annoyingly in the middle of the pathways to mark their yardage or whatever the golf term is for 100 or 150 yards to the hole. The marker was a two-inch metal tripping hazard that my shoe seemed to find at dusk, about every 300 yards or so. It was a nice evening stroll, nice temperature, nice view, nothing too demanding. I didn't try walking with my backpack on, as recommended. I used my trekking poles once and didn't care for the click clacking sound on the pavement. I didn't try too many hills because, well, they were hard. I did do one "major" training walk.

One Sunday after church, Dave drove home while I decided to just walk home. It was about seven miles and mostly downhill. How hard could that be? Surely I wouldn't have that much trouble. So, I set off. About two blocks into my trek, I kind of had to go to the bathroom, so I made a detour and stopped at the Blackhorse Golf Course. I had also somehow lost my water bottle between the church and the golf course, which is about half a mile away. Dave called from home to see how I was doing. I told him about the lost water bottle and the bathroom problem and he said he'd be right there to walk home the rest of the way with me. So, he had David drop him off at the bathroom, er, golf course and we walked just fine. He had also managed to locate my missing water bottle in the gutter and brought it to me. He took my day-pack from me and strapped it on. We walked a couple of miles, downhill, through Seaside, stopping to look at a couple of houses for sale. Then we went through Sand City and stopped to do a little shopping. I'm always up for a little shopping. Besides, we were looking at "serious" hiking stuff. Sale stuff. And delaying the rest of my walk home. Sports Authority had a sale and we both picked up a few things for the trip – rain gear and such. He carried our new stuff in the pack. Now this was my kind of Camino – shopping along the way, Dave carrying my pack, a hot dog at Costco...

We continued walking down along Del Monte and came to Sloat Avenue. We were close to home – probably a mile away. I was getting tired and my knee hurt. I stopped to complain for a minute. We decided to call David to come pick us up because we didn't want to, you know, overdo it. I thought that sounded like the best strategy – I don't want to get hurt a week before we were leaving. I looked down and there at my feet I saw two perfect white plastic shells! Like pilgrim shells! How amazing! I took that personally and was sure it was a sign from God – confirmation that our pilgrimage was the right thing! We were pilgrims! We were going to have a great trip! This was meant to be!

And then a man shouted out of the second-story window at us – "Hey! Those are my daughter's!" And then a little girl's head popped up and said, "Those aren't mine." So, we asked if we could have them and the man said sure. It's a good thing. They were already in my pocket. I wasn't giving up my sign from God.

David finally drove up, we climbed in the car, and he chauffeured us home. What a long walk.

Yep. I had proof we were pilgrims! Now I just had to do the walk.

Dave made himself a neckerchief for the pilgrimage. He hand-stamped it with a shell design, using a technique he learned from Native Hawaiians when he was on sabbatical.

I find my shell – it is a sign from Heaven.

"We're Off to See the Wizard, er, St. James."

Tuesday, October 14, 2014
Monterey, California to Madrid, Spain
(3,998 steps)

We both had a restless night and were up at 4 a.m. Ready or not, here we come. The first time I ever flew anywhere, it was to Madrid. In 1976. I spent three glorious weeks in Spain when I was 17. Didn't know about the potency of sangria back then. Didn't care much for the food. Didn't like the bullfighting. Did I say glorious? I was terrified about a lot of things back then. I was terrified about a lot of things now — thirty-some years later. At church the Sunday before we left, Father Tom called Dave and me up to the altar and blessed us as we left on our journey. He squeezed my head really tight. I hoped it worked. There were sure a lot of people who knew about what we were doing by now. I guess we couldn't back out. I also hadn't come down with Ebola – my backup escape plan. According to the media, everyone was going to get it. Note to self: Do not believe media.

We checked in at the airport to fly to Los Angeles on the little commuter plane. The flight attendant was in training and this was her last day. Her supervisor was right there, making her nervous. She was making me nervous, too, and I wasn't being graded. We arrived at LAX and I think the stewardess passed. Yay for her. We stopped in at the United Club and were able to switch our flight to Newark to an earlier time. We had been scheduled to leave at 11 a.m. but now could be on the 10:06 flight instead, which was good because we had a tight turnaround time in Newark to catch the Madrid plane.

I had spent the last few days contemplating our journey and the pilgrim spirit. I packed and repacked. Less and less. Less is more, right? One of my favorite beliefs. You wouldn't know it by looking at my house, but hey, a great thought. Two nights before our departure, we took our backpacks with what we thought we were taking to REI to be checked over and to make sure we knew how to adjust everything properly. Backpacks these days have lots of belts and clips, ropes, pulleys, all the bells and whistles – yes, my backpack had a whistle. So many things to yank. The same hard-of-hearing salesman "helped" us who sold us the packs months ago. For some unknown reason, he didn't remember us, even though we had told him all about our upcoming Camino and he told us that that was his dream trip and he and his wife planned to do it someday. Geez, we shared intimate details of our lives and he can't remember me? I remember him!

He pulled on our straps this way and that and declared us ready. He didn't remember (no surprise there) exactly how we attached the trekking poles to the bag. We said we'd figure that part out later. When he was adjusting my pack, he told me to fasten the waist strap and then lift up the pack an inch and a half over my hips so I'd be carrying the bag higher. (I later learned he'd told Dave a different technique, which involved inching the pack lower, so when I'd put my pack on and think it was right, Dave would "adjust" it to help me and I'd find it not right and readjust it, and so on, and so on. But that comes later on...). We had 50-liter packs, which seemed to be the right size. They could hold a lot more stuff. Like the stuff I saw in Spain and couldn't live without. Spain is known for leather. And lace. And ceramics. "Less is more" be damned. The salesman had thought we should go with 35-liter packs, which were tiny and they would have been extremely hard to pack. We thought it was better to go with extra space, so we did. Air doesn't weigh much, right?

My pack weighed 14 pounds. That night. Not bad, I thought. Of course, I still had a few last-minute items to throw in. My toilet kit, medicines, a couple other things. One pair of shoes. How much could those last few additions weigh? (About 10 pounds I believe). Finally, pilgrim spirit be damned, I threw in the Givenchy fucshia lipstick. That would make me feel better since I wasn't taking any "makeup" to speak of. Oh, and the Clarin's pink camellia stick, too. And, well, hell, the mandarin color looks good on me, too, especially with the coral-colored jacket, so I added the Smashbox lipstick, too. Heck, I wasn't taking blush or eye liner or anything. And I did actually see a girl using a lip liner while I was there. I wasn't that bad...

So, as I said, 24 pounds later, I was still fidgeting and repacking. I finally decided to take the fleece blanket. If it did get to be too much at 2.5 pounds, I'd just ditch it in some albergue over there. It's from the PX and cost less than 20 bucks, so no biggie. Dave decided to not take his fleece (dun, dun, dunnnnnnnn). He thought I'd share. Uh huh.

That night at REI we picked up a couple of duffle bags to put our backpacks in to check for flying. It did make it easier to keep all the equipment together but then we had to also fold up the duffle bags and carry them with us for the return trip, and they each weighed about two pounds. Weight was everything. We had the space, but not the strength.

So, back to people-watching at LAX. A girl passed by in white "hot pants" or shorts or something like that. Sadly, the seam was ripped out in the rear. Fascinating and unable to look away.... We decided to pass the time instead by playing a game. We called it "Who says first..." and we compiled a list as follows, though the answers are still up to debate for a few of the statements:

I think I made a huge mistake (K, D, K, D, K, D...)
Tell me again why we're doing this? (D)
Let's send our bags ahead by cab (K)
You said it wasn't going to rain (–)
I'm glad I brought these poles (K, and D later on when he was down to one)
I'm leaving this, too (–)
This was "in the movie" (–)
I have to go to the bathroom (K)
Again? (–)
You said you'd be in charge of the trowel (–)
Are we there yet? (D)
Which way do we go? (K)
This ATM doesn't work (D)
You're so annoying (–)
I need more wine (K)

And then:

Who gets hurt first?
How long til David spends all the money we left?
Who needs something from the pharmacy first?
When does Jim hear from the VA?
How many pieces of Matt's glasses are left?
How much weight do the dogs lose?
How much weight do we lose?
Which foot blisters first?
When does Dave's back go out?
How beautiful is the niece?
Is the beautiful niece living at our house when we return?
Who's still left on Survivor?
Do we run into Mark and Susan?
When is our first cab/bus ride?
How much does this trip cost?

The flight to Newark is sort of bumpy. We left at 10:30 a.m. I think the movie "Maleficent" is on. I'm seeing the screen of the person in front of me between the crack in the seats. It looked pretty good, when my eyes were open. Of course, the dialogue that I didn't hear could be all crap, but the pictures were intriguing.

More bumps. Time to distract myself with some music. I spent a lot of time preparing a couple of play lists that I planned to listen to as I walked. I had one special play-list that consisted of "requests" from friends (more about that list later), and I did my own (better) list that entailed culling my library of songs on my computer down to the best 600 or so of my favorite, peppy but inspiring tunes I could think of. I turned it up loud now as it helps me forget about the turbulence...

At the airport in our pilgrim fleece. First selfie; nice lipstick I think.

Pretty Fly for a White Boy, then Pumping Blood, All About That Bass, Help Yourself by Tom Jones, Save me San Francisco, Good Life, Love Runs Out, Let it Go, Life is Beautiful theme, I Look to You, In Dreams by Roy Orbison, Ticket to Ride, How to Save a Life... and so on.

Before long, hah – it was six hours – we landed in Newark.

And, hey, the flight to Madrid is completely full. We're supposed to leave at 7:40 p.m. and we took off close to the scheduled time. I'm in the middle seat as usual, Economy Plus with our so-called Elite Status, Dave on the aisle, and a very large black girl sits next to me by the window. She warns us she'd be getting up a lot because her legs swell, she has to go to the bathroom, she needs to walk around, etc., etc. Luckily, she was soon out like a light and slept nearly the whole way. She was sleeping when they brought the meals. Didn't have to get up once for her. Or see her swollen ankles that she pointed to. United surprised us and served Dave his "special" meal he had ordered. First he'd heard of it. Apparently, he's on their list for extra-special vegan people and they gave him a tray of couscous and some other suspicious-looking stuff. I kept my eyes on my own cheese lasagna or whatever it was they served that was "non-vegan."

"Follow the Shells on the Road"

Wednesday, October 15
Madrid to Leon, Spain
(15,446 steps/6.75 miles)

The winds were with us and we landed early – at 9:15 a.m. We walked forever through the terminal and finally reached Passport Control and then got our bags. They seemed to have gained weight overnight and overseas. Boy, were they heavy! They were very ungainly, too, trying to lug those backpacks concealed in baggy duffle bags, especially with the trekking poles in there, too. Oh, and my hiking shoes. Thumping around. So, we found the shuttle bus outside, asked the driver if it was the right bus, boarded, and made it over to the next terminal – T4 – which happens to be about half an hour away. The great thing at this point is that we are under no time constraints whatsoever. Doesn't matter if we take our time. We have no reservations from here on out and can get wherever the heck we are going whenever we manage to show up. Right?

The sort of difficult part about this situation, however, is that now we were in a foreign country and one that doesn't speak a lot of English. So, from here on out we would depend on me – I had four years of high school Spanish! Thanks, Mrs. Swanson! Although now that I think of it, we spent a lot of time at our desks just listening to Spanish music – "Guantanamera," etc. (Isn't that in Mexico, by the way?) It was, of course, a couple years ago, but I was confident I could always locate the bathroom (bano), or the wine (vino tinto).

We had planned to take the bus to Leon, which was a six–hour ride. The ground transportation was all located over here in T4, so we milled around and tried to make sense of it all. First, we found an ATM to answer our biggest question – would we have money while we were in Spain? Our bank, Navy Federal Credit Union, assured us that there would be no problem. I had no confidence in that. Call it past experience. But, lo and behold, after a couple of language–based misfires, the ATM shot out our daily allowance of 300 euros. We were set. For a day or two. Hopefully.

Next stop, bus ticket. A lot of confusion later and we had train tickets. Trying to read the signs and find some help, we dropped our bags in the middle of the huge corridor and Dave went to ask about buying two Renfe tickets, which turned out to be the train, not the bus. Fifty euros each. Apparently, Dave was told the train was faster, and at nearly the same cost. The bus to Leon takes about six hours. The train – just about four hours. He came back with two tickets that had assigned seats and a scheduled departure of 11:05 – from the main train station, Chamartin. Not the airport. It's 10:15. Where, you ask, as I did, is the train station? Oh, and please disregard what I said just a paragraph or two above about no time constraints, can take our time, etc., etc. Panic was setting in. Fast.

Well, first we had to get ourselves to the commuter train that takes us to Chamartin, and which left in, like, five minutes. Hoisting our god-heavy bags we went to one turnstile, which turned out to be the wrong place, and we were directed to the farthest turnstiles down the length of the building – to Renfe! We managed to get the tickets accepted in the machine and rushed down the hall and down the escalator. The train was there. We quickly jumped on board, banging our duffel bags, and dropped them on the floor. The train was nearly deserted but it left right away. Like as soon as we stepped foot aboard. Doors slammed shut. Just in time! Relief! We made it. At the time, I had thought this was the actual train to Leon but soon learned it was just one train that leads to the next train. We sat and had a ten-minute ride to Chamartin. Behind us was a girl with a backpack. Hah! Our first peregrina sighting! She spoke a little English and we chatted for a minute. She was also going to Leon to join her boyfriend who was there, but she was scheduled to leave on a later train to Leon. We told her about our tickets for the 11:05 train to Leon and she was going to try to change her reservation, though apparently without success because we never saw her again.

We reached Chamartin, one of the main train stations in Madrid, and got our bags out. We trudged down the long platform and then up the escalator. Wow, it really was a huge station. People were everywhere, rushing around. We went to try to find the right platform for our train that left in about 20 minutes. It was very confusing. Trains in, trains out, very hectic. We learned that it wasn't until about five minutes before your train was to arrive that they assign it a platform and then the rider has to rush (run!) to that platform, or be left (holding the bag, or shall we say my heavy bag?).

We stood under the lighted sign, poised to run. Our train finally showed up on the neon board and we ran to the noted platform, which meant down a ways and then down the escalator, under the tunnel, down the hallway, and up a flight of stairs. But, the train hadn't arrived yet and the sign there did say the train would be going to Leon, as well as other points. The train glided in and we found the right coach and our seats. It was nearly empty. We left our bags in the luggage rack and relaxed for the first time in, maybe six months – since we decided to do this excursion/vacation, uh, let's go with adventure.

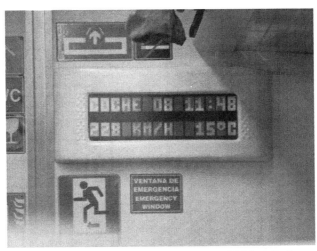

Train speedometer - quite zippy at 228 km/hr!

So, this was one of those fancy, European fast bullet trains with the funny-shaped nose. Not Amtrak! We left at 11:05 a.m., as promised. We were scheduled to arrive in Leon at 2:40 p.m. The train was electric and rode very smoothly. No bumps, no clickety clack. We went very fast – at times – and very slow at times (close, but still not Amtrak[4]). I think we reached 125 mph at times. I know this because there was a sign at the front of the car that said so. Well, it was in kilometers, so we guessed. Well, I guessed – Dave was probably pretty accurate with his math background.

The track didn't follow a very scenic, pretty route. We went through the sad part of town and then picked up speed, watching the countryside go by. We noticed the skies darkening. It was cloudy and seemed to be threatening to rain. But, but, but, it wasn't supposed to rain, I was thinking – this is fall – you know, leaves changing colors, cool and crisp air – no rain. We'd had some debate at home months ago about whether or not we should pack waterproof or Gortex shoes, gear and all. That stuff is much heavier. Surely it won't rain on our pilgrimage. That might ruin everything. So, it won't. That was my persuasive argument. Dave, on the other hand, checked weather reports, statistics on precipitation, etc., and concluded we were going to be wet. Very wet. Well, the view turned to drizzle. Are these windows tinted with a coat of gray film? I was feeling a little anxious and a sense of doom was sinking over me. What if we don't like it? What if we do in fact get wet? That doesn't sound like so much fun. Could we just stay in Leon? A three-week vacation in Leon? Not walk? What would we tell people? This was my first feeling that maybe this wasn't going to go well and we were in trouble...

---

[4]Yes, I was thinking back to the time Dave and I took our three sons from New York to Seattle and back on Amtrak, with a stop in Minneapolis. Now that is another story. A long story.

The poor naive fool ready to walk the half-mile to the hotel.

Anyway, we're a little hungry. I would also love a Diet Coke. With rum. But, I wasn't going to push my luck. Dave went in search of the cafeteria car. He came back with a Coca Cola Light and a Coke Zero. All they had. And apparently they cost about 2 euros each. He was not pleased. I didn't mention the rum.

The train stopped at three or four small stations and then we finally reached Leon. It was close to being on time. We got off, the train zoomed off, and we looked around. Think Bolivia (a la "Butch Cassidy," LOL). The rain had stopped but it was a little dreary looking. We took our backpacks out of the carrying bags. I struggled to put mine on, get situated, have the poles adjusted right, change shoes, fold up the duffle bag and store it. Well, that's not too bad. How far do we have to walk to the hotel?

Our one consolation was that we had booked ourselves a room at The Parador (a five-star hotel, originally a monastery founded in the 12th century to provide lodging to pilgrims on their way to Santiago) – we wanted our first night to adjust and to be able to get some sleep before starting out on the amazing journey we were going to have ... tomorrow... (short aside – when we told Father Tom that we made arrangements to spend our first night on the Camino at The Parador in Leon, his incredulous response was – "The Parador?" GASP)

We only had about a mile to walk (15 minutes?) to the Parador – a few city blocks, across the river, a few more blocks down by the river, and there it was! A huge, imposing, old building, which I guess is what 12th Century

Our first Pilgrim shell on the road. And the yellow arrow.

would mean. It's magnificent and indeed one of the most beautiful renaissance buildings in Spain. And – it was in The Movie! "The Way!" What a way to start our Camino. We stopped to take a few pictures. To the left of the Parador was a wide bridge leading over the river. There we saw our first pilgrim shell.

Tomorrow we would walk across that bridge and take our first steps on the Camino – one of millions of other pilgrims over centuries. Popes, apostles, actors, Shirley MacLaine. In their footsteps. And next year would be a Holy Year – we beat Pope Francis to The Way. The shell figure is ages-old and the symbol of the pilgrim. People (believers) used to just walk out of their homes throughout Spain and walk to Santiago, and then walk back home again. The fanned-out lines on the shell symbolize the various routes there are, all leading to the "pointy-end" of the shell - Santiago! And the yellow arrows are supposedly everywhere. I'm not sure who is in charge of painting those arrows, but what a great job someone has. We would also be able to tell we were on the right path by the piles of rocks people left, old shoes, articles of clothing, all kinds of debris.

Anyway, we checked in and right away got to practice our Spanish – hola! The place was amazing. They told us, I think, about our room. We showed our passports and then – we got our first peregrino stamp on our credencial! The Parador! Not sure about the five-star hotel stamp being first, but hey, this is Our Camino! Who cares what people think? Right? Two months ago when we booked our airfare and were "committed," I ordered two authentic

Statue in San Marcos Square, outside the Parador. His hip locked up, too. Note the sandals. We thought this was cute, not foreboding. Little did we know.

credencials online (from Ivar) so that we would have them from the start and not have to be looking around Leon for the right Pilgrim's Office to locate them.

We were glad to get those backpacks off. They were heavy and not packed right. I think the contents may have shifted during flight – that happens you know. Our room was on the third floor – down three or four long hallways and then at the end of another long dark hallway. The "Peregrino" rate I guess. I think the room cost 100 euros. Worth every cent/penny/peseta/euro, whatever. Our room was impressive. We had two windows in little alcoves that looked out on the river and the bridge across it. It was getting darker out and threatening to rain again. I'm sure it would have been beautiful if the sun were out. The bathroom was wonderful – all granite, with a zillion amenities, including a hair dryer. There was a light switch that was not on an automatic timer, which I would come to appreciate. There was a canopy over the bed. Dave explained the purpose of canopy beds to me. I didn't know. In the dark ages, back before people could install a really good roof, sometimes critters would get inside the eaves and either fall from the ceiling or their droppings would. The canopy was there to catch that kind of stuff. Yuck. Protect the king of the castle, or the queen. The princess. Yoshi. Whoever had a canopy I guess. We only had a partial canopy (it came out only a foot or so) – covered your head/our heads. "Peregrino" rate, again, I'm

Arriving at the Parador.

thinking. The furniture in the room was, as usual, made for tiny European ancient people, but nonetheless, it looked really nice. I didn't see any critters creeping around.

We rearranged some things and freshened up and then went out to explore. First, we looked around the hotel. Lots of arches, high ceilings, old stuff, doorways, statues, a big square courtyard, big heavy doors, tapestries, weird old velvet furniture, one grand staircase, floors with steps of varying heights designed to trip the unexpected jet-lagged pilgrim, and basically the typical old European five-star-hotel stuff one sees all the time... We stopped to check out the pilgrim's menu (menu of the day) in their fancy restaurant and were shocked to see they wanted 50 euros from each poor pilgrim for the dinner. We passed. We went out the front door and started to wander. We were looking for the Cathedral and wanted to check out the area. We walked and walked through neighborhoods. This is a cool Spanish town. Most of it was locked up now of course as we were in the middle of "siesta" hour. But, it was nice to explore and walk and stretch our legs. We got turned around but eventually found our way to the ancient part of town, Old Town, and reached the Cathedral. By this time, it had started to rain. Lightly at first but then kind of steadily. It was getting gloomier by the minute.

We went inside and looked around. Very cool. Very gothic. Very impressive. We had to pay something like 5 euros each to go inside and Dave picked up one of the devices that gives you pointers in English about all you were seeing. The church was completed late in the 16th Century and is one of three major cathedrals on "The Way" – Burgos has one, Leon has this one, and then there is the one in Santiago – 200-plus miles away.

We spent about half an hour to 45 minutes inside and then went back out to try to find something to eat. It was still drizzly but we were running on adrenaline and relief, plus excitement to be starting our quest. Well, okay, my

The nice room in the Parador – note the canopy!

The courtyard in our modest lodgings.

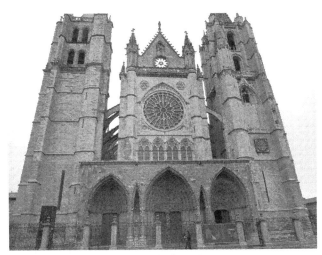

The Cathedral in Leon.

quest. All of the restaurants were closed until 8:30 p.m. or so. Spain has some funny rules. Different culture. We were reminded of that for the following three-and-a-half weeks. We headed back toward the hotel and eventually did find a bar that was open. We got a small glass of wine and a grilled cheese sandwich (Spanish style), and they provided an "hors' d'oeuvre" which was a Spanish type torte/omelet kind of slice of "pie." Not French Silk, or even pumpkin. Drat. This food ended up being our dinner for the night and, at a total cost of 7 euros, was not a bad meal.

By now it was raining hard and we walked quickly back to the hotel. We got pretty wet. We showered in the magnificent bathroom, I dried my hair with the hair dryer, and we repacked our backpacks. We weren't in the mood for going back out to find something more for dinner. We were satisfied. So, we were certainly in bed early. We were so tired after the long flight, train ride, and walk around town, that we conked out right away. Didn't even look for bed bugs! We were asleep by 8:45, after our Facebook posting, of course... Even old hotels have Wifi!

My Facebook post for the day:

> *Wed update: Flights all went well and landed early. Squished, tired, but not sick. Made quick chg of plans and got bullet train to Leon instead of bus. 3 hrs and 125 mph at times. Cool. Off in Leon and walked a mile to Parador, yes starting out right with 5-star hotel. It is amazing. Went out and walked all over, toured Cathedral – wow – and found one bar open at 6 for a ham and cheese grilled sandwich with small glass of wine. Started raining hard but back in room, cleaned up, repacked, and Dave conked out. So far so good. Had my doubts this afternoon... What the hell are we doing? I think i made a huge mistake. Well, not there yet but might be uttered tomorrow especially if it's raining.*

The grand peregrina (suddenly upgraded from "poor naive fool") on the grand stairway.

How we suffered. The hallways weren't even heated!

"Not the Parador"

Thursday, October 16
Leon to Villar de Mazarife
(30,090 steps/13.14 miles/112 floors)

    I woke up a few times during the night. Anxiety, perhaps. Mice? We were up by 7 as desayuno (breakfast) started at 7:30. Peeking out the window was not reassuring. It was dark, dark, dark, and looked to be raining lightly. We organized and dressed. We had now changed into evening-shower people instead of morning-shower-ers. We went down a floor to the Peregrino Café – breakfast was included with the Peregrino rate –they had a long dining room and there were a lot of people eating breakfast. From their dress, I was fairly confident there were no other pilgrims, or not many. Unless maybe some were going to start walking in business attire. It was hard to tell, though. Some wore nice clothing with hiking shoes.
    They had a huge spread of breakfast food – selections of anything you could want. And so we ate. Dave was very happy - he had a full breakfast including bacon and eggs, toast, fruit. I was more reserved and concentrated on the muffin-and-doughnut selection. I didn't want to have any issues with having to find a bathroom right off the bat. Only one cup of coffee. We made one more stop up at our room to collect our things, we checked out, and we were on the road by 8:30. Pitch dark, by the way.
    We had put on our rain gear, which consisted of rain pants and our rain jackets, supposedly waterproof and breathable. My jacket liked to breathe rain. I also wore my waterproof hat. Yeah, right. Also adding to the discomfort were the money belts we were wearing tucked into our pants. They dug into my stomach and made bending hard. I'm usually much more flexible. But, they were necessary to keep our passports, money, and credencials dry and safe. However, the whole trip they were an uncomfortable presence. Plus, Dave had zipper issues with his belt... that turned into swearing issues.
    The rain changed to pouring rain. Later in the day it turned to sheets of rain, and then to driving rain. But, those first moments were exciting. All that gear on, plus the backpack, balancing myself on the two trekking poles. I was a pilgrim! That lasted about ten minutes. We crossed the courtyard in front of the hotel, saw our first yellow arrow and the Camino shell. It pointed across the river over the bridge. We were off. Click clack, click clack. Are we

Walking through the outskirts of Leon in the rain.

there yet?

We were several blocks into our pilgrimage when we heard it. "Buen Camino." Someone was speaking to us. As they passed us. "Um, yeah. Thanks, uh, you too." We quickly caught on and were "buen camino-ing" right back atcha! Or, "Gracias" will do, too. We walked through busy city streets for an hour. We became aware of more pilgrims around us. As the morning progressed and it got a bit lighter out, more pilgrims in parkas and raingear were all around us. All of us going the same direction for centuries. And then, all of those other pilgrims were passing us. I found out that I am a slow walker. A really, really, slow walker. At home, I consider myself to be a fast walker. But here, backpack, poles, rain, uncertainty, I am the slowest pilgrim ever. I could feel my legs turn leaden and I couldn't force them to go any faster than they did. The whole time, I was very wooden, plodding, slower than I wanted or could do anything about. Slow but steady. Just really, really slow. One foot in front of the other. It was almost like something was pressing me back the entire way – I was not going to be able to gain any speed no matter what. So, I settled into my rhythm.

Dave, on the other hand, apparently did not have this walking problem. He was in the mind to walk quickly. We had our first little "tiff" shall we say, or, um, discussion. He at first was terribly disturbed by the fact that everyone was passing us/him to be more specific. Everyone. We weren't going to be passing anyone. I was holding him back. Making him look bad. I told him that first day over and over that he should just go ahead and I'd catch up,

The first hour. Dave is mostly happy and still mostly dry.

but there was no way I could walk any faster. I just couldn't. He relented and slowed down. We heard all the time that you go at your own pace. It's not a race. You walk your own Camino. Well, you hear that but you maybe understand something else. You're slow!

And then it rained harder. This was getting to be miserable. My legs hurt. My left hip hurt, too. Dave's feet hurt. Everyone was faster than us. We weren't anywhere near our destination for the night. After about two hours, well, at 10:30 a.m., we finally were out of the city "suburbs" and found a small café that was open, so we stopped to rest and have a coffee. We shook our backpacks off and set them outside the café. We then had to take off our rain jackets and hang them up. We couldn't drag all this water inside. I took off my hat. It obviously had not done its job and my hair was soaked. I was soaked through everywhere. It was chilly. The one good thing in all this weather, though, was thanks to my waterproof shoes, my feet were dry! The Merino wool was working, and my feet did not hurt. They were feeling okay. It was a miracle that the boots were doing their job and my feet stayed dry the whole day. I felt a huge consolation being able to concentrate on the few positive things so far this morning. My feet were warm, dry, and blister-free. Not bad.

We went inside and sat at a long table. It was a small place and there were only two tables. Newspaper was spread all over the floor. Dave ordered a café con leche and I had a Coca Cola Light (the Spanish recipe for Diet Coke, which is not the same as the U. S. version – it's much sweeter) and we split a croissant 90/10 (hey, I'm telling the truth here – it wasn't equal I admit). It felt great to sit down and rest. To be inside where it was dry. To be getting warmer. The girl behind the bar took our picture. A couple of drowned rats, but smiling. A little later several other pilgrims wandered in, leaving their wet gear outside, too. We sort of had conversations, even with

First break. We are soaked. Note the Merino wool which kept us warm even wet – thanks, REI, the expense was worth it!

the language barrier. We tried. We learned from three or four others that they were headed in another direction from where we planned to go for the day. I guess the road split into a couple different ways up ahead. As I was standing in line for the bathroom, one girl pointed to her head and said she was ugly. Or else she said I was ugly. I agreed. Wet!

After visiting the bathroom, we dressed to leave and were on our way at 11 a.m. It was not as rainy at the moment. However, the wind had picked up. Dave had torn the map we were following for the day from the guidebook. It was soaked. Right past this café and the town of Virgen del Camino is where we had to make a choice. You can go in either of two directions – one path goes along the east side and stays close to the highway. The other alternative route is on the west side and is relatively isolated. It is also supposedly (dare we say allegedly?) the more scenic route. Our guidebook has it as the primary route. It's a flat plain that crosses several canals. We choose isolated – the path that apparently no one else decided to pick. We didn't want to walk along the highway. So, we headed out of Virgen and stopped to look around and again mull our choices. We passed an interesting sculpture/statue at a church on the way out of town. We stopped to take a picture and have one last look behind us at the town – civilization was disappearing. The scene up ahead looked to be a little desolate. We stuck to our guns and picked the shells that pointed to the left. They led right away through a muddy field. Uphill. "How muddy can it be?" Ha ha ha (insert demonic laughter and crazed look in our eyes here). Really muddy. ("If all I have to do is walk, how hard can it be?" was echoing in my head).

We were headed for Villar de Mazarife. It is 22 km from Leon to Mazarife, but Dave tells me that that reading is from the other side of Leon and we are really much closer since we started walking from The Parador on the near

Choices. We took the road less traveled, marked by the dashed lines. Possibly a huge mistake.

side of Leon... There were only a few alarm bells ringing in my head at that moment. That's about 14 miles, and for our first day, we hoped for a bit of a shorter go of it. Breaking in and all that. Plus rain. And now wind.

So, we trudged on, through a lot of red mucky mud. Rocks. A few hills thrown in. More mud. Muddy mud that coats the bottom of our rain pants legs, from the knees down. No one else is in sight, which I sort of think is okay because if anyone was going this way, they would be passing us and I didn't want any more of that to happen. However, ding, ding, ding, if no one else had chosen this route, why was that?

Again, the way we had chosen was supposedly more scenic – ha ha ha. This is according to our guidebook written by a noted authority. Ah, a book that will go down in history. At least in this version of history. Our first day out and we should have known right away that ~~this guy is just a downright liar~~ his book may have inaccuracies[5]. Much mud later and we are still walking. We think there is a café for a coffee stop in three miles. Wrong! There is nothing for six miles. We are so tired. My hip hurts. Really, really hurts. We adjust my pack a lot. Higher, lower, up, down. I just can't seem to get it adjusted right.

Dave wants to help me – he says if he can give me some advice, it's "drink

---

[5]The editor has toned this down, here and later in the book. The guidebook itself warns about pilgrims blaming the book for their difficulties. Although as you will see, a few inaccuracies in the book caused us great distress.

By ourselves in the mud and rain. Note carefully the "scenic view."

a lot." My response – "I'm trying, but there are no bars open yet." The only time I laughed today.

I am writing this memoir from my notes and at this point they read: "So tired. Hip hurts. Have to go slower and rest. Uphill. Mud. Rain. More wind. Bleak scenery. Awful." Both Dave and I are wondering what in the hell we were thinking when we started out on this idea. Which leads to, whose idea was this?

We do see about four or five other pilgrims along this stretch of hell, er, camino. Actually, I see a pair of women pilgrims approaching at light speed from behind. Their voices really carry. They are carrying on a very peppy conversation. Complaining about men is the gist of it. In English. And walking. Through mud. Impressive. How can they walk and talk at the same time? I never found that possible. I look behind me to check their progress and I am surprised to see that one of the women has pulled off the path to heed "nature's call" whatever that was. Ahh – so people really do go in the "woods" if they need to. I found that very comforting. Not that I had to go. Or would. But, bathroom stop and everything and these two women were soon overtaking us. Talk talk talk. Wow.

At 2:30 we reached the next bar and stopped for a glass of wine. Ahh, an upbeat moment. Lunch was non-existent today but I was okay with moving directly onto wine. No way am I calling it "Happy Hour." There is a wide porch and we take our backpacks off. Dave takes the time to care for his feet. I had bought some cream from a store in Carmel that you put on your feet which supposedly wards off blisters and foot injuries. That stuff was awesome. I used it every day, and Dave used it and Vaseline, too. So, we went inside the bar and there were four or so other pilgrims there, too, resting. All were drinking a glass of wine. What a great custom! We met Helena, a girl we had noticed on our train to Leon the day before. She is from Hong Kong and this

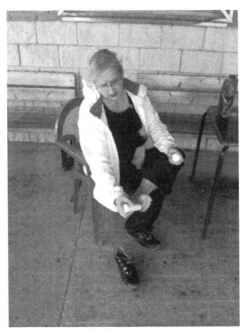

Tending the tenderfeet

was her first day. She is walking alone and appears to be about 21. Her feet were giving her a lot of trouble and the other two women, who had passed us, were helping her out. They had an impressive array of foot supplies and first aid laid out. They knew what they were doing. One was Sue, a woman about 65 years old, from Toronto or Montreal — somewhere like that in Canada. The other woman was Beth, about 55 years old, from Palm Springs. They were friendly and we chatted a bit. This was Sue's second Camino and she was quite proud of it. I was still proud of my feet – so far no issues. They left soon after and said they would probably meet us at the albergue up ahead. We were all going to the same town for the night.

   We ordered a glass of wine from the unfriendly bartender man. We still had apparently about three more miles to go until we reached the town we were headed for. My hip was just killing me and I was not happy about having to strap that backpack back on. It's so heavy and uncomfortable. We tried to ask the bartender about having a taxi come to take my pack the last three miles. He explains, we guess, that a taxi would have to come from Leon and it would cost 25 euros. We decline. We go back out on the porch and start to get ready to walk some more. Suddenly, a taxi pulls up in front of the bar! Providence! Dave goes back inside and asks if that taxi could take my bag. They say it could but it would cost 10 euros. Deal! What a bargain. I hand over my pack and the extortion rate and they say they will leave it at the albergue – the first one on the left. We trust them to do it. Frankly, I don't care if I ever see it again. My left hip was still very painful but my mood

"Not the Parador"

improved. I couldn't believe how that worked out. A miracle! The Camino provides! I don't think I could have made it three more miles, especially in the afternoon with the wind gusting up to 45 mph, in pain. Surely it had already been 15 miles today! A hard first day. But, it's not even close to over yet!

So, after greasing up our feet again, we are off. Only three more miles. How long could it take? God, forever. We are both so tired and in pain. Dave has blisters forming and my hip is very bad. We're gonna need to buy more Advil. The wind seemed to be pushing us harder and harder away from the town. We are fighting it and it is a battle. Finally, finally, we arrive at the small town of Mazarife. We see a sign for the Albergue de Jesus. I'm shell-shocked. The sign advertises a "pool." We walk into the courtyard where Jesus may have stayed. I'm willing to bet he was born there in the courtyard. (Well, I don't actually SEE any mangers laying around...) There are clothes drying on lines. Other pilgrims are doing their laundry in tubs and bowls on the side. The "pool" is a rectangular above-ground plaster container that I don't think I'd let Misty[6] have a drink out of.

We enter the door of the place. Several impressions – first, there's my backpack sitting right there on a chair! Yay! Thank God! Good God! What's that smell? Who's cooking such awful food? I suddenly felt so nauseous and sick to my stomach. Three or four other pilgrims were sitting around. There's one big, long, sticky communal table. There's a card table to the side of it with some folding chairs. There's a guitar hanging on the wall (uh oh), there's a bulletin board in Spanish with lots of papers announcing things and services available. A large woman comes in from the "kitchen" and motions that she will check us in at the card table. I sit down, wet, sweaty, shocked, and peel

---

[6]Misty is our Golden Retriever, who I am sure is lolly-gagging around at home, laying on my bed right at this moment.

The swimming pool.

my passport and credencial out of my pants to hand to her. She prints our information in a notebook. That will be 5 euros. Each. Must pay now. She says dinner is at 7:30 in the other room, but you can cook your own if you want – there is a kitchen. She says she will do our laundry for us if we want.

Registered now, she motions to follow her so that she can give us a tour of the place, and she points out several doors and rooms throughout the shack, er, albergue. There is a bathroom downstairs. Here's the kitchen. Dining room. Back door, and down that way is the town with a grocery store. We're upstairs. Watch your head on the ceiling – very low clearance. Dim lighting. People (for centuries?) have written and drawn on the walls – encouraging words? Hard to tell since it's in different languages. I plan what I want to write...

The woman continues, here's your room. We did "luck" out and get a private room. Just our two twin "beds." Here's the bathroom. Here's the shower. What the hell have we walked into? The lighting is dim. It's dingy. The floors are wood and they creak and are uneven. The doors don't shut right. The beds are straight out of "Cool Hand Luke." The smell rises from the kitchen. What the hell is that? I think I'm gonna throw up. Where's the bano again? We're left alone in our "room." Five euros? Each? That's ten euros for this place? I'm having trouble finding my pilgrim spirit. Yes, it was five euros, and overpriced at 5 euros each – outrageous!

First things first. Shower. Clean up. We unpack our bags as we need just about everything in them. Step 1 – spray the beds with the bed bug spray. Step 2 — set out our sleeping sacks. Step 3 — Find clean clothes and shower supplies. Step 4 – investigate shower. So, Dave goes first. He comes back and tells me the sad story. The shower is actually just a shower nozzle. There are no hooks or any place to hang your towel or your dry clothes. There is no place to put your soap or shampoo. So, now it's my turn. I have Dave

Checking in. Thunderstruck. "What in the hell did I sign up for?"

We now have two stamps in our credencial. A tale of two albergues...

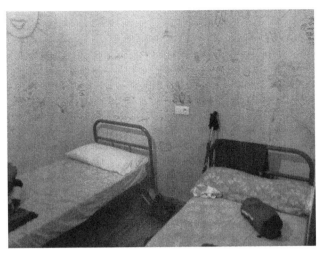

Our suite.

stand outside the door holding my clothes and towel. I go in, quickly take a lukewarm shower, setting my combo soap/shampoo on the floor. Done, Dave hands me my towel. What a worthless piece of s... cloth. I had gotten one of those high-tech travel towels – size "large" (lies!) but about the size of a cookie sheet. Supposedly, they dry fast and soak up the water on your skin. Ha ha ha. Did the guidebook company make this towel?

So, I dried (ha ha) off and Dave handed me my clothes. I scurried back to our "room" to finish dressing. I combed my hair and put it back up in a ponytail. I hung up the wet "towel" on the iron bed frame. We set our dirty clothes apart in the "laundry bag" we had brought. Dave took it down to the woman to wash and dry for us. Feeling slightly better, we decided to locate the town's supermercado to find wine. Fast. It didn't take long to find it. One bottle of Peregrino wine for three euros. The owner opened the bottle for us since we did not have a corkscrew. Note to self: always pack a corkscrew. That's just common sense. It's raining hard again. We did see a couple other albergues on the way, though, and quickly concluded we had picked the "wrong" shack for the night. Obviously, our newest friends, Sue and Beth, had chosen more wisely. We figured we would never see them again. Anyway, we went back to drink our vino tinto at Motel 1-1/2. We got out our collapsible bathroom cups, mine blue, Dave's red. We sat down at the long wooden sticky communal table to mix and mingle with the other peregrinos. Oh, my.

There was a group of six or seven Koreans there. Older mom and dad and their children (in theirs 20s), or something like that. There was an American girl from California there, too. Friendly type. About 25 years old. Trying to bond with the Koreans. Oh, dear. They were the ones who had cooked something in the kitchen. Korean something. They were eating and sharing. Asked if we wanted some. No, gag. They did have a light green/whitish

Communal entertainment at the Albergue de Jesus.

colored melon and asked if we wanted some. No. Dave had a bite. I chewed my Pepto Bismol discreetly.

We talked and they discussed their bed-bug bites. They laughed. Hmmmm. I had read up on the subject and if you had bed bugs, you had to wash and dry all of your stuff in your pack and in a very hot dryer. You had to kill the bugs. They thought that was funny. The American girl was saying they should do that and the Koreans just laughed. The Korean woman had bites on her arms apparently. I was glad Dave and I had our own private room. And I thanked God for the bed-bug spray. And that we were only allowed to stay here one night. As awful as the walking was today and the hip pain and the rain and the wind and the mud and the miles, and though we were safe for the night, I was ready to move on. What a horrible first day.

I was feeling worse. The Koreans had finished their dinner but the dining room didn't open until 7:30 with their menu of the day for pilgrims. And then I felt worse. From a minute ago. The American girl had noticed the guitar on the wall. She got it down. She started strumming and asked if the Koreans knew any songs. The older Korean man pulled out a harmonica.

They were well into American folk songs and way down along the Swannee River when I couldn't take another minute. I had to go lie down a bit before dinner and have a nap. So, I went up to our room at 6, thinking fondly about The Parador, and it didn't take long before I fell asleep. Dave stayed downstairs bonding with the other peregrinos. And checking his email. Mostly the last thing I just said. This place did have Wifi. Dave later came upstairs with our now-clean clothes. I woke feeling slightly better and went back downstairs. There was still wine left, so I had a sip for medicinal purposes and tried to check Facebook to let everyone know I was alive. Barely.

I discovered that Dave had posted several pictures and had described

The medicine is working.

our situation. So, the night improved with lots of comments and sympathy. Allison noted that our room looked amazing, as in "now I know what prison looks like." I posted that, "...bottom line, this sucks..." We laughed. That's twice today. The Koreans had stopped singing. And cooking. They were doing the dishes and Dave and I moved into the dining room to eat and watch Spanish TV, which turned out to be Wheel of Fortune or the news or something. This was our first experience with the menu of the day. It goes like this:

Order something from Course 1 —soup, macaroni/pasta, salad, or something else they are offering. Then order from Course 2 – a meat of some sort which is always accompanied by French fries, then you get bread usually, and wine, and dessert. So, on this night I chose pasta, which turned out to be spaghetti with meat sauce (luckily not tuna today – they do love their tuna), and then chicken. I ate some of it and the fried chicken cutlet and French fries were bland and not too bad. We got ice cream for dessert. Dave had some sort of soup and then a steak. We chatted back and forth via my iTouch and his iPhone and on Facebook. Delusional. Still in shock, in pain, and stunned. The humor helped. "Hawaii 5-0" came on. Dave and I agreed that next time one of us had a great idea like a pilgrimage that we will go to Hawaii instead. Or just take a cruise. Lie down til the feeling passes. Now "Password" is on. I'm sure it is helping my Spanish vocabulary. More Facebook – it helps to have contact with "home."

I'm beginning to suspect the Camino is not all it's cracked up to be. In fact, I am wondering if there is a conspiracy. Today was spent focusing on my body and the weather. There was nothing else – no praying, no profound thoughts, no epiphanies. Maybe they come later. I hope so. Right now, it was confusing and not at all like I thought it would be. Also, I appear to have lost my rock. For the Cruz de Ferro. Maybe it'll turn up. Right now, I

Menu del peregrino. Pretty good, especially if you are burning 5K calories a day.

don't care. I do still have Isaac's rock he gave me. The big one.

We are off for bed at 9:15. Surprisingly, the place is pretty full of people but it is rather quiet overnight. We do hear some sounds and some snoring. The doors and floors all squeak and when people move about, we hear it. My Fitbit says I took 29,181 steps today, though Dave's says he took 35,000-plus steps. Mine must be broken. It also says we did 112 flights of stairs, too. I can't adjust the time on mine, though, and it starts over again at 0 steps every day at 9 a.m. Not real accurate.

We've taken more Advil and are soon asleep. My hair is still damp.

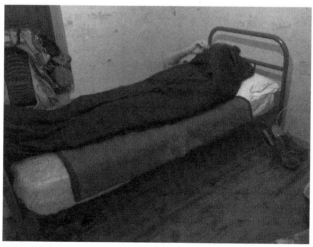

Dave zipping up to go to sleep in the Albergue de Jesus.

"I've Grown Accustomed to Her Scowl"

Friday, October 17
Villar de Mazarife to Santibanez
(31,464 steps/13.74 miles/26 floors)

Ow.
Ow.
Ow.
Oh, my God. Ow.
Ohhhhh. This isn't good. Ow. Ow. Ow. Ow.

I was attempting to get out of bed. So sore. Oh my god my legs hurt. My hip hurt. My hip hurt bad. My feet were swollen and it was hard to stand. Ow. Ow. Dave offered some encouragement to me from the bed on his side of our cell – "Wait, let me get my camera. I need to get a picture of this..."

It was 7 a.m. and it was pitch dark outside. It was quiet and no one was up. "I thought we were supposed to be out of these albergues early?" I hobbled to the door of our room. Squeak, squeak, squeak, creaaaaak. I yanked open the door. Ow. Ow. Ow. I crept down the dark hallway and, squeaaaaak, pulled opened the door to the outside of this shack because the bathroom was, you know, outside on the second floor. In the cold. And the dark. Cold toilet seat. Light on timer. Back to our room. Freezing.

We turned on the dim light that illuminated the dirty drawings on the dingy walls. We dressed and packed in silence. Well, except for the groaning. It was hard to shove everything back in our backpacks. Every single morning was a struggle because the packs are not made to stand upright. They fall over. They go lopsided. They fight you. Pulling on strings to loosen the bag. Stuffing the stuff bags inside just so. Pushing and pushing. Thunk. The pack falls over and to the side. Again. And again. Frustrating and no way to avoid it. Swearing.

"Do you have my long-sleeved black merino top?" Dave asked me. "I gave the woman two of them to wash yesterday and I only got one back." No, I didn't have it. "Where is it?" We squinted, looking for the missing shirt. "It's not here." And the saga begins. No, the shirt did not turn up. Dave

Breakfast.

asked downstairs, gesturing wildly about the shirt, the laundry, not getting it back. Apparently, it was gone for good because no one knew anything about it or could find it in the "laundry room." Grumbling, Dave put on his other warm shirt. That shirt was expensive. And now he was down to one. "Not happy!"

We ended up back down in the dining room for breakfast. It wasn't too bad but it was not Parador-worthy. Orange juice, café con leche, some toast and butter/jam. Advil. It was still quite dark out and though it was quiet, more people were moving around. Dave noticed a black shirt draped over a chair in the other room. "Is that my shirt?" He went to investigate but it was not his shirt.

And it was now, on Day 2, that I had a scathingly brilliant[7] idea, brought about by that handy taxi from yesterday. Maybe we could just send my backpack on ahead to our next albergue for the night. Today. Just for today. There were ads in the other room for just such a service – Jacotrans – they transport the mochilas (backpacks) for pilgrims. We picked up an envelope, threw in six euros, attached it to my backpack, and left it for the guy in the van to pick up and deliver to our destination. We checked our map and decided where we would stop tonight. Twelve miles today. To Santibanez.

It was a better day, as in not rainy or as windy. I carried our green daypack with what I thought I'd need for the day. Lipstick. Essentials. Dave added my rain pants and jacket to his pack and carried it for me. I still carried a lot of stuff with me – took me quite a few days to realize I didn't need much of it and then just left it in my bigger backpack to be transported. Dave caught on later, too, and stuffed a lot of his heavier things in my backpack, which suddenly weighed about 40 pounds...

Lightened up, we escaped out the back door of the place. It was still

---

[7] See *The Trouble With Angels*

Happy to be traveling lighter.

dark but we were beginning to see some light. It was about quarter to eight. No one else in sight. We click-clacked our way through town, following the yellow arrows. Soon we were back on the road, walking on the shoulder, and out into the country. We passed field after field of dried and withered tall sunflowers and stalks of dry corn. Black, burned, or picked crops. Hay. Lots of strange-looking buildings, too, some in an odd design with bricks and little openings in the bricks. We thought they were maybe for keeping bees? We later learned they were for storing hay or feed and the design helped keep rats and mice out. That's what we were told. Not sure I believed it. Our guidebook may have said it. Allegedly.

My hip hurt a lot in the morning – for about the first two or three hours. Then it seemed to feel better. Must have worn the groove in or something. A few pilgrims started to appear. And pass us. "Buen Camino!" Yeah, whatever. "Is that guy wearing my fleece?"

But then, something incredible happened. We passed two people! If you want to be technical about it, they stopped to make a phone call, but still, we never saw them again so you have to consider it a win. For us. For Dave, really. And just on our second day of walking – I knew all my training would come in handy. I was in shape. Yeah, right. Other technical details might include those two people being the only people we passed in all our days on the Camino, but hey, it was a great ego booster!

After six miles, we stopped for coffee. I believe we were in Villavante. I had a Coca Cola Light and a ham & cheese croissant. Brief rest over, we

Marching west.

Scowling through a break. Not amused. The thrill of traveling lighter has worn off.

Bridge entering Hospital de Orbigo.

walked our way to our next stop, in Hospital de Orbigo. This was a slightly larger town and had the requisite cobblestones in the street along with an aqueduct - a cool bridge that stretched a long ways. There are 19 arches, though the river flows through only three. We were looking for an open bar to get something to drink and rest for a bit. We finally spied one down a side street and went in. It was dark inside but we went to the back of the place and it was fairly modern. They had a big bar, TVs playing, and there were a lot of tables. Taylor Swift was up there in a ballet costume in a video singing her latest song. Dave got us two vino tintos from the bar, which came with a dish of something I called to myself "croquettes." Four small round breaded something or other. I was not brave enough to try one. 1.40 euros. The price was right. For the wine.

We gathered our strength and suited up again to leave. Click clack, over the bridge. The afternoons were hard walking. I faded in the afternoons. My energy, my drive, my mood. The distances just didn't add up – seemed like we had walked at least twice of how far we should have, according to our trusty guidebook. And, so it begins. I start my list:

1. The guidebook
2. Martin Sheen (this is nothing like the movie – one scene after the characters were in Leon, they were marching into Santiago – it took us another 20 days...)
3. Father Tom (you MUST go on the Camino – neglected to mention anything about rain, wind, hills, rocks, sweat)
4. Jane Christmas (author of the first book I read on the subject)

The list shall continue later on...(and I eventually find my way onto Dave's list.)

It's now late afternoon and we had one last hill to go, I think. We started

A much nicer room.

down a hill into a long valley. The colors were really nice, it being Fall and all that. Long sweeping views of trees and pastures. Light shining down. No rain. It was actually almost maybe lovely.

It seemed to take forever to walk down into the valley and then into the town and then through the town. We finally saw a couple pilgrims sitting outside against a wall. Yes, there was an albergue right there. And there was Helena, the first person we saw from Hong Kong. We greeted each other. She seemed very happy to see us. She hugged us. We asked about the name of the albergue and it seemed to be where we were headed for the night. Albergue Frances! Yay! Our walk was over for the day! I felt so happy, too. Elated. Another day of walking done! We went inside to check in and Helena walked off. She was going on even more for the day. She was headed to Astorga for the night – just another 12 or 13 kilometers for the day. You've got to be kidding me. No way could I go another step.

We entered the courtyard, which was actually in fact very nice. Impressive. The typical clotheslines were strung around. I saw a few tables. We went inside the restaurant area and found a girl behind the bar. There were also flies buzzing around everywhere inside. They had the heat on, too, and it was quite warm. We were really sweaty from walking, too, but now it was very hot. We asked about a room and the girl signed us in. Thirty euros for the night. Again, we got our private room and with a bath to ourselves, too. Inside the room. Yes, my backpack had arrived. The young girl hefted it up and carried it for me. She led us to a marble staircase but first had us remove our shoes and leave them on a rack outside.

Upstairs we were in a nice enough room with two twin beds. We collapsed for a minute. And then Dave's bed collapsed. The mattresses were on slats and not really up to having people actually, you know, sit on them. "I wonder where my shirt is?"

Karen resting and watching the world go by. Drinking. No shoes. Giddy.

Turns out, we were the only people staying here. This was a new, modern albergue. However, the location was not one of the end stages of that liar's guidebook, and we were walking in the off-season. Astorga was the endpoint for today's page. Santibanez was in the middle of the page. We decided we liked avoiding the bigger points, and the longer distances. Our guidebook seemed to think 30 to 40 km a day was suitable. We were trying to keep to 20 km. So, it took us about twice as long to keep up.

We cleaned up. The bathroom was fine. No hair dryer but I was getting used to it. After we felt better groomed, we went downstairs and into the restaurant/bar area. We had a glass of wine and got on the internet. All was well. We then took our drinks and sat outside, against the wall like the other pilgrims had been earlier. No action going on outside. There was another albergue, the municipal (icky) one just across the street and down a few feet. We met the guy who had been sitting outside earlier, Joe, and he was staying over there. This was the typical albergue – about 5 or 10 euros, no more, and you were in the big room, bunk-bed style, with everyone else. There weren't many people staying there, either.

I was so happy to be done walking and drinking wine, I couldn't contain it. I walked down the street a little bit to see what was there. We were on a "main" street and just down the road was the church. I walked back and then went up to take a nap. I didn't feel great but slept for a bit and got up at 6:15. Mass at that little old church was at 7 and we wanted to go. Well, Dave wanted to go. I still didn't feel so great but went along, too. There was

Walking to Mass.

a "pilgrim's blessing" supposedly. We entered the old place and sat in the back on uncomfortable wooden benches. There were about a dozen elderly Spanish women scattered around to also attend Mass. A few men thrown in. I think there might have been two or three other pilgrims, too, in the back. It was cold inside and I was concentrating on not throwing up. Very nauseous. I chewed on another Pepto Bismol tablet. I was going to have to get some more of that somewhere.

The priest entered. Not a happy-looking guy. Mass started. Mass ended. What was that – about 15-16 minutes, tops. No homily. No music. Just the barebones basics. In Spanish. He did throw in a pilgrim's blessing from what I could discern. We tromped out and back to the albergue. Dinner was being served at 7:30. We sat down at a table and were handed the pilgrim's menu. Several of the old women from Mass entered and they gathered around a table. Apparently, they were making a night of it. Lots of commotion. Other people joined in and it was a pretty lively place.

Tonight I had the macaroni for my first course and then chicken. A huge amount of macaroni came on the plate, covered in tuna. I picked at it but, feeling sick, the tuna was not helping. Smelled like tuna. I tried to gesture to the waitress that my tummy didn't feel good and that is why I couldn't choke down the huge platter of food but she wasn't too happy me sending all that macaroni back. "Me gusta but me tummy is sick-sick" – Park Center High School Spanish IV (I got an "A"). (I missed "Guantanamera!") Lo siento! But, the bread was good. The chicken was not too bad either. Last night it

Dave and Joe, our new Italian friend.

had been coated and fried but tonight it was baked - more tender and moist, and actually rather tasty, if bland. The wine was starting to kick in. And then Joe walked in and asked if he could join us. From that point, our night picked up.

Joe ordered his dinner and we had a very enjoyable conversation. He's 22 and from Rome. Very personable, handsome, outgoing. He was very interesting. He is living in London and working as a waiter. He's been there about a year and a half but is thinking about moving to Spain as he likes it so much. He loves the food and the people. He kept his eye on the young girl behind the bar and was planning to chat her up later, I believe. After we left and went up to bed. Joe's English was very good and he was very talkative and wanted to practice his English. We found him very entertaining. As most pilgrims start their conversations, they discuss their day, where they stayed the night before, their feet, where they are going, etc., etc., and Dave mentioned his sad experience with his lost black shirt. Joe sympathized, saying he had lost a pair of underwear so far, but he was hoping to restock and pick up some more things in Astorga the next day – the biggest town around that would have clothing and such. After Astorga, there wouldn't be a place to buy equipment or clothing.

I was feeling better by now – the food helped, or the wine helped, or the engaging young guy helped. We ended with ice cream, helado, and that was tasty. A last check of our email, etc., and then we went up to our room. We were in bed and sleeping by 9 p.m. What a day. What a night.

And, the titles we tossed around earlier for our upcoming Camino book all seem to be appropriate:

- "There's no Nordstrom on The Camino de Santiago"
- "I'm Gonna Need a Lighter Rosary"

- "Do You Know the Way to San ... tiago?"
- "Are We There Yet?"
- "The Camino They Didn't Walk"
- "Are You Kidding Me?"
- "I Think I Made a Huge Mistake"
- "Why Are There no Benches Along Here?"
- "Is Anyone Else Hot?"
- "My Hip Hurts"
- "I don't Feel Like Walking Today"
- "Where's The Bus?"
- "Just Kill Me Now"
- "How do you say "taxi" in Spanish?"
- "What the Hell are We Doing?"
- "The Soul of a Pilgrim[8]"
- "There's No Licorice in the Albergue"
- "Murder on The Camino"

and, my favorite —

- "Bottom Line – This Sucks!"

---

[8] A la Diane Chambers – soul of a dancer speech – from an early episode of *Cheers*.

Nightmare

Interlude

"It's 6:30. Time to get packed and have your backpack downstairs to be picked up."

Dave spoke to me from his bed. We had asked about sending my backpack on again in the morning and they wanted it downstairs at 7. Sounded very early to me.

I got up and dressed. I started packing my backpack. Shoving stuff in. Crap, the thing kept falling over. It was pitch dark. Stumbling around, I was still so tired. It was going to be a long day.

Dave spoke again. "What are you doing?" I said I was packing. Dave said, "It's only 11:30."

"What?"

So, apparently, one of us was crazy, talking in our sleep, misunderstanding, or something. I was just glad it was still only 11:30 p.m. and I could go back to bed. I was still dressed but I laid down and conked out again.

"¿Donde Es Don Alvaro?"

Saturday, October 18
Santibanez to Castrillo de Polvazares
(33,639 steps/14.69 miles/66 floors)

Ow.
Ow.
Ow.
6:30 a.m. (again) and now it's time to get up. Again. For real, this time. Ow. Ow. Ow. Again. Besides the packing-in-the-middle-of-the-night episode, I woke up several more times throughout the night. My legs ached and that kept me awake. The swearing didn't help, either. Dave's bed collapsed in the middle of the night. He eventually just put the mattress on the floor and slept there. I tried not to move much so my slats wouldn't collapse.

Pitch black again. I was already packed – hah. I finished dressing, moving gingerly. Dave lugged the backpack down the stairs in the dark. I joined him downstairs for breakfast. It was a little after 7 and we each had a donut and a café con leche. Hey, we actually had two. "I can't survive on breakfasts like this," Dave stated. He started adding sugar to his coffee for the extra calories. There were flies everywhere in the room. Annoying. I'd be glad to be moving on and away from the flies in this town. I mean, how many flies could there be? Surely there couldn't be flies all the way to Santiago... right? Today we were headed for Castrillo de Polvazares – 12 miles or so away, at least according to Liarley. One last use of the Wifi and I posted on Facebook:

> *Yesterday (day 2) was much better. But ... Body achy but at least not hurt. Weather mucho better – threatening but did not rain on us. No wind. No mud to speak of. 12 miles. 6 hrs walking. I'm slightly faster. There's poop everywhere ... Dog poop, deer poop, other stuff to avoid, as well as tons of rocks. Don't know why we brought rocks over here. Spain is full of them. Roosters are thriving over here too. And they don't stick to crowing in the morning – they do it whenever they feel like making noise. Keep hearing them.*
>
> *But. There are moments ... Like walking into town (downhill) where we were staying last night. Very nice albergue. Dinner last*

Sunrise.

night with 22 yr old guy from Rome – a highlight. 12 more miles today – through Astorga and then to albergue 6 miles past that town. Can Skype here and kids are good. VA came thru for Jim – a relief – David and Isaac good – sent picture of Isaac asleep in our bed – cute. Matt hopefully got his new phone. Time to get moving.

We checked out at 8:30 when it was a little lighter and better to start walking. It was a nice sunrise. We walked and walked across fields this morning. We saw pumpkins, lots of pumpkins, cows, sheep. Lots of cows. Evidence of cows. Geez, how many cows does Spain have? The evidence was overwhelming. And the flies. Wow. Really annoying. They flew about your face and your arms mostly. Trying to breathe in was difficult – trying to catch a breath without catching a fly, and also avoiding the smell of the country – those cows. Gag. We were really in rural Spain this morning. I couldn't wait to walk out of this area and away from the smells. How far could it be?

We had walked for several hours and were on a downhill patch, very wooded when suddenly those two café con leches kicked in. I had to go potty. The guidebook was no help — he advised we had miles to go before there was another stop available. And so I pottied in the woods. Just back from the path. So there I was, going potty in the woods and feeling good that I did it without making a mess or anything because, you know, I didn't practice this at home. I didn't get to this procedure in my training (ha ha – I'm just putting this in to give Dave a jolt when he reads the part about me training). So, again, there I was triumphant and about to rejoin Dave on the road who was standing guard when he yells at me, "Do you need the trowel?"

"No!"

Yes, Dave is a bit fastidious and insisted on carrying a trowel in case of

Lots of cows. Lots.

emergencies. I said that if I needed to go in the woods, I would not have time to use the trowel and I didn't care about not using a trowel. (Side note — that trowel is now back at home in my "garden" to help with my flower-tending duties – it was never used, by the way.)

It was a long day walking 12 miles. Or 13. Or 14. Or 15. Who the hell knew? It warmed up and there was no rain, so weather-wise, it was not bad, but there were lots and lots of rocks. They exact a toll on your feet no matter what footwear you have on. I had switched to my light hiking tennis shoes and Dave was now in his Teva sandals. I settled into my slow stride. I had a flashback to another movie we had seen about the Camino called "Six Ways to Santiago." One of the pilgrims being filmed was Annie, a middle-aged woman from America. I could now really relate. She was slow. Very slow. Plodding. Just one foot in front of the other. She knew it. I knew it.

Before getting to Astorga, we walked through lots of fields. We came through a patch of trees and up ahead someone had set up a makeshift "café" — a stand offering lots of different foods for pilgrims. All for a donation. There were a couple of "outbuildings" there, too, where this guy offered massage and what looked suspiciously like other services to me. Nothing looked too appealing but, at any rate, there was a bench where we sat to rest for a few minutes. A few other pilgrims walked by. No one was really in the mood to chat and we didn't bond with anyone.

About five minutes later, we steeled ourselves, stood up, and took off again. It was fairly sunny and we took a few photos of our shadows. Cool. Right? We agreed that this was the right time of the year to be doing this trek — the colors were really beautiful. The trees were peaking with their colorful leaves and the sunlight accented them. Throughout this area we saw lots of stands of trees — interesting landscape. And we couldn't imagine doing this pilgrimage in the summer. I'd die. Really. I really would. And next year –

There were many small shrines and statues along the way.

A much nicer walk in sandals. Note the shoes clipped to the pack.

A friendly respite area in the middle of nowhere.

Approaching Astorga.

Statue on the outskirts of Astorga.

2015 – was a Holy Year – I believe they were expecting record crowds, plus I think the Pope himself was going to be doing part of the walk, so 2015 was for sure off the calendar for consideration. Not that I was considering any more of this walking stuff. I was getting it out of my system now. I was especially hoping we would not have any trouble finding lodging for any nights – when we reached our destinations each day, I would not be able to keep walking if all the hostels were "completo."

We reached Astorga about 1 p.m. We saw the cathedral spires from a distance. They looked awfully high up. As in, high up on a hill. Dread set in; I knew what that meant. I was right. As usual.

We walked through a lot of the town and then the arrows pointed up, as in up the hill. We climbed and climbed. We finally got to level ground. I was feeling sick again and very tired. We stopped for a "Diet Coke." We then went into a pharmacy to buy some sort of Imodium-type medicine as I had sent my pills ahead in my backpack and I wanted something to take now to avoid any unwanted references to the trowel... I went in by myself as it was a small store and Dave didn't want to risk going in with his big pack on and he didn't want to "disrobe." He also likely did not want to be seen with a peregrina who needed Imodium.

I clearly stated my problem and what I wanted to the non-English-speaking pharmacist. After a bit of gesturing, which might have been amusing to passersby, he checked his computer for the "equal" medicine and sold me something he said was "just like Imodium." I paid and stuck the box in my pack. For emergencies. Like the trowel.

We trudged ahead, knowing we had miles to go past Astorga before stopping today. Astorga was one of the bigger towns on the Camino and Dave wanted to try to find a waterproof hat since the one he had was useless in the rain. We walked through the big plaza and there were lots of people out

Like many Roman towns, Astorga was built on a defensible hill. A big hill.

and about. We picked a place to sit outside at one of the tables and Dave ordered a beer and I had a vino tinto. The drinks arrived with a small dish of nuts. This was the typical appetizer usually served with a glass of wine – you got a small saucer of mixed "nuts," which included kernels of corn and dried crunchy stuff – think Deer Park in Park Rapids, Minnesota – you put a quarter in the machine and held your hand under the spout and you would get a handful of "corn" that you could feed the deer and bunnies. Yum. The woman also brought us the usual small plate of potato chips. The "hors' d'ouerves" and I use that term lightly, were tasty – I was craving salt. We were right outside the pilgrim-stocking-up shop and Dave went in to find a rain hat. He returned a while later, successful. But not happy with the price he had to pay. 60 euros, but that's a secret. He also had a present for me – a Survivor-type buff – Santiago! I loved it! I wrapped it right around my wrist – it proved to be very useful to wipe the sweat away from my forehead, and my nose, too. Very thoughtful! Of course, I washed it often! It was my turn to go into the store and I was looking for another merino wool short-sleeved shirt. I had just brought two and they were the only tops worth wearing here, so I was taking turns wearing the green-striped one and the black one. It only took a day (less actually) to get all sweaty and uncomfortable. But, no luck – no merino wool around. I'd be wearing my black top again tomorrow, smelly or not.

 We moved on and passed the Cathedral. It was closed. Impressive-looking but we couldn't go in to check it out. We stopped at an ATM and got out more euros – 300 of them. Thank you Navy Federal Credit! Then we passed a bread store and bought a baguette. For the road.

 And so we walked some more. We made one more stop at another café and sat outside in the sun. Felt great to rest again. So tired. So hot. So sweaty. So thirsty. We weren't quite sure of the road to take to get to our

The Camino buff!

albergue – it was off the actual Camino and we had to detour a little bit. Dave went over to ask a man seated at another table. He was a British man from Nottingham, dressed in typical business-like attire, slacks with neat sweater vest, all tidy and all. He was very happy to talk with us. He joined us. He gave advice. He stayed for about half an hour with us. Giving advice. I had to take out my journal and take notes. He said he had done this pilgrimage about 20-some years ago (in 1994, according to my journal and what I wrote down). He did business over here in Spain now and was very familiar with this area and for some reason, all the bars and cafes, and he knew all the owners (especially the women) throughout northern Spain. He had something to do with hospitals and I wasn't sure if he was a doctor or surgeon. He mentioned when he walked years ago, he did it as a fundraiser for some hospital or cause. So, he gave recommendations where we should stay in practically every town until Santiago, and then Santiago. I dutifully wrote them all down, with his opinions, and his thoughts about the food, the person running the place, and the best route to take. We finally extricated ourselves from the guy. He was on his way back to Astorga and had apparently walked because when he finally left us, he started walking the way we had come.

Dave went in to pay for our two wines – 4 euros! It was outrageous. After all the cheap wine we'd had, this was a ridiculous price. Dave's still talking about that place/that price. We began to doubt the accuracy of the British man since he really liked this bar and the woman who ran it. We agreed to take his recommendations with a grain of salt.

Home of the most expensive wine in Spain.

Still a long way to Castrillo de Polvazares.

Map of Castrillo de Polvazares. Note 'C' – location of Albergue Don Alvaro!

We had 2 km to walk until we reached Castrillo de Polvazares. Hah! Lies! We walked on the narrow strip beside the main road. It was a nice day. Sunny. Warm. Traffic was moderate on the road and we had to step off onto the median to avoid cars. I was ready to collapse in our albergue, which we should be approaching at any moment. Finally, finally, we came to the turnoff and saw that this town was sort of a "renaissance-type" place where people came to visit. Old Town. Buses dropped people off. There were lots of restaurants here. The streets were made of huge cobblestones – more rocks of course. There was an uphill path. Of course. Lots and lots of ancient buildings. This town is very important due to its history – something to do about the Spanish rebelling and fighting against the French.

We stopped at the bottom of the hill and checked the big map. We were staying at the albergue Don Alvaro. There it was on the chart, up about two blocks and then to the left and down. Number C on the map. I took a picture. Don Alvaro. We followed the instructions and walked round and round in circles. The place was a maze. We couldn't find the name Don Alvaro on any buildings. We couldn't actually find any albergues in the area either. We asked some people gathered outside one restaurant where we thought it should be if they knew of Don Alvaro. They had no idea what we were talking about.

We went in one of the restaurants and asked about the albergue Don Alvaro. No clue. We wandered about some more. We went back downhill to check the map again. There it was again. Back uphill and we went to the exact location. The building had a different name. We went inside, all pil-grimy and everything with our packs and trekking poles and exhausted sweaty bodies. The haughty host grimaced when he saw us and then when we asked "Don Alvaro?" Again, he said "non exist!" Does not exist? He was

"¿Donde es Don Alvaro?"

unhelpful to the nth degree.

Panic. Setting in. Quickly.

We had sent my backpack that morning to Don Alvaro, according to ~~That Goddam Book~~ our guidebook. We were going to stay there. What now? We had passed a municipal albergue a few streets down. We went back there. It was deserted and all locked up tight but there was a sign that I'm sure said ("Guantanamera...da da da Guantanamera...") to call a certain number and there was a house number, Number 7, to go check in at. We attempted to find Number 7 but all we saw were Numbers 3, 4, 5, 6 and 8. Non-exist??? We headed back again, past the same group of people standing outside the restaurant. We pretended we knew exactly what we were doing. This was the fourth or fifth time we'd passed them. We went inside a nice looking hotel/restaurant right across from the non-exist Don Alvaro place listed on the damn town's own map. There we asked the hostess if she spoke English. She didn't but she motioned the elderly bartender over. He was the nicest, most helpful angel in the world. Well, sort of. We explained our problem and he said that unfortunately his hotel was full. It was Saturday night and all of the places in this town were full. However! He said he would call over to the municipal albergue and see if we could stay there. We were very grateful.

We turned around to wait and, lo and behold, right behind us on the curvy stairway leading up to the rooms, sat my rose-colored backpack! A miracle! I was so, so, so happy. I hadn't known how we were going to track it down. The man told us to sit on the steps and wait and he brought us each a beer. Oh my god – the relief! He then said the woman from the albergue would be over in about ten minutes and we could stay there. She'd let us in. Oh my! A flood of emotions, but mostly just relief. And exhaustion. And man that beer tasted great. And then the woman showed up before we were finished with the beer and we had to leave it! Ugh. But.... Okay. We followed her.

We come to rely on the kindness of strangers, which is a major Camino lesson. Call me Blanche. Or is it Stella?

Karen is blessed, as well. Ok, she can be Blanche. Note the *Survivor Camino* buff on her right wrist!

Our second Camino miracle, after the appearance of the taxi on the first day. First we find a saintly helper and then we find the mochila.

Not so pleased and no-speaka-the-English, but she motioned for us to come with her. Dave picked up my backpack and carried them both down the street, past the same rowdy party across the street, and then down the side street. She held out a key the size of her fist and put it in the ancient wooden door. This used to be a castle. I think she was trying to tell us some of the history of the place. The door creaked open and we entered into a small, very tiny, courtyard, and then another key and we entered into the apparent kitchen. The woman signed us in, stamped our credencials, had us fork over 5 euros (each), and then with another huge key showed us upstairs via an uneven spiral staircase where we'd be able to stay the night. There were seven cots there in a very cold room, big windows, two tiny bathrooms. We had the place to ourselves. It was not so nice, but we were so grateful.

She explained several times how to lock up, where to leave the keys (very important), and then she left. We picked two of the beds and spread our stuff out over most of the other five beds. We decided to shower and clean up first. Dave went in one bathroom to shower. He had understood the woman to say it took about five minutes for the water to get hot. I understood her to say not to take longer than five minutes in the shower or the hot water would run out. I was right. Of course. The water started out hot and then didn't last long. We changed and fixed up our beds for the night. There were some well-worn blankets folded up on another bed but there was no way we were going to crawl under those.

The man at the hotel had said to come back for dinner. They were having a closed, private party, but it would be okay for us to come and he could feed us. What a saint! He really was a life-saver and a compassionate, wonderful man. So, looking a little better, we went inside and up a few steps into the restaurant. They were indeed having a large party – about two dozen men

Sanctuary! So happy! Our own castle!

"How much would YOU pay for seven cots in a castle?"

Dinner was wonderful. We had an enormous tureen of soup to slurp through – we couldn't finish it.

and women in their 20s and some younger. Not sure if it had to do with a wedding or baptism or other event. There was a baby there. They were all seated at a large table and even though it was only about 6:30, they were about done with their dinner. Dave and I sat down at a table nearby. The waitress came and shooed us away and to a table in the corner of the room. Okay then. Bring back the bartender...

We didn't have a choice about dinner although she asked us to choose a soup to start. I believe Dave chose a squash soup and I had cream of onion soup. We then shared some sort of "provencal" chicken dish that came with French fries. They brought us wine but it wasn't great tonight. It was a little fizzy. It wasn't a great dinner but it didn't matter so much. For dessert Dave asked for fruit and they brought him a sad plate of, well, fruit. A bruised banana. Potentially a Spanish kind of pear? I think. Maybe something else. Couldn't really tell what type of fruit it was. I think I passed on dessert. The bill was 28 euros.

The entertainment consisted of discussing our day, planning the next day, groaning about our aches and pains, and watching the antics of the dinner party across the room. A lot of the young people had moved outside and there was a lot of drinking going on. A lot. Several of the young boys were really drunk and getting sick. They brought one boy in and the waitress said he could lie down on a couple of chairs. There was a lot going on in the back room and in the bathroom. It was noisy and fighting was starting to break out and there were a lot of impatient kids lined up at the bar waiting for more drinks. It was starting to get a little frightening.

We paid the bill and left, hobbling back to our own castle for the night. The bartender had said we could bring my backpack back over the next morning and the transport guy would come and take it to our next destination,

Happy to have a place to sleep. Author Note: Dave took this at 6:30 a.m., and I had no make-up or even lipstick on at that hour. Editor Note: She looked marvelous anyway!

according to the ticket we filled out. He said to bring it over and leave it in the back of the place at 8:30 a.m. He also told us that it was supposed to be nice weather for the next 12 days. What a great guy!

We were back and locked in and in bed by about 8. It was freezing cold and I slept in my down vest, my warm jacket, the sleeping sack, and the fleece blanket. Brrr. But very, very relieved.

"Those Annoying Walks"

Sunday, October 19
Castrillo de Polvazares to Rabanal
(23,139 steps/10.11 miles/73 floors)

Ow.

Ow. Ow.

Ow. Ow. Ow., etc.

Why am I doing this to my body? I like my body. Why am I doing this, period? Good question and one I ponder today.

We didn't sleep very well – it was very cold and the place was not heated. We got up at 7-ish, dark outside, no activity at all going on. It's a different rhythm of life in Spain with sleep, work, and eating all carried out at much later times. We never get used to it. I do like the "siesta" afternoons, though! We dressed quickly and repacked. Thunk. Thunk-thunk, pack falls off the bed. Dave carried my backpack down the street and left it behind the hotel to be picked up later in the morning. Trust. Someone will pick up my bag and deliver it to the right place. All will be well. Today's destination is Rabanal, a shorter day but it looked like we would be walking steadily uphill. We were basically at 900 m and Rabanal was at about 1100 m. It would be one thing if you just walked and climbed up the 200 m, but no, you had to go up a ways and back down and then do it again, over and over. We crossed a lot of rivers/riverbeds and when you went down to the river, you had to climb back up on the other side again. Sigh.

We left Castrillo de Polvazares around 8. There was nowhere to have anything to eat yet, so we made our way out of the town, downhill. We had to walk our way back (up) to the actual Camino since we were somewhat off the trail. We walked through a lot of country to finally reach our first stop for a coffee and croissant about 9 a.m. Our next scheduled stop was El Ganso, a few more kilometers down the road. I wasn't feeling so great again and when we finally reached the little village I had a Coca Cola Light. And Pepto Bismol.

We met a man named Chris along the way and he also stopped and sat with us. He recommended that we get a Spanish cognac – a sweetened brandy. He always did. He assured us it went very well with one's morning café con leche. We declined but made a note of the info. He is from England and

We had put an hour under our belts by the time it was daylight.

was friendly enough. His married son lives in Seattle, though, and he had visited there and so was happy to talk about the States, etc. However, the first thing he brought up was a question – he was very puzzled about his son. Apparently, the son used to be a big drinker (though not an alcoholic or anything like that – heavens, no) but suddenly the son just stopped drinking. Just like that. No discussion or anything and he won't talk to his dad about why. The wife still drinks. But, why would someone do that? We had no comforting answer for him, I could tell. We ran into Chris a few other times along our way and he was still thinking about that. I guess it bothered him quite a bit.

One of the things you experience here is the "accordion" effect. You meet people and then start walking and you think you'll never see them again, but at various stops along the way, you do. People walk and spread out and stop where you don't know and some you think are way ahead of you turn up behind you. You come together again. And, it's funny but when you see someone again, it's a great reunion. You're so glad to see them again. We met people we thought we'd never see again but we did, and then we hoped to see some people and thought we would at the end, but we never ran into them again. You wonder. What happened?

Anyway, our short break was over and we got up to walk some more. We only had about 7 more kilometers to go until we reached Rabanal (if you believed our guidebook). Sounded pretty good. It was hard going. We walked and walked and headed up some steep inclines. There were a lot of flies buzzing around and it was rather sweaty, though a cold, dank sweat. We reached a patch where we were headed up, it was wooded, and there were trees around. Footing was difficult with big sharp rocks pushing this way and that on the path, and along the side was a very long wire fence. Woven into the fence were sticks fashioned into the form of crosses. All different shapes

Arriving in the first town of the day for our morning coffee break.

and sizes. Other materials, different colors. And thousands of them. Dave picked up a couple of sticks from the ground and bent them into a cross and then stuck it in the fence. We stopped to rest, er, to look at the crosses quite a bit. When I lagged behind too far, Dave would stop and insist I take a big drink of water. He was carrying both our liter bottles of water. It was a good reason to stop and it looked better than having everyone just pass us. He was still concerned about our speed, or lack of, and I was still insisting he just go on ahead and I'd catch up. Eventually. Probably later today. Maybe. He never did get out of sight, though, and I never did get any faster. The amusing part was that with each pilgrim that passed us, Dave was looking him over with a keen eye – is that my fleece?

It was hard going. I may have said that already. I was having a lot of serious thinking going on in my head – no, not about anything important, no profound thoughts, no epiphanies, no praying, nothing I thought I'd be doing or pondering. Disappointed I wasn't thinking important thoughts. No, I was still stuck on this stuff sucks and why the hell am I doing this again? What a stupid idea. This is the worst thing I've ever done. This is the hardest thing I've ever done. I'm not feeling any spiritual or religious fuzzies. I don't get the feeling that thousands of other pilgrims have done this before. Why did other people do this? This is crazy. It's so tiring and exhausting and painful, and for what? I don't get it. I just don't get it. This is a conspiracy – no one else can like this! This is everyone saying how great it is and telling all their friends, yeah, you should do this, too! It was great! Well, I can't wait for this to be over. I really want to be done. I'd quit but I don't know how. I don't want to do this.

But – a big but – I was also feeling so glad I did this. I would have regretted not doing this Camino for the rest of my life. That's a true statement. I would have thought I was missing something great. Now I won't have to regret it,

Crosses on the road to Rabanal.

and I wouldn't have known how miserable it really is! At this point, it's all lies.

I started to pour all this out to Dave and, surprisingly, he was kinda sorta really actually thinking the same thing. But, he went a little farther – "Whose idea was this?" Yes, yes, yes, it was my idea. (But he was the one who insisted we must do it now! Now I say! Before we get any older and more frail...) And I asked – people are doing this pilgrimage because St. James' bones are buried in Santiago? Yeah. Right. Wink, wink. I highly doubt that. Sure they are. And we do this to, what, get some sort of special get-to-heaven-quicker card when we die? No, I guess that's not part of the deal. And other people told me that some people a long time ago used to do this pilgrimage on their knees. You've got to be kidding me!

Resting.

So, the quickie version of this pilgrimage – the why and the what the hell is that St James' bones supposedly are buried in the Cathedral in Santiago. You can see them. Well, you can see some bones. Well, actually you can see a box that allegedly contains some bones. I read that James was an apostle – a great saint, trying to get people to believe way back when, but he doesn't do such a great job there in Galicia, Spain, so he takes the two or three other guys that he did manage to convert back to Jerusalem with him, but unfortunately, he is quickly beheaded by Herod. The thanks you get... So, he's a martyred saint now. And no one is sure exactly what happened to his body or bones and such but hundreds of years later and with a lot of hocus pocus, some priest finds some bones/relics in a field and declares them to be James. Takes them to Santiago, a small village at the time, which turns into a big venue then with the sacred new bones and all. Go pay homage to the martyr. And that's why people are doing this pilgrimage. Yeah. Right. Wink, wink. So, I'm a newcomer to the Catholic game, er, religion, and I'm not so great at math but they want you to believe that a plus b equals c, but even I know the correct answer is e – not enough information...

So, back to my question. Why am I doing this? True, the scenery is pretty spectacular. True, I'm pretty sure I'm losing some weight. True, if this isn't helping my blood sugar numbers, then I just give up. But, is that it? I haven't listened to any music – it doesn't seem right. I really don't want to have songs going on in my head. It's not like my brain's busy with philosophical thoughts or anything, but music just seems wrong for the moment. I haven't focused much on praying, except for the "please God get me through this day," or the alternative, "please God don't let me die" – and we've seen a few gravesites already along the Camino. We haven't made any great buddies. I can't walk with anyone because I'm slower than every other person out here, and that includes some pretty old guys – though most everyone is a lot younger than us.

And, we've certainly noticed that when we start to talk with other pilgrims, the most common first question you are asked is where you started and our answer of "Leon" (not St. Jean Pied de Port – the correct answer) is not popular. "Ohhh. Well, bye." Most people started there at the beginning, and a few started even farther away. However, a few did start later in either Pamplona or Leon, and we have heard stories that people have taken buses or taxis quite a bit, and that is something we don't plan to do, so "score" one for us! Although...I had a thought. Maybe one of us could hurt his leg, turn an ankle, or something. Then, we'd have to take a bus, or taxi, or quit, or something. It would be terrible but we just wouldn't be able to continue – couldn't risk permanent injuries or anything like that. I mentioned it to Dave and told him I felt quite guilty hoping he fell over in a ditch. Sigh. He seemed to be doing fine.

My next daydream involved us just hopping a bus, maybe to Paris, and hanging out there for the next three weeks. I was wondering if anyone back home would notice. We could still post updates and such. I'm sure I could make something up that sounded dreadful. While I was sipping my café au lait and eating my fresh croissant, gazing up at the Eiffel Tower or walking along the Seine. I made a note to ask Dave what he thought about bus to Paris, etc. – next time I caught up to him. I may have been dawdling.

So, today was a thoughtful day, not what I wanted to be focused on, and it was a hard day, and it was another day when I felt sick to my stomach, and it was kind of a down day because I'm not feeling what I expected or thinking what I thought I'd be thinking. But, we did get to Rabanal about 2 p.m. – so that is shorter than previous days. We reached the town and of course had to walk a steep uphill incline to get to the center. Cobblestones. Quaint. Brick buildings lining each side of the one street. But suddenly something caught my eye that cheered my disposition. Right there walking down the center of the street toward us was a St. Bernard (or a similar breed) female that was obviously lactating. And that alleged St. Bernard had a full-size baguette in its mouth. She was just slowly walking toward us, bread in mouth, and not caring a bit.

I was very hot and sweaty and still feeling nauseous. Per the British man we met a day or two ago, he recommended the Hostel de Refugio, and that's where we were staying. We continued walking uphill, panting, when we walked past the Benedictine Abby. Dave stopped to look at the bulletin board outside and translated that there was a Pilgrim's Mass and blessing tonight we could look forward to. He thinks. We added that to our schedule and kept walking. There was an odd man there in the street, looked like a gypsy in dress and by the flute-like thing he was playing. We gave him a wide berth. Then we noticed that our hostel was actually right across from the church and we doubled back and went inside. We were in the restaurant area and asked a woman tending bar where the "recepcion" was for the hostel. She pointed next door as the two places were connected. We walked through

St Bernard. Allegedly.

and she followed. She checked us in. And, best of all, my mochila was sitting right there in the hallway!

It was expensive – 50 euros for a private room. She led us upstairs and showed us our room, small but neat. The room reeked of insecticide, which I'm not sure is a good thing or not. We opened the window to air it out a little but flies were coming in, so we closed it again. We hadn't eaten, so we went back to the bar and Dave ordered a beer. I felt like I was going to throw up, so I asked for a lemon-lime drink (7-Up or Sprite, which they didn't have) but the woman brought me a lemon drink from a can. I tell you, it tasted so good. It really soothed my stomach and was the best thing I ever drank. In my life! I had two.

With our drinks came the requisite hors' d'ouerves – this time a plate of potatoes in a zippy paprika/oil aioli. Patates Bravas I believe is the technical term. They were wonderful. Tasted really good to me. I polished most of them off in no time and asked for another plate, please. Dave ordered a chorizo bocadillo. The woman said she would do our laundry if we could get it to her right then, so we gathered all our stuff together and brought it down. There was no dryer, so when she brought it back at 4 it was still wet and we hung it outside upstairs on the patio to dry. We sat in the lounge area upstairs trying to get Wifi but it was not working well (to Dave's great dismay), so we went back to our room, waiting for the clothes to dry.

Dave decided to go look for some fly or bug spray but he didn't have any luck, though he did have an ice cream while he was gone. Dave did tell me something encouraging, perhaps. He had talked with a pilgrim woman who said she was on her 29th day and she didn't start to feel good until Day 21. Wow. I guess I have some days to go.

I went up to take a nap, which would have been great except the gypsy outside had found two friends and they decided to camp right across from us

Best. Drink. Ever. – In Rabanal. Pre-shower (also pre-death)!

on the street, each playing an instrument. One had a flute, one got his hands on a guitar, and the other had a harmonica. At least they weren't singing. Oh, but the gypsy also apparently had a dog, who was howling to the music as he also seemed to object.

There were a lot of flies, inside and outside. The room still smelled of pesticide. We did manage to nap until about 6:30. The Benedictine Monks' Vesper Service across the street is at 7 to 7:40. We plan to attend and afterward have dinner. So, we shower/clean up and, dressed in our only finest clothes, walk across the street and go inside the ancient church. It's cold. It's filling up with people – where were all these people before? We haven't actually seen very many pilgrims walking the Camino. Pretty deserted really. Most of these other people must be staying at the municipal albergue that is on the other side of the church. We sit in a "pew" – hah – hard bench toward the back. There are two monks. One is talking in Spanish – how frustrating! I catch on that he is saying not to take pictures of the monks but to pay attention instead. It hasn't actually started, so I take his picture. Finally, the event starts and the two monks begin chanting. There are booklets that we picked up and we follow along. It's a long "show" but is quite moving. There is some sort of rhyme and reason and service they are following. I recognize parts of the Catholic Mass, in Spanish and Latin. There are some sing-songy parts. It ends.

Everyone files out. Dave and I recognize the two women we had run into a few days before – Sue and Beth. They are with a couple other people. We ask where they are headed for dinner and they ask us to join them up the street at a restaurant. We go in and get a table for six. It's Dave, Beth (from Palm Springs), Mark from Erie, Pennsylvania who we learn has just beat third-stage cancer and is doing this pilgrimage as a thanksgiving, and then me, Sue (from Canada), and a girl from Australia, Roz, with whom I

Rabanal laundry

hit it off right away.

Our dinner is very interesting. This is our first chance to interact with a bunch (flock?) of other pilgrims. Over a meal. Everyone speaks English to begin with and is in good spirits. We hear Mark's long story about his cancer and all the details. We hear about Beth and how she wanted to do the Camino alone and had to tell some of her friends she didn't want them to come with her. We hear from Sue that, again, this is her second Camino, with an explanation – two years ago she did this but had to take a bus and only walked partway from Leon due to injuries or something, though she did finish, and this year she had started at St. Jean (of course) and had finished her first Camino at Leon and was now on her second Camino from then on. Or something like that. She remembered we had started in Leon. "Oh." She said she was so sad that we were almost done – only another week or so to go and I just blabbed, "good." She looked at me appalled! "Good?" I went on to explain about how I was having a hard time getting into it and the spirit of everything, the rain, the first night, Koreans singing with harmonicas, Swannee River, etc., etc., and how hard it was and my body hurt, and I just didn't get it. She looked at me again and I think moved her chair a little to the right.

Roz, on my left, completely agreed with me. She wasn't "drinking the Kool-Aid" either. She was doing much better, though, and wasn't still feeling like me, but she did understand my point of view. She had started from St. Jean (well, good for her). She said she was now starting to feel better carrying her backpack, which weighs something like 30 pounds. We laughed together and shared a lot of stories. Sue ignored me. But then the conversation changed, as it does, to children, etc. Sue had children but "they don't live at home." She spoke up loudly, "I think it's bad for kids to live at home." "It's not right." Beth agreed – she had kids and one granddaughter but she lived

Dave's Ice Cream

over an hour away. Dave and I had been pretty quiet but now, after the wine was served, I piped up a little. "Oh? That's too bad. We have a grandson – our greatest joy! What a sweetheart – we see him all the time and he's at our house about half the time. We love it!" And then Roz asked me more and it came out that all three of our kids are at home. "How wonderful!" and so on and so on. And then more stories come out and Roz ends up saying she can't hear very well and she thought Mark had said he was from Transylvania and not Pennsylvania – mucho laughter all around. Then she said people were talking about the walk and for a long time she was thinking "wok." We agreed that walking is hard and Sue is in denial. Love that girl!

But, Dave had the best line of the night here. He spoke up when we were talking about how hard it was and our experience so far and blurted out that for us the Camino has been a "series of fun dinners interrupted by annoying walks!" Sue actually laughed and loved it – asked if she could use that again and she wrote it down. More laughter.

Dinner turned out to be very good that night. My first course was the pasta with meat sauce and it actually had a lot of flavor tonight – in a positive way. No tuna to be seen. Or smelled. I ate most of it. Second course was pork chops, which were bland but tasty. Ice cream for dessert and, of course, wine throughout. My nausea went away and I was happy. All for 11 euros.

We finished up with dinner and went back to the church for the pilgrim's blessing at 9:30 p.m. It lasted about half an hour. Again, we referred to the booklet and paid attention. This time, we sat near the front. I was in a

Camino Chamber Orchestra

better mood, feeling much better. I was getting into the spirit at the moment and relaxing, and letting go in this setting was awesome.

At 10 we hugged everyone goodnight and went across the street to see our hostel all closed up tight, locked, dark. Doors would not open. Hmmmmm. We tried at the restaurant/bar door. Closed tight. We walked back to the church but it was now deserted. No one in sight. Everyone had really scattered quickly – like a bomb went off or something. The streets had emptied and we were alone. Starting to panic again. We headed back to the hostel and tried banging on the door. No response. I was beginning to think we would be sleeping in the street when Dave came down from up at the bar entrance. He said the manager had come to the door and would let us in. Ahhh, relief. We went up to the second floor, collected our nearly dry laundry from outside and retired to our room. Today had been a shorter day – only nine miles. Tomorrow would be uphill to the Cruz de Ferro where we would place our rocks. My body still hurt and I was still lacking inspiration. Maybe tomorrow would be better.

And then a light bulb came on! A distant memory of one of my favorite sayings – "bad decisions make good stories." And then I knew this was going to be a doozy and I looked forward to putting it all out there – the truth! The whole story. I was going to write a great book!

Vespers at the chapel of the Benedictine Monastery in Rabanal.

Rabanal dinner. Coming attractions: note the group of French pilgrims at the long table in the background. We will see them again in Ruteilan!

The Day We Catch On

Monday, October 20
Rabanal to Acebo
(28,600 steps/12.49 miles/99 floors)

Ow. God, it stinks in here. Ow. Ow. Ow. Phew. Thank God, though, for small favors – Dave's bed did not collapse. I slept through the night. I woke up. Ready for another day...

Up at 0-dark-thirty. Again. "How is your blister doing?" I asked Dave and peered down at his feet as he was greasing them up before putting his socks on. "Hmmmm, doesn't look too bad" I said. I guess we'll be able to keep walking today. Sigh.

We wandered downstairs for breakfast, which consists of orange juice (freshly squeezed, of course, here in modern Spain), pan tostado (toast) and café con leche (of course). A few other pilgrims appear in the breakfast area. "Is that my fleece?"

Thunk. And, my backpack is left for the mochila-carrier. Best seven euros ever spent! Today's destination is Acebo – pronounced "A-Thee-bo" – about 18 km. Up a big hill. Down a hill. How hard can going downhill be? Insert foreboding "dun dun dunnnn" sound here.

We left Rabanal at 8:15 in darkness. Duh. It was always possible to trip over all those rocks on the path in the dark. I clung to that hope, sort of. Alas, our bodies were in control today and actually maybe even getting stronger. We walked uphill for two hours to Foncebadon. The day is going great! It was hard in the morning going uphill but since it was morning I was not too awake or alert. Still hard. I'm getting better, though. Stronger and faster. We made 3-1/2 miles uphill in 1-1/2 hours. Wow. The views are getting good. It's always nice watching the sun come up and seeing the light spread to the trees and fields. And flowers. And watching our shadows appear. I have been taking a series of photos of my shadow. It's an interesting perspective. Well, to me.

We finally reached Foncebadon, or the sign that declared we were in Foncebadon. We got a picture of me collapsing on the sign. But, we still had to walk to the actual town, which generally is quite a distance (and uphill) from the sign that lets you know what town you're almost in. We found Foncebadon at last and stopped for a Coca Cola Light (and Dave a café con

Leaving Rabanal

leche) and talked with other pilgrims at the small café. We saw one pilgrim and his wife walk by without stopping and they had their belongings on a cart with wheels, pulling it up the hill. There was another dog at the café with huge paws. I took some photos. I like dogs. Especially big dogs.

We also saw Sue and Beth here. They had been here for a bit because Sue was eating a bowl of soup and said the food was very good – they hadn't eaten anything as they had stayed at the municipal albergue last night in Rabanal and left without breakfast. Sue pointed at my head and asked, "earmuffs?" and I explained that cold air in my ears makes me dizzy and sick. She had given me a little gruff about wearing lipstick the other day and now the headband? She was not my favorite person at the moment. Beth left without saying anything and I guess went on. We never saw her again. Sue said she'd see us at the Cruz de Ferro. Although Sue was probably 65 or older, she was a fast walker. And talker.

We finished our drinks, used the servicios, and were on our way. It was one-and-a-half miles to the Cruz de Ferro (a big iron cross). Up. More up. Up some more and we finally reached the top. This was the highest point on the whole journey. Over 1500 m. So, it was pretty difficult. All that up. But, rounding the corner in the distance we saw the cross and were moved. Sort of. The iron cross itself is not so exciting. To me, it looks like a tall telephone pole with a thin metal cross stuck in the top. But, this is the monument that means the most to a lot of people. Just reaching the top of this mountain and seeing the tall pole is something. And the rocks. Thousands and thousands

The day dawns. We walk.

Foncebadon. Allegedly. Lying sign. We were only getting to Foncebadon. There was still a hill to be climbed.

Packing after breakfast. Sue is in the black. We see the man in red a week later in Fonfria.

of rocks and mementos that people for years have left in remembrance is moving. Dave found this to be very emotional. A lot of this was possibly because he was about to unload five pounds of rocks he'd been carrying. Or maybe it was something more.

There weren't many other pilgrims on the road today. However, we were waiting our turn to have the mound to ourselves and the one other pilgrim up there was taking his time. His significant other was taking his picture this way and that, and it was getting to be a little much. Dave was working on his patience and I'd say struggling with it. Finally, we got our turn and I went up and dropped my rock (I had found it after thinking I'd lost it) and Isaac's rock – the big one he'd given me from his Big Sur camping trip the weekend before. I know on Facebook in a moment of self-pity I suggested that I might just throw my rock at the Cross but I did practice self-control instead and placed it gently, sort of, near the top of the pile. Dave emptied the bag of rocks he'd been carrying representing many family members. I think he had at least 35 rocks with him. While I had asked for friends' favorite songs to add to my play list, Dave had said he'd do more and carry a rock for them instead that he would place at the cross. He's so competitive – I got 42 songs, but they're lighter. I concede that he got a "heavier" response.

In the movie and in other literature I've read, one generally recites a short prayer when setting their rock or memento on the pile. It goes like this:

> "O Lord, may these stones, symbols of my efforts on the pilgrimage, and of the efforts of those who have supported me and who accompany me spiritually, which I lay at the foot of the Cross of my Savior, weigh the balance in our favor on that day when all the deeds of our lives are weighed. May it be so. Amen."

Karen places Isaac's rock at Cruz de Ferro

The movie version is a little different. The gist is still the same.

Dave filmed his short recitation to commemorate our little ceremony. The German couple who had been hogging all the time up there agreed to take our picture and we had our photo taken together for posterity.

We saw Sue when we got here and greeted her. Since she is much faster, she was done much sooner than we were and she left. We weren't too far behind – after ten to 15 minutes at this stop, we loaded up again and took off. Downhill. The top was 1500 m and from here, today, it was downhill to Acebo. The scenery was great – the weather clear and sunny. Fabulous. You could see the mountains in the distance. It was very nice. So long as you didn't think, well, we had to go over those mountains in the next few days. And today was downhill from here on out. Well, sounds good except I now have lost a couple toenails from that descent. I'm sure that's where it all started. Wow. Who knew? Downhill was very, very treacherous and difficult. Very rocky, easy to turn an ankle or fall. Luckily, neither Dave nor I ever fell or tripped.

We proceeded down for hours. At one point I laughed when Dave decided he should pick up a rock to take home with us from the Cruz! We walked for 1-1/2 miles to the next major spot in our guide, to Manjarin. We planned to grab a bite to eat here and rest up. We were amused upon approaching the "town" of Manjarin, which turned out to be a point in the road that had posted lots of signs for various world-wide cities and their distances, a la M*A*S*H* . There was a makeshift "building" (tents) where we could rest. There was, however, no food or drink to be had or for sale. You could sit at a table under cover and you could buy various souvenirs, but that was about it. No bathroom to speak of. There were a lot of pilgrims here, many who had brought their own provisions and were munching on them.

Dave and I sat outside the covered portion on a wall. It was hot. Very hot.

The peregrinos at Cruz de Ferro

Dave and his return rock.

Manjarin. 222 km to go.

Dave unzipped his pants (the legs - geez) and finished the day in "shorts." There were several cats darting around. We couldn't do anything here except rest for a bit. No water to fill our containers. We were hungry and wondering where we could grab something to eat. According to that alleged liar, our guidebook, there was nothing at all until we actually got into Acebo. We should have stocked up and carried something with us.

And so we continued walking. The scenery at this point was wonderful – spectacular. The fall colors were outstanding and we saw hills, farms, cows in the distance. Red trees, yellow trees, beautiful fall colors. It did help to walk when you were in such beautiful surroundings. We followed the narrow dirt track along the edge of a mountain looking far down into the valleys below. We went around a corner and saw a stand set up for pilgrims – fruit and water available, for a donation if you wanted. We deposited a euro or two and grabbed an apple. There was a bench under a shaded tree. Dave pulled out the dull knife he had bought a day or two before from a street vendor, and sliced up the apple. It was the best tasting, most wonderful apple I had ever eaten in my life. I've never tasted a better apple! Wow. A Minnesota Honeycrisp had nothing on this apple. Sitting in the shade, resting, with the cows and fall trees under us stretching into the distance, and eating the most delicious fruit ever and drinking our water – wow – it was one of the best experiences of our trip. I mean it.

We continued along our way, the narrow dirt path following the curve of the mountain. We descended some more, very rocky, and down, down, down. The tips of my toes were hitting the ends of my shoes. They were very sore already. You had to pay attention to what you were doing and where you were stepping. This took hours. The sun was very hot, too, in the afternoon. It was quite miserable. Again, there were great views but we were hungry with nothing to eat. We were almost out of water. I was not nauseous today

The trail is rocky and steep.

as I began to realize that maybe the queasiness had to do with all the Advil I had been taking for the soreness and achiness of my body. So, I stopped with the Advil. I hurt more but wasn't feeling as sick. What a tradeoff.

We finally reached Acebo in the late-afternoon. Unfortunately, we had sent my backpack ahead to an albergue that turned out to be "non-exist!" Again! Thanks, goudebook, you ~~stupid, annoying, maddening, alleged lying~~ noted reference. The albergue in your book does not exist! And we do have the most recent edition of your guidebook from 2013. So frustrating! There was an albergue that looked very nice and inviting as you entered Acebo at the beginning of the town and they had an outdoor café that was covered to shade the sun, and the place was hopping with pilgrims relaxing. Not hopping, of course after all that walking - just sitting. We looked for my backpack there. No luck. Across the street was another albergue. No luck again. The street continued downhill and while I sat at the top of the hill, Dave went down, checking each place for my mochila. I was hot and miserable. Hungry, thirsty, and really, really out of sorts. My toes hurt. The tips of my toes. So hot, sweaty, tired, really exhausted. And then Sue showed up from under the covered albergue. We talked for a minute, mentioned our missing mochila and non-existent albergue. She was no help, not interested, said, "bye" and that she was going farther today. "Bye, Sue."

Dave finally approached me from down the street. Success! Ah, relief. Sweet relief. The mochila-deliverer had delivered it to an albergue down the way. And Dave had better news – we can stay at the albergue down there

The best apple, ever, about to be cut with Dave's new Camino knife. This was such a good break!

or at the next-door neighbor's house, who offered us a place to stay, too! We walked down the street and decided on the albergue as the neighbor sort of retracted his offer when we spoke. Peace in the neighborhood and all that. So, we checked in and for 36 euros got a private room on the top floor with a shared bath. "Top" floor being the relative word here. We were led on a topsy-turvy route through the restaurant/bar, café, outdoor area, indoor area, stairs up and then up and then up another flight to our room. Flies again everywhere but the room was sufficient. It had a pitched roof and it was pitched in three areas. We had to duck our heads to get from bed to bed and then to the door. I knew Dave would hit his head at least once during our few hours there (which actually did not happen). I guess I don't know everything. Epiphany #1?

We relaxed for a minute and unpacked. There were three beds in this room and we spread out. The bathroom was down the hall but just at the next door. Another couple was staying in the other room on the floor. The shower looked to be broken. It was in a tiny little square that you had to step way up and into. There was a shower curtain. The hose with the attached shower head was dangling in the small tub and could not be fixed to the hook up high on the wall where it would do some good and, like, be above your head. We decided we'd explore the shower more later. We went down the three flights of stairs, not hitting our heads on the lower clearance, and sat in the bar near the door. We were hungry and ordered beers and bocadillos.

On top of the world, looking down on creation.

Did we mention it got hilly?

Attic room in Acebo.

We were about to eat our late lunch when in walked Roz! Happy to see her. She sat with us and ordered her own sandwich. We talked and laughed and continued with the bonding we had started back in Rabanal. She's a teacher, not involved with a boyfriend at the moment, but wishing she was, has a bit of a crazy family, and is a really fun spirit. Half an hour later, she got up and was anxious to get moving. She planned to go on to the next town since she had the energy and was feeling good and felt like walking. So, she left and we never saw her again. Sigh.

Dave and I went upstairs and had a nap. It was sweaty and the air was uncomfortable up there. Afterward, we each took a shower in the broken tub and felt a little better. I managed to spray water all over the floor and I felt sort of bad about that but it's not my broken showerhead. I did sacrifice my towel and use it to wipe up some of the water on the linoleum so the other people wouldn't slip. It was uncomfortable like I said and I wasn't feeling great. I felt sort of sick again and thought I needed more water. I was still tired and my body really hurt. It's hard to sleep when the tips of your toes hurt more than you can imagine those little parts could hurt and it goes deep.

We went downstairs for dinner and sat in the restaurant. The place was half-full but throughout the night it filled up with other pilgrims. We met a couple from Napa, another woman traveling alone, and then were intrigued by a large French group at a big table to our left. About 12 or 14 of them. I ordered the pasta that was not so great for a first course and then the pork chops with French fries. I drank a lot of water, which seemed to help, and some wine but it didn't taste very good to me, so I didn't drink much. Dinner was only so/so. Dave and I agreed that we needed from now on to make a call-ahead reservation at the place where we wanted to stay the next night to make sure it was "existent." So, tonight we asked the owner to please call to make us a reservation in Ponferrada at Hotel Novo. A name we picked out

Hello, Roz!

of our alleged guidebook. A stab in the dark but we trusted the guidebook – wait, maybe I did drink too much tonight... He agreed and secured us a room. That was a relief.

After our dinner, we went outside where it was pitch dark again and quiet. No one appeared to be about. We decided to try our Skype and see if we could reach anyone. We first tried Matthew, whom we woke up and was uncommunicative. Next up, David, whom we woke up and had nothing much to say. We tried Dave's mom, who was not home. We tried my mom, who could only mention that her computer would not let her see a map of Spain so she could not follow where we were, and, it looked like we'd lost a lot of weight but we should keep trying to lose more weight... I then tried Mimi and got a hold of her but nothing much was new there.

And with that, we were exhausted and headed for bed and it didn't take long to fall asleep, toes or no toes.

Today's online post:

> *Monday - a much better day. I'm getting stronger and faster. Left Rabanal at 8:15 in pitch darkness. Walked uphill 90 minutes and then another hour til Cruz de Ferro – uphill some more. Left our rocks. Now time for downhill for several hours, all on rocky steep "ground" – actually much harder. Body really hurts but not hurt hurt just hurting. You know. Dave decided to pick up a rock to take home ... Now in albergue after again sending my backpack to non-existent hostel (feeling anger toward the author who wrote the guide we are following – he is Number 4 on my list now.). Jane Christmas is Number 5 by the way. I have taken up swearing also ... One week down ... Happy though!*

"Can You Read My Mind?"

Tuesday, October 21
Acebo to Ponferrada
(31,567 steps/13.79 miles/35 floors)

We were up at 6. Again, it was dark with lots of stars out, which meant no rain again this morning. I tried to take some pictures with my phone but it didn't work – too dark, stars too far away, incompetent camera-handler. You know. We learned that the owners did not do breakfast here and wouldn't arrive until 9 a.m. The downstairs was all locked up. And dark. Too dark to take pictures, as well. We packed up, paying close attention so we wouldn't knock our heads into the pitched ceiling. We brought our backpacks downstairs (three flights – insert ow, ow, ow, ow, ow – three flights worth here), and left them in the courtyard while deciding what to do. Dave still had to work on his feet, which were developing blisters from the sandals. He sat on the stairs in the dim stairwell. I assisted. Ointment! Vaseline! Scissors! Moleskin! Tape! Gauze! Scissors! And in-between I'd have to run to the other wall to turn the light back on – again an automatic timer that went off about every 20 seconds. Very dark with the lights off. Very energy conscious there in Spain. Very inconvenient and goldarn annoying! My swearing skills were improving.

A few other pilgrims were up, too, from the main bunk-bed compound, er, room and they didn't know what to do exactly either. Some just packed and slipped out the side door – on their way early. Well, not really early but it felt like the middle of the night with all that darkness. Dave's feet prepared, we decided he could just walk my backpack back up the street to the beginning of Acebo and leave it with the other mochilas at another albergue that was open. So, at 7:30 he marched off and I sat in the street and waited with the rest of our stuff. for half an hour. Dave felt compelled to have a cup of coffee at the shop that agreed to hold my mochila for pick-up.

Dave returned and we click-clacked our way out of town. A few hundred meters down the road on the left we saw a brand-new modern albergue on the corner. It was not in our guidebook, of course. We could have stayed

Sunrise leaving Acebo.

there if we'd been willing to walk just a little bit farther the day before. It was lit up and looked like desayuno was going on in there. We kept walking. The sun started to come up around 9. I was actually feeling pretty good and sprightly today and moving quicker than usual. We were walking on the road and going downhill. We were dropping like a rock. Our guidebook promised we could stop for breakfast in about 3.8 kilometers. I looked forward to it.

We continued our downhill pace and came upon three Japanese kids in their early 20s I'd guess – two guys and a girl. The girl was in very bad shape, limping with her left foot twisted in and barely able to move. We asked if she was okay and if she needed anything. She didn't have any poles and neither did her companions. She was really hurting. Dave insisted she take one of his poles. I gasped. He persisted and said she'd need it to get to the next town where she said she planned to buy a pole. Dave said we'd be stopping for coffee at the first place – only about a mile or so according to the authority (liar) and when they got there, she could give it back to him. She finally agreed. Dave let go of the pole and the girl thanked him. We moved on. "You're never gonna see that pole again," I said. "Sure I will. She'll catch up and I'll get it back." Uh huh. Like your black fleece. I said that to myself, under my breath, quietly. Yes, sometimes, I do mumble. For a reason.

So, we walked on. We went down over very rocky slate and steep hills for three to four miles. I know Dave was sort of regretting not having two poles and I know I couldn't have made it without two poles to balance on. It would have been easy to turn an ankle or fall. We walked through one town but no one appeared to be up and no café was open. We walked some more. The guidebook was now number 5 on my list (in addition to being number 1) – it made the cut twice. Each town/village that we trooped through with no desayuno also made my list.

On one downward portion of rough road, we met two men and a donkey

One-pole Dave.

Rocky trails descending from Acebo to Molinaseca. Karen continues downhill unfazed.

Peregrinos returning from Santiago with their pack donkey.

on their way up, but we never did find an open bar to have anything to eat. After all that going downhill, we switched gears and started going uphill. And more uphill. We ascended for quite some time and then went around a bend. Time to go down for a while. We finally came out of this wooded portion of the track and, with a little more downhill, we crossed a road and reached Molinaseca and found it to be a quaint, pretty town. We crossed an historic Roman stone bridge to get into the center of town. We had run into the people from Napa from the night before on the path. They are Paul and Stephanie and they had come into the restaurant for dinner and sat at a table behind us. They are probably in their late-50s, a popular fun age, and he was outgoing and friendly – she was more reserved and quiet – older women tend to be like that. Uh huh. She was thin and happy enough but we learned that Paul would walk on ahead of her because he was faster and she would catch up. They stopped to rest and take in the view and we went on. I would consider that passing someone (two people). Of course, ten minutes later they passed us, but I don't believe that counts.

Dave and I ducked into a corner bar in Molinaseca and ordered "the usual" – café con leche with a croissant for me and toast for him. It felt good to sit down and rest for a bit – our morning break was late. We did after all have to wait for the limping Japanese girl to catch up. But, alas, she did not show up. We asked people if they had seen three Japanese kids along the way, with the one girl very badly limping. A few people said they saw them and they were not very far behind us – they were in the last town we passed; however, most said they had not. "You're never gonna see that pole again." You're more likely to find your black fleece...

We decided to stop at a pharmacy before leaving town to get more advanced blister supplies, as Vaseline wasn't cutting it. We found an open store and the pharmacist was very helpful. She picked out what Dave would need

Molinaseca was beautiful. Simply beautiful.

for his feet. I was browsing, checking out the Spanish drugstore products when – Ooh! I noticed the makeup and most notably the lipstick display. "That one is gorgeous!" I must have it! So we added one stick of rosy gloss to our supplies. "Ooh! Fly spray!" That was Dave. That was an absolute necessity, too, so we paid for our things and left. We went back to the center of the square and sat on a bench in the sun. Dave fixed up his feet and I tried out my new pretty lipstick. We spritzed the bug spray all over. We were both satisfied. We marched on.

We met up with Paul again and he tried to give us some advice about our poles/pole, which he said when they were in Nepal some guru or someone told them that you are actually supposed to have the poles adjusted much lower than at the right angle where the deaf REI salesman had instructed us. So your forearms slant down. "It takes some getting used to, but then it works and feels great." Uh huh. I nodded and left my poles how they were. Dave adjusted his pole in agreement with Paul. Pilgrim solidarity and all that. I wasn't messing with my poles. It wasn't too long before Dave was readjusting his pole to how he had it set previously and swearing at Paul under his breath.

We walked. Now that I look at that liar's book, it seems we went about 20 km today. From Acebo past Ponferrada to Compostilla. A long way. Longer than 20 km. I just know it.

I'd been looking everywhere for Mark and Susan. Mark is my cousin I haven't seen in about 50 years (well, actually that's not true – I did see him and Susan and had dinner at their house in Dallas in February 1982 – but I haven't seen them since and I hadn't seen Mark before that night since about the time I was five). The day before we left on this trip, my cousin Lisa had sent me a FB message. She said her brother, Mark, and his wife Susan were doing the Camino and I'd probably run into them. I wrote back immediately,

At the Molinaseca Pharmacy. Note the lipstick display to the right.

Yes, it may look like it, but I am not having a stroke. Here. Yet. Not really feeling the love at this point.

The scenery is sustaining me.

excited and with questions. Where are they now? How long are they going to be on the Camino? When do they plan to finish? What date did they start and in what town? Lisa was vague and replied "I don't know, I don't know, I don't know, I don't know, and ... I don't know." She said Susan had shoulder-length red hair and to look for her.

I never did run into them and halfway through our Camino, Lisa messaged me again to say they were off the trail now and in Morocco[9]. I was disappointed – I would have liked to hear what they truly thought of the ordeal, er, experience, and what they were thinking. I was anxious to hear what everyone really thought. I wanted to take a poll of everyone who passed us (Why are you doing this Camino? Are you really, truly enjoying it? Is it what you expected? Are you getting the religious fulfillment you expected? Why are you walking so fast?). Support me or not, I wanted to hear some truth. I wasn't believing what I'd read in every book for the past five years. Just tell me the truth. What am I missing? Am I the only one? I don't comprehend – don't understand. ¡No Comprehendo! All these other people we're seeing, passing us, well, why are they doing it? And at breakneck speed? They're mostly very young. Do they not have jobs? Just something to pass the time? Are they looking for something in their lives – for answers? Are they religious and doing it for spiritual reasons? They weren't stopping in churches that I'd noticed or going to the pilgrim Masses. Those were the older people.

Our Camino was not turning out like we watched in the movies and documentaries and You Tube videos we'd seen – we hadn't encountered any big groups of people sitting around, laughing, massaging each other's feet, having conversations and ceremony/mass type congregations. Not once did anyone offer to massage my back. Of course, we weren't staying in the municipal

---

[9]Must have seen that movie, too.

albergues, but even those did not seem to be very full this time of year. The private albergues we were in did not have many staying there, either. We were in a private room but they also had the big communal bunk-bed room. There was no big cooking going on, which we did experience the first night and which I did want to avoid from then on – made me sick to my stomach. So, part of it was the time of year, I'm guessing – we picked the late fall in order to avoid crowds – we wanted to make sure we could get a place to stay. So, other people who were walking then probably had the same thoughts, and we weren't a huge social bunch all out there walking at the same time – no desire to get together and commune.

I was feeling a different point of view now from at first – I had thought the only reason one would do this pilgrimage must be for religious reasons. At this point, I was not feeling any religious tuggings. I hadn't been able to pray, or have any meaningful conversations with myself. I hadn't been able to concentrate on anything. I hadn't had any epiphanies. I hadn't felt closer to God. And I appeared to be the only one who was feeling like this. I was dying to meet someone who was experiencing these same feelings. I felt very alone in my thoughts – I felt kind of dishonest and like I must be missing something. Right then I was thinking a better reason to do the Camino was to commune with nature, do good things for your body – exercise-wise, maybe lose some weight. But, it was early-on still and maybe, just maybe, my experience would change and my opinion would also change.

But for today, after a lot of hard walking this morning, we finally got to Campo and had lunch. We were very hungry. By now we were walking in the sun and it was very hot. The streets went on and on and we could tell we were reaching the "suburbs" of Ponferrada, a larger town. We could also tell by the arrival of the "bread truck." Sometimes when we were walking into a small village we'd see a van come screaming down the road and the driver would hit his brakes, pull over and stop and lean on the horn for about 30 seconds. A really loud sound. The bread's here! He was delivering bread from the bakery to local stores. The horn would go off like a siren and the owner would come out and pick out his bread.

We knew we were staying in Ponferrada, so we were happy to be nearly there. We were having trouble finding places to eat and we finally spied a bar on the right side of the road and we walked over. There was a patio upstairs but you apparently were to go down some stairs to order. So, we did. Walk down some stairs. Ow. Ow. Ow. Hard on the knees.

We entered the darkened bar area and found a young, very tiny, very cute girl tending the bar. She reminded me of my niece Becky – very pretty, long dark hair, smiling eyes, may have had dimples. The place was rather crowded with men and from the décor we discerned that we had apparently walked into a "biker" bar. Also because of all the motorcycles parked outside. We ordered two Coca Cola Lights and then bocadillos for lunch. She didn't have plain cheese (solo queso) so we ended up with the typical jamon. She brought them up to us to eat outside. We sat and took a breath. We were both

Lunch at the Biker bar. Dave is starting to lose a lot of inches off his neck.

Karen at lunch on the patio of the biker bar.

The castle at Ponferrado. Note the dog-friendly Camino shell marker.

exhausted, and we still had a way to go. We were happy we had reservations, though, and it looked to be a hotel – a step "up" from where we'd been staying in hostels, even with private rooms. We didn't have to worry about getting there soon – we could take our time since we were assured of a place to stay.

We ate our lunch and a friendly dog appeared to keep us company. He sat at my feet. He liked me. Or, it might be because I kept feeding him pieces of jamon – I can only take so much jamon before the queasiness surfaced. We finally sighed and got back up again. We walked another hour or so into Ponferrada and, up a hill again, because you know you can't just build a city on flat, level ground. It must be raised so everyone can see it from far away. We crested one hill and then saw the Templar's Castle in the literature and the Liar's book. Very impressive. It was time for another rest, so we found one right across from the castle on a busy street. Dave went inside and ordered and I collapsed at a table outside. The waitress brought out either beer or wine – I frankly can't remember what we drank – but also sugary churros with a cup of melted hot Godiva chocolate to dip them in – that part I do remember! Yum. That really perked me up. Our old friend, Sue, had mentioned that she had had churros dipped in Godiva chocolate along the way. Well, we did too, now. Very tasty.

I watched the people passing by and at this one particular corner it appeared to smell awfully good to a lot of different dogs. To amuse myself, I took several photos of dogs relieving themselves on the cement Camino shell marker across the street next to the castle. If there weren't so many people around, I might have been tempted myself to let everyone know what I thought of the Camino at the moment.

So now that we're in Ponferrada, the hotel's got to be fairly close by. Right? Right? Anyone? We walked and walked and walked forever. The

Churros with Godiva chocolate. Mmmm. Note the happy smile. Not.

book showed 4 km. It took hours. It was so hot – record-breaking heat in October for Northern Spain, did I mention that? We crossed a bridge and then headed out of town and onto other roads. We kept thinking we were seeing the hotel because we'd see a big building and the hotel supposedly was large enough to have 400 rooms, but each building turned out to not be a hotel. We walked through a large park at one point with several historic-looking buildings. We passed a school. At the tennis court, we asked two high school kids, "¿Donde es Hotel Novo?" I mean, how hard is that to understand? They had no idea. They hemmed and hawed for five minutes. Hotel Novo? No idea. That scared me since we had to be pretty close! We must be way off base. But, it turned out they were just two dense students who didn't know anything about their neighborhood.

We continued walking and now were in a residential area. A man pulled up in a car - obviously the owner of the house right there. Dave asked him, "¿Donde es Hotel Novo?" and shoved our Liar's book in his face with the map. The man hemmed and hawed. Geez, does everyone hem and haw in this town? Hotel Novo? He thought for five minutes. He then tried to explain that we had to keep walking – not more than 2 more km – straight ahead – and then on the right. Big building. If you pass the freeway or go under a tunnel, you went too far. "Gracias!" I was sure that was what he told us.

We walked on. Yes, we finally did see the sign and the tall hotel up ahead on the right. Yes, a clue for the clueless – "Hotel Novo (free air conditioning)." It was next to a tunnel and the freeway. And, yes, it was built up and on a

Where's that darn hotel?

hill. We had to climb a steep driveway to get up to the front door. Click, clack, I was really lagging. So hot. So exhausted. Sweaty. Bad mood! It was late in the day and I started to not do well any day after 1 p.m.! It was now about 5 p.m. We were still a distance from the front door – up a flight of stairs – when we could hear a commotion going on inside. What the heck?

We entered a spacious lobby area with a long reception desk but it was full of people, most notably toddlers and babies in strollers, most screaming. To the right was a big room - the bar area - and it was overflowing with people, also making a huge amount of noise. Everyone was "dressed up" according to Spanish standards and this was a wedding. And, according to some Spanish customs, everyone was completely trashing the bar room. There was paper and trash all over the floor. The tables and chairs were scattered everywhere. It was a mess! The man at the desk attempted to check us in over the din. We were appalled at the craziness going on and the noise and the man just shrugged and said we were in Room 216. He pointed to the elevator. Most importantly, he pointed to my backpack behind the counter. We grabbed it, squeezed into the tiny elevator (smaller than the Hotel Columbus elevator in Rome[10]) and went up to check out our room.

This was indeed a hotel, although slightly seedy, but a step up from a peregrino hostel. The room was okay. It was very warm. It faced the front of the parking lot and freeway, and was very noisy. We were on the second floor but could hear all kinds of screeching noises coming from somewhere. I couldn't figure that noise out. We unpacked in our usual fashion – like our backpacks had exploded and regurgitated their contents. The hotel advertised free Wifi, which was non-existent, at least upstairs. They also had huge signs pointing out the free "air-conditioning" but we couldn't get our control to work. When Dave asked later about the a/c he was told that "This is

---

[10]See *Death On the Hop On / Hop Off Bus.*

The Hotel Novo. Finally.

October! No a/c!" (and the implied tone, are you an imbecile?) Even with the record-breaking heat, no a/c. "Impossible![11]"

So, we laid down to rest for a minute on our bigger-than-usual bed. When the reservation was made for us the night before and the owner asked if we wanted two beds or one bed, his wife who was walking by at the time chimed in - "one bed!" Of course! So, one bed it was. Not quite a queen size but bigger than a double, I think, and it was fine. I kept hearing the screeching from somewhere and wasn't able to take a nap. Dave did a little laundry in the bathroom sink and hung his garments around the room. Ahh - just like Rome again! Hopefully, they would dry by tomorrow. We took showers and that felt pretty good. It was a nice shower.

We dressed and then went down to see if we could get a drink in the bar, find some decent Wifi, and check when dinner was available. We found the downstairs area deserted. We walked outside for a minute to see if we could see any other nearby bars or places to go sit and do some Internet surfing, but we were beat and didn't see anything. I didn't want to walk back into "town." We saw that the wedding party had moved to a downstairs room where there was a lot of dancing and music going on. Think "gypsy party" in "The Way." We went back in to the bar and were shocked by what the party had left. What a gigantic mess. Really a disaster and this was a very large room.

We went over to a corner and sat by the windows. We kicked the trash from the floor away and cleaned off the table. Dave went up to the bar and ordered two glasses of wine. They happily arrived with the usual plate of potato chips. I again was craving salt, so munched on them. The wine tasted great. As usual, when we stopped walking and were cleaned up and drinking

---

[11] See my favorite movie, "Dirty Rotten Scoundrels" and the great "jail" scene for correct intonation of "NO! C'est impossible!" by Anton Rodgers as Inspector Andre.

The trashed Hotel Novo – this picture does not do the wreck justice.

a glass of wine, it was paradise! Even in this piece-of-filth bar. Dinner was not served until 8:30, so we were gonna be here a while waiting. I didn't care.

We watched the bartender start to clean up - resigned but apparently used to doing it. And then I heard the familiar screeching sound again - the bartender was moving the chairs and tables back to their designated areas but doing it without picking them up - they made a huge scraping noise on the floor. The sound I could hear two flights up! It was like nails being scraped down a blackboard. You'd think a rational person would pick up the chairs to stop the racket, but apparently that wasn't done here in Spain. At least the mystery was solved. Not satisfactorily, but now I knew what was driving me crazy. And, hopefully when they were all set correctly, the screeching would stop.

We were on our second glass of wine when another pilgrim couple entered – the only other people around. They came over and Dave asked them to join us. They introduced themselves – they were Lynne and David from Australia. They started on their wine and sat with us. We spent the rest of the night with them and had a really fun time – the first time I have used the word "fun" in days. They were talkative and we soon learned all about their lives and family and their Camino experience, and everything else about them. We chimed in, too, but it was more a listening experience. Lynne was a larger woman and apparently had trouble with her knees, so they were able to hike up the hills but then would take a cab or bus on the downhill parts. I also learned that both of them were sending their backpacks on ahead. They were "walking" longer distances than us each day, though.

We all shared our aches and pains and Dave lamented his blisters, which were getting worse. The other David shared his experience with Compeed – a European salve for blisters. He explained how to apply it. First you warmed the Compeed in your hands, then you held it on the blister, keeping your

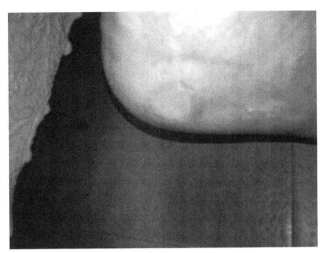

One of Dave's blisters.

warm hands over it until it adhered to your skin. Then you left it in place for two to three days, until it fell off. You couldn't peel it off as it would peel the skin off your blister. We noted all this. We said we'd pick some up at the next pharmacy we saw.

We also spent some time discussing the Spanish healthcare system and how it worked for pilgrims from other countries. Apparently, David had been very sick with a cold or cough or something (hopefully not ebola - ha ha - is that funny yet?) and he visited a hospital or doctor. The cost was covered by Spain and he thought it was a great experience. He was given a prescription, which he took to a pharmacy and they filled it there. They then gave David the prescription back. Apparently, there was no accounting for the medication. We discussed the difference in systems and David said a few days later when Lynne came down with the same illness (I moved my chair farther away from them), they just went to another pharmacy, handed over the same prescription and they gave Lynne the same drugs that he had received. Very nice!

It finally reached 8:30 and we went into the huge dining room. We were handed the typical pilgrim's menu-del-dia menu. I excused myself to go to the bathroom and found the typical light-on-a-timer situation. I went in one of the stalls, finished up, and was ready to get out of there. Unfortunately, I found the door would not open. At all. I yanked. I pulled. The lock would not give. It was stuck. Really stuck. And then the lights went out. The lights that were located outside the stalls. Of course. So, I started banging. There was no one around - the hotel and dining room seemed deserted for such a large place. So, I banged some more. Really loud I had thought. Finally, the door was yanked open. The waitress had just wrenched it open. She looked at me. I looked at her. She left. No word, no explanation, no apology.

I went back to the table. Mad. Like, really really mad. Very annoyed.

The offending trap door.

Dave looked at me and asked if everything was okay. I glared. Lynne looked at me and said she could hear this loud banging. Was I okay? "No!" It took me a good ten minutes to calm down. Locked in the bathroom?! I was at the end of my rope.

But, we all ordered dinner. I had the usual pasta for my first course and pork chops for the second. Accompanied by the usual French fries. More wine. More bread. Ice cream for dessert. Not exactly "real" Spanish food but what they feed pilgrims. I guess.

We said goodbye and went up to our room. We had made our plans earlier for the next day - 20 more km to Villafranca del Bierzo. But now, with no more screeching, we fell asleep.

"Bringing Sexy Back"

Wednesday, October 22
Ponferrada to Villafranca
(31,278 steps/13.66 miles/62 floors)

There are roosters everywhere. You hear them crowing at all times of the day. Lots in the morning, sure, but throughout the day you can bet on hearing a rooster. And you'd see them all over, too. Most families had roosters instead of dogs, I think. Chickens, too, but we certainly noticed a lot of roosters. God, it's like walking through Prunedale... if I'd ever walked through Prunedale. Certainly, Prunedale has their share of roosters, and chickens, and rural, backward county roads.

Today was no different and as we started out, cock–a–doodle–doo. Repeat.

I woke up feeling pretty good. Maybe it was the bigger bed? We were down to just an "ow, ow" or two. My legs were better – the hip actually didn't hurt much anymore. My feet were fine – no blisters of any kind. They felt pretty good – just generally a little swollen each morning but after I had walked up my first hill or two, they were feeling okay. I was worried about the ball of my right foot. It sometimes felt like I was walking on a pebble or hard rock under the skin, but so far it wasn't too bothersome. Dave's laundry was nearly dry. He planned to pin his socks to the outside of his pack and "air dry" as he walked.

I was in a good mood. I started plotting out my book. "I had a farm in Africa...." No, wrong book. Then I start to wonder who will play me in the movie adaptation[12]. Yes, I'm coming around. Laughing to myself.

And then it gets better. Finally. We had gotten some breakfast in the bar downstairs. Just us. The place was still in decent shape. I guess the gypsies, er, wedding party, didn't stay the night. The waitress brought us freshly squeezed orange juice, café con leche, and a croissant. Dry bread but a good start. It was very dark out, still, but we set out, down the hill of the driveway, under the tunnel and along the freeway. Dave had his flashlight out so we wouldn't miss an arrow. We walked farther out into the country, through some small villages. Then, leaving one village we were on flat land and walking alongside a country road. On our left out on the horizon was a

---

[12] Helen Hunt. – Ed.

Roosters!

mountain range. Beautiful. We were approaching a mountain range ahead, too. The sun was rising and there was a mist rising in the fields on our left and our right. Stands of trees with the sunlight made the leaves glisten. More fall colors. For hours. I didn't mind. My body wasn't taking my attention today. The scenery was. It was absolutely gorgeous. The fresh air, the sun, the temperature. All agreed with me today. Maybe I was "getting it." Until Dave mentioned that that mountain range ahead of us was getting closer and "you do realize we have to go over it?"

But for now, we just walked and Dave went ahead a little bit today – not very far but I was lagging because I was taking a picture of every tree and leaf and bit of mist and flower I was seeing. So beautiful. Saw some sheep. Cows. I heard lots of dogs barking. Chickens. Not barking, just chickens. I just couldn't pass it all by. Dave already thinks I am taking a picture of every flower, especially every rose, I see in Spain but, in my defense, they are so lovely and colorful and thriving and alive and I am compelled to capture it all. And, certainly there were a few flowers I didn't shoot. I was also taking pictures of a lot of those roosters, chickens, and animals we passed, and interesting houses, bricks, gravel, trees, and rocks, and I just wanted to be able to look back at all that we encountered. Because it was all amazing. To walk by at a slow speed, to see everything and not rush by in a car, was very appealing. So long as your body agreed. And my Pepto Bismol was holding out.

We stopped for a coffee at a small bar in Camponaraya. We were the only ones there, except for a few locals, for about ten minutes but then we were joined by a rush of a dozen or so other pilgrims. They were all catching up to us now. I wondered where they had started from this morning. We spoke with two of them – Fred and Debbie from Ft. Smith, Arkansas. We chatted and "bonded" over our coffee. They were walking at a much faster pace than

There are hills in our future beyond the early morning mist.

One of the many thousand exceptional flowers that Karen was compelled to photograph. Oh, and a downspout.

A little art with your café, senor?

we were. They'd started in St. Jean, of course. I had expressed my feelings of not quite "getting it" yet and Debbie agreed. She also said exactly what I had thought at first – "if all you have to do is walk, how hard can it be?" So, I liked her. We laughed. Dave asked if they'd seen three Japanese kids (one a limping girl) since she had the pole he'd given her and wanted it back. No, they hadn't seen them. On the wall behind Dave was a large sketching of a naked woman. Very interesting pose. Camera handy, I took a picture.

Time to move on and we got up. As we were leaving, our old friend Sue arrived behind us (ack!), and so did cancer-survivor, Mark, from Erie, Pennsylvania, not Transylvania. We introduced Sue to Debbie and Fred and they hit it right off. Talk, talk, talk. They later passed us at a fast rate, click-clack, click-clack, talking a mile a minute. Lost another friend...Oh, well.

We walked on and in a while realized Dave was going to need to fill up his water container. It was about half full but it was "old" water and he wanted to change it out. We approached a fountain outside with a water spigot. Dave emptied his bottle and put it under the faucet to fill it up. He turned the handle. Nothing. He turned it farther. Still nothing. No water. Dry. And now he had emptied all of his water out. So, he was a little annoyed. That was a good lesson and now whenever we needed to fill up on water (if there was no bar around to be filled at the tap), we made sure it was potable and flowing first. We never did pass any of those free wine fountains where you could fill up on the local vino tinto. Should have started in St. Jean...

Continuing on, and now the scenery changed again. To be even more beautiful. After hours of walking, a lot of it hard-going, we passed into "wine country." We started by trudging for about an hour up a long country "road" made of pebbles/small rocks. It did hurt your feet to walk on it but there was no avoiding it. The sun was beating down already and we were hot.

Beautiful country.

We finally got to the end of the rocky road, crossed a paved road, and then started on a downhill path. There in front of us on either side were fields and fields of vines. Laden with purple grapes. Trees all over with their leaves in bright reds and yellows. Blue sky, sunny, clear, just as beautiful as I've ever seen anything. The grapes and vineyards were amazing. Dave stopped and reached his hand out to a nearby vine and picked off a few grapes. A little seedy, but they weren't bad. Dave was getting a little annoyed again because I was walking a bit slow now but we worked that out. We were back to our routine of him stopping to wait for me, offer me some water, let other pilgrims pass by while we were engaged. Yes, we know and heard over and over that you walk your own pace, your own Camino, and it also doesn't matter where you started. Right. Wink, wink. Leon is a fine place to start. You betcha[13].

We reached Cacabelos, a pretty town, which Dave declared to be his favorite place so far. We were ready for lunch and looked for a place to stop. This was a fairly big town. We were walking down a narrow road, brick, with shops and such on both sides. We spied a bakery and went in and bought some sort of plain bread and a sausage wrapped in bread for Dave. We walked a little farther and found a larger square with more restaurant and bar opportunities. Several were hawking "pulpo" as we were getting into octopus territory. We sat on a bench in the square as the tables were all full of other pilgrims. We saw Sue and Mark coming down the street accompanied by their new best friends, Fred and Debbie. They entered the pulpo restaurant to have lunch. We then saw Paul and Stephanie from Napa come into the square and they wandered a bit before settling on another bench. We saw other familiar–looking pilgrims. We had all managed to catch up to each other at this point and were resting for lunch. The "accordion" effect was in

---

[13] Yes, I'm from Minnesota. Sure.

Grapes left on the vine after the harvest for peregrinos.

play.

We polished off our bread and Dave went to get us Coca Cola Lights. We were working on those when we noticed something even better – vino tinto at the corner bar. They had a counter outside, so Dave went over and bought us each a glass of wine. We took them over to one of the now-vacant tables with the nice red chairs. We sat down and started to enjoy our drinks. We hadn't taken one sip when a man rushed over to us garbling something in Spanish. Finger-wagging. The gist of it was we couldn't sit at the tables (all now empty) because they were for customers from the bar on the other side of the street called "The Monkey." Sigh. We took our wine back to our bench and finished it there.

We waved to Paul and Stephanie and chatted for a minute. I was going to ask them how they fared in Napa after the recent earthquake but didn't get around to much talk. Dave did however manage to ask them – "did you happen to see three Japanese kids with one limping girl" as he had given her his pole and wanted it back. Paul's answer was "Yes!" He did see them and in fact the Japanese girl had mistaken him, Paul, for Dave and she had wanted to give him the pole back. Paul explained he wasn't Dave and didn't take the pole. Gah! Dave wished he'd taken the pole from her. However, it was good to hear the Japanese group was still going, the girl was much better, and she was looking for Dave to return the pole! Hah! Maybe today they would catch up and Dave would get his pole back. He was going to need it when we started over the mountains again! Especially getting up to O'Cebreiro, or so

The pilgrims look happy so it must still be morning. Oh, the vineyards help, too!

Sitting in steerage where we belonged. "No red chairs for you!"

Wine bar. This was such a cool hole-in-the-wall dive.

we heard.

We decided we needed to get back on the trail and start moving. We marched off down the cobblestone street and then Dave saw something on the side of the road and motioned me over. "Look!" There was an old wooden doorway that looked to be a few hundred years old and it was open (looked warped and like it couldn't even close). It was quite dark inside. It smelled very musty and I actually detected a familiar scent – just like Granny's basement in Pittsburg, Kansas! It truly did bring back memories of snooping around down there. Uhhh, shivveerrs. But looking in, Dave had noticed a bunch of wine casks – very old wooden barrels. This was a long, narrow, dark room. Sixth sense or something, but Dave went inside and I followed. We walked down to the end of the room. There, a wooden bar was set up and a wine tasting was going on. Very authentic. About 8 to 10 elderly men were standing around while one behind the bar was serving the local red wine. 40 cents for a small tumbler-full. Nothing fancy. And he was cutting up authentic-looking (i.e., scary-looking) sausage or some sort of Spanish meat – likely jamon – and putting it on a plate for "appetizers."

Dave ordered us up two glasses of the wine and the man was happy enough to pour us a tumbler-full. Ohh. It was very good. Very, very nice. What atmosphere. It was a fun experience. Hey, there's that word again. "Fun" – it hasn't appeared much during our trip and I wouldn't describe our Camino in any way as "fun" – yet – but it was a very cool, memorable half an hour. We weren't in a hurry anyway. Turned out to be one of our best experiences in Spain.

But now, wine-in-the-afternoon time over, I learned it really is not best to drink and then have to walk, especially in the sun, in the afternoon when I am not good or happy after 1 p.m. It was a struggle. I was tired. Exhausted. Hot. And we still had to go about 10 km before we could expect to find our albergue for the night. If you could believe the guidebook.

We had a very long uphill road to follow. The scenery was gorgeous but I was not so impressed at this point. More vineyards and mountains everywhere. It was a beautiful afternoon but the sun was hot. We were climbing that hill on the road forever. And then I heard click–clacking behind us. Sue! And her new friends. Boy, they were annoying! Boy, were they marching at mach-speed! Dave and I were finally about at the crest of the hill when I thought I was going to die but we saw an open bar on the left and we went inside. I just had to rest. I put my feet up on a chair. The scenery looked better from this position. Dave ordered us a Coca Cola Light and we sipped on that and rested while the rest of the pilgrims kept marching on upward. Apparently, they were not affected by the hill or the heat. Even after a week of walking and all the hills and the heat, I still can't keep up. Whatever. There was some great Spanish guitar music playing – I could picture the flamenco and the bullfighting, and there was a breeze, so all was good. For the time being.

From Cacabelos to Villafranca we had been steadily climbing – we had to go up about 300 meters to reach the peak. It continued to be hard-going but we finally reached the town and the municipal albergue at the beginning of Villafranca on the hill. We continued on the street and then went down several steep roads and some stairs. It's a cool town and we wandered a little bit before asking and finally locating our hotel – the Ultreia Hostel. It turned out to be very nice. We entered on the ground floor into the bar. A girl was working there and she checked us in. My backpack has been delivered safely. I am sweating buckets and very exhausted. I don't feel so great, either. I just want to rest for a while.

The girl led us out of the bar and up the street to the back side of the hotel. We entered through a big heavy door with a huge round door knob in the center of the door. We were in one of the rooms, the first one on the left, down the one hallway. It's nice! We really like our room. It has a dark wood–beamed ceiling and there are two wide beds pushed together. The bedspreads have a black and white fuzzy design on them and they are comfy! It is a rustic looking room. There is a nice bathroom. There is an interesting alcove window with shutters that juts over the street. I feel better already. Our backpacks explode and we sit to catch our breath. 45 euros is all it takes.

My legs are very, very sore. The shower feels great. We do a lot of our laundry in the sink and Dave takes it outside on the terrace to hang on the clotheslines there. We get to use our clothespins that we've been carrying. We have a lot of clothes hanging out there and hope they will dry. There is no wind and it is not sunny anymore. We leave the laundry and decide to explore the town. Really sore legs. We walk uphill a block and then have to descend some stairs. We find Plaza Mayor in the center and it is ringed by various bars and places to eat. We keep walking to see what is a little farther down the street. We walk up some more stairs to see if we can get a look at

Karen out the window – "¿Donde es mi pantalones?"

the church right there but it is locked up tight. We go back down the stairs and back to the center plaza. There's not much to see.

We decide to have a drink and choose the bar on the corner, closest to our hostel, though all of the bars seem to offer the same menu of tapas. We each get a glass of red wine and order our own tapas. Dave asks for the platter of meats and I go for the patatas brava. These are potatoes cooked in a spicy sauce (oil with paprika). Mine were good. Dave says his meat is good and it does look impressive. I abstain. We have another glass of wine. We watch the activity in the square. Various other pilgrims arrive. We recognize a lot of them. There is one girl, German, I think, that we see at the table next to us. We've been following each other since Acebo. We see Paul and Stephanie at the end of the plaza. Later, we see Sue, Mark, and their new best friends, Debbie and Fred, enter and they sit at the bar across the square from us. Laughing, talking, ordering food. Ignoring us. I don't really want to be part of their party but it does sort of bother me to be excluded.

We decide we've had enough gawking and meat and go back to our room to check on the laundry and perhaps take a nap. This was a lot of food and it turns out to be our main dinner. Dinner, later, turns out to be ice cream. Fair enough. The clothes were still not dry, so we left them hanging. No one had stolen my merino wool ("bringing sexy back" as the tagline promised) underwear. They really are very comfortable – I wish I'd packed my wool bra but I just didn't have enough confidence in the advertising campaign. I laid down and slept a little and Dave went back downstairs in the hotel to the bar to get some better Wifi. At 8 p.m. we both decided to go downstairs and see about dinner but they didn't do dinner or a menu of the day, so we decided we'd just have the ice cream instead. We ended up each having two ice cream cones. And that was "fun!" We've learned that when restaurants offer ice cream for dessert, it turns out to be an ice cream cone from a freezer.

The platter of meat. Wow.

The kind Isaac likes. Nothing fancy or special. No sprinkles, but tonight it sure tasted great.

We also had a glass of wine that turned into two glasses of wine. As a treat, the hostess brought us a plate of pulpo. How considerate. It's probably still sitting there. We sat at our high table in the corner and the place was nearly empty. We watched the TV mounted up high above us. There was a Spanish game show on. We tried to decipher what the contestants were supposed to do. It involved two teams, trivia questions, a rainbow–like display of wires, wire–cutters that are given to one team member, and some sort of confetti or spray or goop that goes all over the team member if they cut the wrong wire and give the wrong answer to the question. Intriguing actually. The waitress also brought over a dish of nuts – the selection like we've gotten before – nuts/corn/crunchy things – just like Deer Farm. I ate those. Baaaa. The salt tasted good and helped my nausea go away. The wine probably helped, too. Maybe the ice cream helped – the trifecta of dinners!

Today's posting during a break at a cafe outside town:

> *Today is the most beautiful day ever! I mean it. Great scenery and weather. Last night got locked in the bathroom at dinner but eventually waitress let me out. Heard me pounding. No Internet yesterday. Three miles left to go today to Villafranca. Wonder who will play me in the movie ... I had a farm in Africa ... No, wrong one. Doing much better.*

We're in bed by 9 p.m. Exhausted. Sore legs. Great bed, though. Dave again mentions that we have big hills to go over tomorrow. He keeps bringing that up. I tell him I'll think about that – tomorrow. Call me Scarlett.

The laundry. Dave counts his shirts.

Our dinner menu.

Karen rides in a car. Allegedly.

Thursday, October 23
Villafranca to Ruitelan
(31,431 steps/13.73 miles/69 floors)

And so, our group has deserted us. Abandoned. We/I can't keep up. Talk, talk, talk – can't keep up with the conversation, either. I can't say I really care but it does bother me. That's it – we don't see Sue, Mark or Debbie and Fred again. And all I have is a photograph, a la Ringo Starr.

Today, my legs are still very, very sore when we wake up. We are up at 6:30ish. We pack up in silence, sleepy. Dave goes to collect his laundry that he left on the line overnight, drying. It is still damp but it should dry during the day swinging from the back of his pack.

Surprisingly, it is quite cold this morning. Most mornings have been chilly but it is downright cold today. I'd say 45 degrees Fahrenheit. We leave my backpack out in the lobby area of our second floor to be picked up later by Jacotrans, and leave, going by Plaza Mayor. It's dark and we stop and go inside a bar for breakfast. Café con leche and a pastry – dry croissant. The usual. There are a few other pilgrims out and about. At 8:15 we start on our way. We have a choice of three routes today and choose the "easiest." We plan to hug the road, which is not as far, not as hilly, and the better choice for us. The route to the right is quite hilly and the route to the left is shocking – much farther and much more up and down. We leave in darkness, my headband in place, and make our way out of town. We follow along the river and the highway. We ease into the day's walk by taking a few hills. Just as a warmup I think. Then it levels off as we follow a river for most of the rest of the day.

This route reminds me strongly of growing up in southern Minneapolis along Minnehaha Creek and the hill at the end of our street. We played out in the "woods" all the time – the packed mud, leaves, wet rocks, trees. It smells like fall and my footfalls on the earthen mud is a reminder of my childhood. I think often of Meg, Sara, Teresa. Friends from my past, old friends, friends I haven't seen in years but have recently reconnected with

Leaving Villafranca at first light.

through that good-old Facebook. It reminds me of my freedom, of going out to play in the mornings when I was young and not having to always be checking in with home. Being free, doing what I pretty much wanted, being outside, having fun. It reminds me of the seasons and especially fall, with all the fallen leaves, the colors, the big trees, the rushing waters of the river we are following, the waterfalls, the rocks we have to balance on at times and step on and off. In the back of my mind, I do have a vague recollection of once falling into Minnehaha Creek – it was shocking, wet, cold. Again, it's slightly dank, cool, humid. Rather uncomfortable here but I am back, playing in the woods, walking on the dirt, the mud; no one knows where I am.

The tips of my toes hurt today, too. They are swollen. When I wore my waterproof shoes, they were slightly tight and pinched my two toes beside my big toes. My light tennis shoes are bigger but maybe my feet are slipping around in them too much. They are more comfortable but I will try to re-lace them a little tighter. We walk and wind our way for a few hours, following the highway and the river to our left. We finally are able to stop for a rest at an open café and we have coffee and a chocolate-covered donut. It is so good. With this activity, the coolness, the hunger, and the pain, when you finally get to eat something, it often tastes like the best thing you've ever eaten in your life. This was no different.

And then we walk some more. We are shadowing a river up an impressive valley. We pass a logging area. We go through another small village that the guidebook promises has a café. Wrong. Again. We continue walking. We stop to sit on a bench overlooking a river. Pretty. Hungry. We sit next to two girls that we speak with for a few minutes. They are from Seattle. Youngish – both just finished college there. Neither has a job yet. Both started in St. Jean. Walking quickly. Not quite sure why they are drawn to the Camino, but no job, nothing going on in their lives yet, why not? We see several

Paralleling the river. And climbing.

kittens playing across the road. Cute.

Up on our feet again. We seem to walk and walk forever without any chance for a stop to eat and have lunch, or anything at all. That ~~fricking~~ guidebook.

We run into Chris the Brit again for a bit on our walk this morning. He is walking with someone else at the moment but we talk for a little bit and then he goes on. Finally, finally, we see a very large truck stop on the right side of the freeway and Dave and I take the opportunity to cross the road to see about food. It reminds me of a stretch of road coming into the suburbs in Seattle, from the east – still in the mountains but there are a few truck stops along the way.

We sit outside – I can barely move anymore at the time – and Dave goes in to investigate. The restaurant itself is not open but we can order bocadillos and so I have the best cheese sandwich I've ever had in my life. And Coca Cola Light. Great bread. Nice cheese. My feet up. I am happy.

On the road again. Willie Nelson. Now we see a group of young guys walking. One is carrying a skateboard. Dave comments and the young kid says that yes it comes in handy – on the downhill parts.

We finally reach our destination for today – Ruitelan – about 3 p.m. It's located on a nice stretch near the river. And there are the roosters. Chickens, too. We continue along the road until we see the albergue – Pequeño Potala. It's located in a bend in the road on the right side – the building looks old and kind of shut-up. We see a sign and it says to enter "from the rear." Which is up the hill. Of course.

We go inside and a Spanish man comes over. It's Luis. He signs us in and calls for Carlos. The two of them run the place and are very friendly. Carlos appears and says he will take us to where we are staying as the room is in a different building – back down the road from where we came. He has my

We are grateful for the small things, like a donut. Everything tastes so good!

backpack, which has luckily arrived and is leaning against the wall. They ask if we eat "everything" and will join "everyone" for dinner. We say, sure, or "si." I wonder what he means by "everything" and a sense of dread comes over me. And, who is "everyone?" I don't see another soul.

So, I make my way down to the road again, Dave following, and Carlos has retrieved their very old car. He opens the door, and I get in. He puts my backpack in. He motions for Dave to get in the front, but Dave says he will just walk back. Then Dave whips out his camera to supposedly take pictures of my alleged trip in a car, but he is too slow and manages to get a picture of the front of the car and not the back seat, so he is out of luck for blackmailing purposes. Of course, though I allegedly got in the car, I was just following orders and we were going backward as I had already walked that distance. So there.

Carlos drives his car back down the street about a quarter of a mile. On the left is a more modern red brick building. We are in a room upstairs. As in up the stairs. Ow, ow, ow. It's a nice room. Nice bathroom. A little chilly inside, but it will do. The heater works. We catch our breath for a minute and then Dave washes up a few more items – mainly his socks – and he hangs them outside to dry. We wander down the street the way we arrived into town and come to an open bar. We order a couple of beers. Large size. Oh, they taste good. They come with a dish of potato chips. No surprise there. Dave goes in and buys us a package of almonds. Oh, wow, they are good, too. The salt is great and I am craving it. We sit there in the sun, talking with a couple other pilgrims for a little bit.

We finish up and then we go across the street to check out the little park area there that apparently appeals to chickens. Dave decides to soak his feet in the river for a second – it is quite cold. I take a picture of the chickens. And

Another pilgrim offered to take our picture on the side of the freeway, before passing us.

Dave's feet. Of course, when we return home weeks later, Father Tom tells us about a friend of his who had soaked her feet in a river on the Camino, which infected the sores on her feet, badly, and she had to be medivacked home. Luckily, this didn't happen to us and the possibility wasn't even on our radar. Ebola was on my radar, but so far, so good. It's back to our room and I lie down for a quick nap while Dave decides to walk back to the "main house" to use the Wifi.

Around 5:30 or 6 p.m., I believe, I'm up and have showered (great) and feeling good in clean clothes. I'm wearing my very light, gray, down vest. I've started the habit of just wearing my leggings that I use for pajamas as "dining clothes" – why the hell not? Very comfortable. And I'm always wearing my Jambu light strappy sandal shoes at night. Much better. I start to walk down to meet Dave and he is already walking back to check on me. We go back to the main place and Dave tells me what he's been doing. Apparently, the big French group is staying there – we ran into them in Acebo and apparently before that in Rabanal (though I didn't notice them at the table behind us). I do have them all in my pictures. They have been taking showers, sitting outside writing and talking, etc.

The Wifi is not good, though, so Dave and I walk down the street to the next place, a nice bar – modern with nice wooden features and wooden ceiling. We have a glass of wine there that tastes wonderful! Best ever! I think I have two. We also get the platter of potato chips. So good! You forget those things. I try making a couple phone calls. I do reach Mimi and talk to her for a while but have to leave a message for my mom. We work on our email/Facebook/Internet stuff. But then it is time to leave and go back for dinner at 7.

We go inside and enter the long dining room to join everyone for the

Dave samples one of the hundred million chestnuts he has seen (and been stepping on) along the trail.

communal dinner. Besides the 12 French people, I meet a couple others staying there. One memorable person is Bruce, a former Royal Army medic from London. We hit it off and talk (in English) – perhaps that is the secret? Language. He tells me one thing that stays with me the entire time of my Camino. We start by mentioning our apologetic beginning – yes, we only started in Leon... and he interrupts and says that you can say whatever you want. No one knows the difference, or if it's even the truth. Interesting concept. I hadn't thought of people being deceptive or lying. But now.... Hmmmmm. Food for thought. So, now I wonder if he is really a medic. From London. (I'm also instantly reminded of my favorite "Mad About You" episode – where Paul and Jamie go on vacation and pretend to be lots of different people, which turns out to be very fun, until they are caught in all the lies...)

We take our seats at the long table. Carlos and Luis are serving. There is music playing. The room is warm. Everyone is happy, friendly. We are amongst the French. Some of them speak a spattering of English and we do communicate. The first course is a soup. Carlos brings out three or four huge tureens of soup. Steaming. It smells great. I was leery, of course, at first. We all ladle the soup into our bowls. And. It. Is. The. Best. Soup. I. Ever. Had. In. My. Life. I mean it. So good. I had two bowls. It was a creamy, pureed potato type of soup. No lumps of anything. No vegetables. No odd tastes. Tastes like cream of potato soup. Except it might not have been potato. I don't know. But the seasonings were so wonderful. It did not taste salty, but it was salty. There were flavors that were amazing. Was it the atmosphere? The night? The hosts? The hunger? The company? Or just the soup? The recipe – I must have it! The next course is the antipasti – they set out huge platters of lettuce/salad and other vegetables. Bread is

The sign outside the most fun albergue ever, in Ruteilan.

passed. Wine is flowing. It's great.

We talk with the French woman opposite us and the French man next to her. We learn that this group has been doing a portion of the Camino for the past nine years. Every year they walk for a week or two. They started in Bordeaux, France. They have a couple days to go this year – and they will reach Sarria before they have to return to their homes in Normandy. Next year they will reach Santiago! Wow – how special. This is a church group. They say they are taking their time and each day they do religious activities and pray and sing and along the way they stop and have conversation and discussion about religious aspects of the trip. Wow. Amazing. Tomorrow they plan to just go to O'Cebreiro – only about 7 km. We say we plan to go about 10 km past that. They tell us it is very difficult and they are staying at the top of the mountain. I start to wonder about our decision...

The main course is spaghetti carbonara. And it is amazing. They dole it out and I am suspicious at first so don't get a lot. I regret it. It is wonderful. And for dessert there is a créme brulee. All of this is handmade in their ancient kitchen by Carlos.

Our best night so far of our Camino ends and we walk back to our room. We are in bed by 9:30 and out like a light. It was a good day.

Soaking Dave's feet. It felt great!

A very pleasant afternoon.

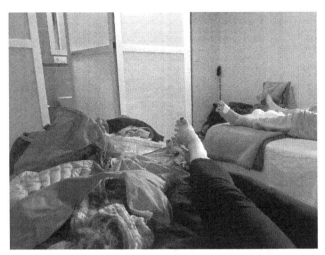

Resting our feet before dinner. "Aaaah."

Karen is as happy as she has been so far. Her clothes are a "tad" big by now.

Preparing for dinner with Carlos, Luis, and the French pilgrims. Bruce, the alleged medic, is at the left.

The best spaghetti. Ever. Thanks, Carlos!

Just Call Norwegian Cruise Line

Friday, October 24
Ruitelan to Fonfria
(30,181 steps/13.18 miles/260 floors)

A summary from Facebook about yesterday and today:

I take it all back. This was hardest day of my life. But, we made it for the night. Five or six hours straight up the mountain to O' Cebreiro and then more hours of walking. Rocky uphill most of day. Avoiding horse droppings today too. Would have liked to catch a ride but never saw the horses. Stuck my iPod in my bra and sang my way to the top – first day listening to music and it helped. Last night was great dinner – food amazing but couldn't get recipe for the soup. Didn't understand. Pasta carbonara. 12 French walkers there – for past nine years they have walked a week or two. Next year they'll finish. Hard hard day. Up 300 plus flights of stairs. About half a mile an hour. Don't know why I'm doing this to myself... But happy I am making it. Should be easier from now on. But, next time we'll take a cruise ...

From the beginning, when we got up about 6:30 this morning, I thought I knew we were in for a hard day. But I didn't know. We packed and walked down to the main building of the albergue, carrying our backpacks. I left mine to be picked up and driven to our next location. We joined everyone in the dining room for breakfast. It was very, very warm inside. There was juice, coffee, and lots and lots of toast, made on a skillet on top of the stove, which means a little blackened. The French were up. It was dark and warm and early and sleepy. The music was playing, pretty loudly actually. Suddenly a song came on that apparently appealed to one of the French couples. It's "Always Look on the Bright Side of Life" and instantly this couple was up on their feet and dancing up a storm. Everyone loved it! Clapping and laughing. They were spinning and twirling to that song, which apparently is from the play Spamalot! It was very funny and the song was infectious and peppy. It

Karen realizes it is a long way up today. Better have a second cup of coffee.

was "fun" watching this couple who was obviously happy and in a very good mood.

What I was really thinking, though, was how can they expend all that energy whipping up a frenzy when we had to climb a huge mountain today – in an hour or so? I sure couldn't do it. I would have picked dancing, it's true, but I didn't have the luxury of choice on this morning with a mountain looming in my path. However, let me tell you, it was a highlight of our entire trip, watching the couple dance. I need to incorporate more of that spirit – that freedom – that love of life – into my own life. Maybe I needed to learn this lesson. On the other hand, what do French people know?

We left at 8 a.m. On the way out, we stopped in the hot kitchen to thank Luis, or Carlos, I don't know which one I was talking to. I tried to express my thanks and appreciation for dinner last night. Most importantly, what I wanted was the recipe for that soup! "The recipe!" "Por Favor!" "The sopa!" "Me gusta!" Si, si, Luis/Carlos replied. "Recipe!" Si, si. I gave up. It was hot and we had to leave. I planned to email them when we returned home since Dave informed me that this albergue does have a website.

My journal is full of entries for today. Mostly one line entries. Most say: "more up." We walked. Up. We started up along the road. At first, we thought this wasn't so bad. We went through a small town in darkness, Herrerias. This was the town that had "horses" advertised for help getting up to O'Cebreiro. But it was early and too early for anyone to be up and selling

Our companions from France start the morning with a quick jitterbug. Talk about *joie de vivre!*

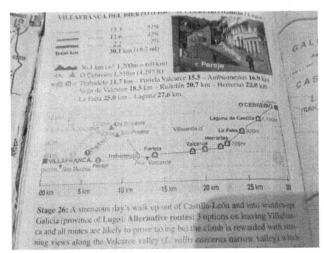

The guidebook shows the magnitude of the impending climb to O'Cebreiro.

The hardest day of the Camino. Up, up, and more up.

you their horse. We saw a couple of skinny horses in fields. I wondered if those were the poor animals they were renting out. After the town, we started some more serious hill-climbing. Lots of switchbacks. Never reaching the top. We were still on the road and so the surface was not too bad. We watched the sun rising behind us. It was a nice little break to stop, turn around, look at the sun coming up, and catch your breath. According to the Liar, Herrerias is at 705 m and O'Cebreiro is at 1,330 m. So, that is a climb. It's at least that much.

We went uphill for hours. We were walking on rocks now. It was so hard. The views were great but it was difficult. This was "Sound of Music" land here. The hills kept getting more awesome and beautiful and higher and higher. We also had to be on the lookout for horse poop which was all over the place. Obviously, a lot of people took advantage of the alternative transportation. If I'd seen a horse, I would have taken it. Stolen it. Whatever. At any price.

Dave was ahead of me. I slowly made my way up. We made it through dank, cold, sweaty forest going up that turned into a plain rocky path going up, into the narrow dirt path going up. You kept thinking you were getting to the top, but you'd turn a corner, round a bend, and find more "up" ahead. I took a lot of pictures but my camera just could not capture the grandeur of all this. I was impressed. Both by the scenery and that I was doing it. I did reach a point, not halfway up, when I thought I just couldn't do it. My heart was pounding, I was sweaty, and I doubted I could do it. Usually there

We were ready to pay for horses, but they couldn't be found for love or money at that hour of the day. So we walked on.

was a point every morning when I felt kind of sick, like I couldn't walk any more, like I was going to faint. I was dizzy. When that feeling started to appear, I would drink water. A lot of water. That seemed to help. But, I still felt that icky dizziness every morning. This was it. After drinking some water, I decided to try something else. I got out my iPod and plugged in my headphones. It was strange but every other day I had not wanted to listen to music. It wasn't just that I thought it would take something away from the experience, but I was really loathe to listen to anything at all. I didn't want to. But today I thought I'd give it a chance.

I didn't have a convenient pocket to put the gadget in, so I stuck it in my bra and turned up the music on my own playlist folder. I hit "shuffle." And volume. Louder. And then I was at that point when I'm riding on an airplane and there's turbulence and you just don't care if you make it anymore, so I turn the music up even louder, and then I start humming and then singing aloud, loud. And you know, it helped. Actually, the only songs that helped had to be peppy, fast, popular tunes. So, I stepped quicker and moved up that mountain. Toward the top, I thought, I needed to go to the bathroom and we had reached a Sound of Music field stretching out over the world, so I found a spot and tried. There was no one around. "Well," says Dave, "do you need the trowel?" "No!" I was on top of the world. But, I changed my mind and decided I'd try to wait and use the bathroom at the café where we were surely just about to reach. According to that son of a bitch you-know-who.

We finally, finally, reached a small café. It was a tiny bright blue building and, surprise, standing right outside was our "friend" the hobo/gypsy from Rabanal who had been playing the annoying instruments outside my window while I was trying to take a nap. With his dog. Hola! How'd he get there? We went inside, ordered a café and croissant. I used the bathroom. Things

The music is helping, but not much.

were good again. We rested.

But. We weren't done yet! After leaving the café, we started up a road, trying to reach the highway as we thought we'd do better following the major road. However, we couldn't find it and the man we attempted to ask seemed to say there was no highway right there. So, either he or the guidebook was wrong. You know who I was believing. Not the guidebook!

So, we circled back and tried it again. Back to the path. Up. More up. It was so hard again. We gained altitude and gasped and panted. More water. More resting. More out-of-this-world scenery. We did eventually reach another café somewhere along there and stopped for a Coca Cola Light. A short break but necessary. And then we got back out there again and walked up some more. It really did take us five or so hours to reach the top. Seven kilometers. That's less than five miles. Hardest thing I've ever done in my life. Period.

We reached O'Cebreiro and I was so happy that that had been the hardest part of the Camino and it was over. We had walked into the Galicia region now – where the weather is unpredictable. According to the guidebook. We had our rain gear handy but didn't need to change into it, hallelujah! I had read in one of other my Camino books that Galicia is known by a nickname, which is "The Land of One Million Cows." I could believe that. And horses, too, today.

I was very, very proud of myself. Of course, we weren't done for the day, but it helped. If I were French, I'd be done for the day. But I was not, and I had to keep going. We stopped and looked in the church right there. Dave had given up on getting his pole back any time soon and saw some for sale. He caved and bought one. He also bought some Camino "bling" – a small pin of one of the yellow arrows. I wore it, trying to keep it from sagging. We decided it was like a mood ring of old – could give off my mood. It usually

At the top, but only a third of the way done for the day. Who planned this?

Reaching Galicia.

O 'Cebreiro is also about the halfway point for us.

pointed upward, so, like a mood ring, was not all that accurate...

Next, we found lunch. We went in one of the places built of stone right outside the church. There were only two I could see and we picked one. It took a while but the waitress finally took our order. Bocadillos, of course, and two Coca Cola Lights. It tasted pretty good. It felt even better to just sit and rest.

But all good things had to come to an end and it was time to stand up. Oh my God. So hard to stand. Ow. Chris the Brit showed up again as we were leaving. We greeted each other in passing. We hobbled outside and down the rocky path through town. The view on the other side of the mountain was impressive as well and we started off. We had reservations in Fonfria – just another 10 kilometers away. How hard could it be? We were at the peak, right? We were done going up, right? Right? Right?

Oh for God's sake, let this torture end! We went up and down and up and down for miles. It was hot. It was sweaty. We reached a downhill patch and came to the town of Linares. We thought we might get some water at a well since we were nearly out of water in our containers hanging off Dave's backpack. We came to the big water trough and found a group of guys already there. One was standing in the water itself in his speedo trunks. We passed on the water.

We continued up. I was not amused. This had been the longest day ever. We started following the road itself. Across the road we saw one of the big statues – one of a pilgrim fighting the wind or rain. I could care less at this

How's your mood? The arrow knows....

The church at O'Cebreiro. We did not know until later that we could have gotten a Compostela there, too. When we did find out, there was no going back.

Keep pushing.

point. I had thought this particular statue was one that overlooked Santiago, but this pilgrim was just overlooking more mountains. Sigh. Took a picture and moved on. I must say, though, that for all my exhaustion and anger, at least we weren't fighting bad weather. We had lucked out in that regard.

And so we walked. Another couple of miles and I was dying again. We finally reached a town with a big population of cows, that were apparently allowed to walk through town on the streets, and they must have fed those cows terribly organic food. But, we found an open bar and went inside. We fought the flies and went to the back. We ordered Coca Cola Lights and tried to relax and enjoy them. It was boiling hot inside and the flies were so annoying. We finished up, used the bathroom, and got on the road again. According to that Liarley's alleged "guide" book, we had only 3.5 km to go. Right. I hate him. I hate him. I hate him.

I attempted to try listening to the soundtrack to "The Way" today to see if that helps. It Does Not! And I reviewed My List in my head: Martin Sheen is still 2nd. The guidebook is on it at least four times, starting at Number 1 and at the end, and several places in between. The town of Acebo makes it to 5 for not having an open café for breakfast on our way out of town. The following several towns after Acebo are 6, 7 and 8. No open cafes? Come on! Father Tom is still 3. He somehow neglected to mention a few details to us when insisting that we do the Camino. He has some 'splaining to do! The way it stands now:

1. The guidebook
2. Martin Sheen
3. Father Tom
4. Jane Christmas
5. Acebo
6. Town of Riego de Ambros
7. Town of Puente
8. Suburbs of Molinaseca
9. The guidebook
10. Woman who sold us two small glasses of wine for 4 euros
11. The cows of Spain
12. The flies of Spain
13. The guy in the water trough in his speedo
14. The guidebook
15. God
16. The guidebook
17. Bicycle gangs
18. The guidebook

(Lengthy aside: I had posted my list on FB but it mysteriously disappeared. Like the post I did when I told everyone that, "bottom line, this sucks." Not sure where some of my daily posts went, but I can't find them now to copy and paste into my "memoir," let's call it. Were they really so objectionable that FB took them down? Did they really not post when I thought they did? Did I dream it? This whole trip? I'm now seeing that apparently a lot of my daily posts are not showing up on my FB – they have disappeared. I think someone may have complained and they were taken down. That's a little annoying – I know I had written up some sort of daily update to amuse everyone back home. I had planned to copy those into my book but now they are gone.)

Is this it? We had reached the top of another point on top of the highway. The altitude sign read 1,335 meters. NO! But, there was another albergue right there with a café and lots of outdoor tables. I'm sitting. So, we sat to rest for a while longer. Dave got us two glasses of wine. Free wifi! (okay – so you now know what motivates us – Wine? – Karen; Free Wi-Fi? – Dave) Dave is interested but who the hell cares anymore? The only evil amusing part to this was that we had stuck to the road instead of the true Camino path, which led the other poor pilgrims through a wooded up-and-down hot trail, ending at this café with a very steep incline to get out of there. We watched several pilgrims, sweating, gasping, tearing their way up out of hell, er, the Camino path below.

Rest over, Dave promised me that "our" albergue was just down the road, just about half a mile away. We were almost there. "Promise!" Reminder – This is not my time of the day! Grudgingly, I slowly trekked on. We found Fonfria after another hour. We walked through the tiny village and saw the albergue, Reboleira, on the left. It was a nice, modern place. There were a lot

Albergue A Reboleira.

of pilgrims staying there. We again got a private room and it was not bad. We paid 26 euros for it, which did not include sheets or towels. The mattresses were covered with "bed bug" coverings though. There were wooden floors and the room was okay. We had our own bathroom but we'd need to use our own travel towels.

We dropped everything and went back to the front of the place, where the bar was located. We ordered a glass of wine. Of course. It came with a plate of potato chips, as usual. It was great. We did some email and enjoyed not walking. We recognized a few other pilgrims staying here. We asked for more potato chips. And more wine. We finally adjourned to our room and tried out the shower. Okay. It was nice to change clothes. I put on my light Jambu sandals. And nice comfy down vest. Things were improving. There was a nice lounge area in the center of this place where other pilgrims were sitting doing email, etc., but we just sat in the bar. The communal dinner was at 7 p.m. We learned it was held in another building – downhill and across the highway. So, a little before 7, we started our walk to dinner. Ow, ow, ow.

It was a nice building and had lots of long tables set up. We took a place at a table on the upper floor. There were about two dozen people eating here tonight. We introduced ourselves to who was sitting next to us. On Dave's right was Teri, an older woman, and on my left was the girl who had arrived late in Ruitelan. She was walking alone, is from Iran or Iraq – not sure. She didn't speak much English. She was very pretty with long dark hair and pretty eyes. She was taking extensive notes in a journal. I thought she was

The separate building for dinner in Fonfria, about 100 yards downhill from the main albergue.

doing it all in shorthand but Dave pointed out it was probably in Farsi. I guess that just shows my age. I was trying to transcribe what she was writing in my head (without appearing to be nosily looking at her notebook) but it didn't make any sense...

There were some interesting older men across from us and by older I mean 70ish, and I don't really mean interesting – I'm just being nice, and Bruce, the so-called maybe medic from London, allegedly, was also here and across the table. One of the older men said Bruce had worked on his feet that were suffering with horrible blisters but now they were doing better. Sounds like malpractice, possibly.

They served soup first and it was terrific! What a surprise. It had beans and leafy stuff and the broth had a very good flavor. Loved it. Again, I wish I knew what seasonings they were adding because it was salty but did not taste like salt and I never swelled up like I had too much sodium. I had a couple of bowls. Second course after a long, long pause in the serving was rice and meat – sort of like beef stroganoff or bourguignon. I didn't care so much for the beef, or the rice, but ate a little. Dessert was torte de Santiago (again) – Spain's national dessert it would seem.

And, with dinner finally over, I knew what that meant. We had to walk back across the street and uphill to bed. After sitting for at least 90 minutes, my legs had tightened up and it was a little hard to make it up the path. But, made it and we were in bed not long after.

Conclusion: I Am Not a Goat!

The dinner group at Fonfria.

Another excellent soup, especially if you like unidentified green stuff floating in a mystery broth. But it really was tasty!

"And With Your Spirit"

Saturday, October 25
Fonfria to Triacastela
(15,820 steps/6.91 miles/2 floors)

I was dreaming:

> *I awoke, refreshed. I bounded out of bed, eager to start another day of walking, communing with nature and giving thanks to the Lord for this day. After an hour of "centering prayer," I decided to carry my backpack today and heaved it on my strong back. I was the first one out the door, even though the sun was not yet up. I had enjoyed a full breakfast of French toast and crepes, served with bacon and eggs, and strong coffee. I was ready for the day and so happy to spend the time praying, singing hymns I remembered from heart, and rejoicing in a grateful spirit. My energy is overflowing! Bring on the hills and the challenges of this day! If it be your will, let it rain! I am an open vessel and a true pilgrim!*

Um, no. Although I've read nearly those exact words in every other book I've read on The Camino, those thoughts never crossed my mind. Lies. Lies, I tell you! Back to reality:

And, let's coast. It was supposedly going to be a downhill day. I'm still flying high, so proud of myself for making it through yesterday, so today can't be that bad, right?

Slept well but woke a lot because my legs ached so bad. The tips of my toes are still sore and very, very painful. It's an odd feeling - really hurts but just on very small parts of my body and feet. Tingly, stinging, but pain. I'm probably going to lose a couple of toenails. But, when I get my shoes on, my feet and toes don't hurt at all. And, I am feeling so lucky that I don't have any blisters. I do have some itchy places on my ankles that are annoying. My feet are the only place that itches.

We were awoken early today – bang, bang, bang. What the hell is that noise? Click clack. Turns out our room is on the wall next to the hallway where everyone has to walk to their rooms and all of the walking sticks are

Working our way downhill today. It is still lovely country.

supposed to be stored in a barrel against the wall – against the head of my bed. Geez, a lot of people left early today.

We planned deliberately for today to be a lighter day. We weren't going as far and were going to take it a little easier. I had to rest my legs and my toes and my knee, which was now starting to ache. Dave wanted to rest up to let his blisters heal. They were both still quite "icky." We got up at a reasonable time and dressed. We joined the other prisoners, er, peregrinos in the bar area for breakfast at 8 a.m. You know, years ago people who walked the Camino were in fact prisoners. They would receive the "sentence" to walk the Camino in lieu of being jailed. Interesting. I apparently did not heed that fact when I was considering my own pilgrimage. Also a fact – wealthy people used to pay others to walk the Camino in their stead, thinking the good deed or whatever would transfer back to them when the poor person completed the walk for them.

It was still dark out. Most everyone had left. There were a couple of the old guys still hanging around and we still had Teri there. She was an interesting (well, I don't mean interesting but don't know exactly how to describe her – let's go with peculiar instead) woman. She is probably about 65-ish, lives in Seattle, has no family there, is an odd duck, and this is her second Camino. She says she's not in as good of shape as she was last time and last time she had trouble. She is having difficulty both physically because she is sick and her legs hurt, I think, and she is also trying to change things about herself and her life. She keeps saying she is not in very good shape and she takes a lot of buses from place to place. She's not Catholic, doesn't have kids, or a husband, or a family really. She has worked at various jobs but is now considering moving to this part of rural Spain and she told us someone she ran into had offered her a job here. She seems to have a bad cold or cough and she asked us if she kept us up the night before with her coughing.

I guess she was in the next room. We didn't hear her. Dave and I have been very, very lucky this entire trip to not get sick. I believe that's because we stayed in private rooms and were not exposed to all the breathing and germs of everyone else, but for that I was very grateful and really happy we came out of this without any sickness. We are also really happy to not have to listen to all the snoring that we hear is going on in the big rooms. And, of course, we are being thoughtful by not subjecting others to our own snoring. And Dave's other noises.

Anyway, Dave and I finally got on our way and started walking downhill along the road. It's a smelly portion of the Camino. Poop everywhere. I'm constantly reminded that this is rural Spain. It's primitive, backwards almost. We wonder how much the Camino is keeping these towns alive. There are no young people here anymore. The residents are older people who farm and I guess like cows a lot. And chickens. Like the personal ads say, "Must like chickens." Cock-a-doodle-doo. Cows and more cows. Every once in a while we see a donkey.

After walking downward for probably two hours, we finally reach a small town - only a few buildings but one is a modern, new café. We stop in and want to order our usual breakfast when Dave sees a sign (with pictures) and quickly translates that he can get bacon and eggs here. So, he orders that and I get the café con leche with a cheese bocadillo. Very tasty. And then Teri arrives. She comes over to sit with us. She orders something to eat, a torte de Santiago - says she loves them. She admires Dave's bacon, so he offers her a piece of bacon and she leaps on the offer. We sit outside at a table in the sun for half an hour. There are other pilgrims stopping and it's a popular spot. I have a hard time believing that every pilgrim follows the exact same path and goes over the same ground. David and Lynne from a few nights ago had to walk by here? Sue and Mark did this area? The pope did? Martin Sheen? Shirley MacLaine went by here? Did she have bacon and eggs? Did she used to be a chicken? And so on.

We finish up breakfast and get moving again. We leave before Teri. We continue the path downhill. I've found each day is either hard on you and you're experiencing physical exertion in walking uphill, or hard on your body extremities with walking downhill. I don't know which I prefer. I guess variety is the spice of life, so you get to take turns with how your body is hurting each day.

We're going from probably 1,200 meters at Fonfria down to 670 meters at Triacastela. So, that is a significant drop. The scenery is very nice again today and I am not feeling too bad. I am buoyed by the fact that we will soon be in to our next destination and we can rest, do laundry, and rest - I know I already said that.

And, we are, in fact, in by 1 p.m. We have booked a room at Casa David. It's at the far side of town and on a side street. We check in at the small café in front. They say my backpack has arrived. The woman takes us around the building and up the stairs to our room. Marble staircase. It's nicer walking

It was really a delicious breakfast!

upstairs on marble by the way. Nice furniture. She unlocks the room and it's crowded but nice – cluttered with a lot of furniture, dressers, tables, and three twin beds. There are chandeliers above the beds. We have a nice bathroom. Marble throughout. Doilies on top of the dressers. Granny-like, you know. We sacrifice the middle bed and throw our stuff there. Dave sits on the end of his bed. The other end flips up. Good grief. Not a good start. But, there are no slats underneath – he checks.

First things first, we decide to do our laundry. The woman had pointed out the "laundry room" downstairs and Dave thought she had said it was free. It wasn't. Use of the washer/dryer was expensive, so we went out around the back of the building and found the washtub. We turned on the hose and washed our things ourselves, and then hung them on the clotheslines. It was a sunny, breezy day. They should dry in no time.

We next decided to find something to eat. We went back around front and ordered two beers. Six euros each, so not a bargain, but they tasted good. The woman brought us out a nice little "treat" - two pieces of bread with some sardines on top - the fish were cut in half and were "whole" shall we say. Oooh. We stared and they stared back.

We also got a nice little dish of corn mix a la Deer Farm. Okay, baaa, I ate that. We watched the commotion in the street. This was a busy place at the moment. There was a small dog that was annoying everyone. He was barking and darting around. Dave threw him a piece of sardine to calm him down. Yeah. He ducked that and ran away. The sardine was left in the middle of the street, right out in front of the open door to the café where the owner could see it. Untouched. Damn Americans. It's probably still there.

Dave went inside to ask for the Wifi code. Yes, they have free wifi. But not until 3 p.m. And, if you want to confound Dave, that would be how. "No Wifi? Until 3? What in God's name could be the reason for that? You've

Dave does the laundry.

Hors d'oeurves ala Triacastela.

got to be kidding me! That's the most ridiculous thing I've ever heard of." And so, useless, we went up to our room to take a nap from 2 to 3. Or, try to take a nap. It was noisy. There were a lot of men out in the street. I suppose without Wifi, there was nothing else to do. We heard dogs barking, men shouting, guns going off. A pack of wild dogs? Shootings? It was incredible what the lack of Wifi drove the locals to do.

We got up at 3 and took showers. There was a hair dryer. Wow. It was great! Dry hair! I used to have nightmares about going on a trip to Europe and forgetting either my travel hair dryer or the electrical converter gadget, and not being able to use the hair dryer. Now look at me – I was living every day without one. But, life was better with a hair dryer, I must admit.

So, we turned on our iPods (iPhone/iTouch) – me, I'm barely in the 21st century – just look at my flip-phone – and checked for Internet. The Wifi was really bad. It was time to move down the street and find a location with better service. And buy some vino. So, we first checked on our laundry, which was not yet dry, and then continued up the street. We found an acceptable place that was open and it was very large. We sat at an outside table and ordered wine. It arrived in large glasses and we received the requisite bowl of nuts. Baaa. The Wifi was great, said Dave. I couldn't get in. But, I didn't care. I sat and watched the world go by. Drank the wine. Nibbled on corn. More wine please.

And then something amazing happened. And not in a good way. Apparently, a bus of Camino tourists must have been dropped off because the street was suddenly full of people, a variety of sizes and ages, all wearing little daypacks and swinging walking sticks this way and that. They trooped down en masse, all found chairs and tables, and sat down at "our" restaurant. They all got drinks and such and talked and laughed for about half an hour. Then, they all got up and marched away. I discovered I don't like casual Camino tourists who don't know anything. This is supposed to be hard! Hard, I say! After all, we started in Leon, by God!

So, another glass of wine later, more nuts, and I was calm again. We also ordered some little appetizers to hold us until dinner. We got a plate of French fries. Best of all, the total for our six generous glasses of wine and the fries was 8.5 euros. Plus all those corn nuts – that could feed an army of bunnies. A bargain! And the waiters were friendly and handsome.

Farther down the street we had passed a church and they were having a Pilgrims' Mass at 6 p.m. We planned to attend. That quickie blessing Father Tom gave me and the other couple of Pilgrims' Masses we had attended were wearing off. I needed a touch-up. So, we walked down the street to the old church and went inside. There was only one other couple there. The old priest arrived and he gestured, asking if Dave and the other man would do the readings. Dave would do his in English and the other man would read in Spanish. That left me and the other woman for the "audience."

Mass started. Mass ended. Fifteen minutes tops. Priest gave his readings, other man did his, Dave did his, and basically it was about over. I took a

Dave reads the Epistle in English at Mass, while the priest glares at your photographer.

picture. The priest glared. One other woman walked in toward the end of the Mass and the priest glared at her, too. Quick communion service. And also with you. Oops - and with your spirit too. Done. Blink and you were done. I could attend daily Mass if it was always like this[14].

So, we wandered back to the same restaurant we were at before to have dinner. We were gone for maybe half an hour – tops – and now the place was full. Most of the tables were full outside and they had brought a big-screen TV out to the patio area, which was turned on to soccer. We sat in the back, almost in the street, and looked at the menu. For ten euros each, we had the menu of the day. I had the pasta to begin with and it arrived covered in tuna, which I ignored. I then had the pork chops and fries. Another dog showed up at my chair and we made friends. The dog liked tuna. Dave had the paella, which he said was quite good. More wine. Bread. And, of course, ice cream. The good kind this time, a wedge of vanilla ice cream with chocolate interweaved in it. Like an ice cream cake.

We tried checking in with the kids. Talked to David and learned Matthew had driven to San Francisco to do something with his friend Robbie. I also managed to talk a little bit with Mimi.

We finished up and went back to check on our laundry. The clothes were dry by now and we took them upstairs. We were in bed fairly early and out like a light.

---

[14]Weekday Masses at home **are** about 25 minutes, which a certain someone might know if she had ever been to one. – Ed.

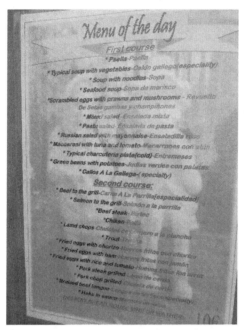

Menu del dia, with English first. This is a sign of a tourist restaurant.

A pair of gnomes supervise Dave as he does his email in Triacastela.

A Pocketful of Peppermints

Sunday, October 26
Triacastela to Samos
(19,342 steps/8.45 miles/38 floors)

Surprise! Europe apparently changed their clocks last night and moved them back an hour. We gained an hour. We were up at 7:30 and it wasn't dark out. What a huge difference that makes! We got about 11 hours of sleep. Felt great. I did have a nightmare around midnight though - something about alligators and snakes and mice crawling on me. I woke up a few times during the night. Heard that pack of wild dogs barking like crazy at times. Even though we are sleeping in private hostels, we still weren't trusting the sheets and were sleeping on top of the beds in our sleeping sacks. Those are not the most comfortable bags. I really don't like the feel of them, the decreasing size of them at your feet, and they are cold. It always feels a little creepy or scary sleeping at night like you are a mummy. I think I can feel bugs and things crawling on me. I still have the itchy feet and bites on my ankles. I've deduced they are likely bed bugs but at least they are limited to my feet.

We dressed and were downstairs for desayuno at 8:15. We lugged my backpack downstairs to wait for pickup. We encountered Chris, our friend from England, sitting in one of the little booths in the café. He had spent the night here, too, just down a couple rooms from us. We sat with him and waited for our breakfast. He was almost finished, eating his gluten-free biscuits. We asked where his Spanish brandy was and he said he skipped it this morning. He left and we ate our usual breakfast fare.

We were on the road soon after and had planned another shortened day. We were stopping in Samos today. Here in Triacastela one can choose two routes - either the right route or the left route that encompasses Samos, which has a Benedictine monastery that is cool to visit. It's longer, but we still chose Samos. I've come a long way, baby.

We left in the daylight and walked the six miles to Samos. It was mostly along the road and was a bit boring. The weather was nice again and we really, really appreciate it. Thank you. The day heated up and there were some

Stopping for coffee. We were off the beaten path a bit, and the locals were curious about us.

uphill portions that were exerting. We trekked through some picturesque villages. We crossed a few bridges, saw a few babbling creeks. Cows were evident, as usual. We stopped for coffee in one little café a few miles into our morning. It was San Cristobo, I believe. Unfortunately, today I was having some tummy issues and I was happy to arrive as soon as we did. No! I didn't need the trowel. I'd been trying to save the last half sleeve of saltine crackers I had and they were in the top of my daypack – by now all crumbs and kind of stale. Every once in a while I'd reach in and scoop up a handful of cracker dust. And, I was sucking on peppermints I had salted away in my pockets. Those helped a little.

We finally crested one hill and saw the monastery below us. It was huge. It was indeed very impressive and we took several pictures. This was the sixth century Monasterio de Samos. We then followed a tree-shaded path downhill all the way into town. We learned the monastery is 1500 years old – one of the largest and oldest in Spain. There are 24 arches surrounding a courtyard and all are different sizes but the bolts are all the same size. That seems like a boring fact, but that is what I picked up.

We crossed the bridge into town and went up the street to see the monastery, which dates from 665 AD. The bells had just chimed noon and we knew Mass had started. It was Sunday, so we hurried to make it. We went inside and sat toward the back. There were a lot of people in attendance. Almost all the monks concelebrated the Mass. It was actually very cool. Afterward, we wandered around and I took some pictures. We went into the gift shop right next door and I bought a small glass painted cross that you can put on a chain for a necklace - blue and yellow - for six euros. The first thing I had bought really since we'd been in Spain. If you don't count wine. A souvenir.

Coming into Samos.

The Benedictine Abbey at Samos, from above, as we came out of the hills.

The monastery from downstream. Note the shell patterns on the bridge rails.

Souvenirs from Samos. I bought the one in the center on top – blue and yellow.

Mass at the Abbey.

We now decided to locate our hotel and plan the rest of our day. The owners of the Casa David had made us a reservation the night before and didn't give us a choice where to stay. We weren't sure we liked that idea but they insisted and we were booked into the Hotel A Veiga. It turned out to be on the far side of town. We registered and forked over the 35 euros they wanted. They stamped our credencials but didn't need to see our passports. That was my first clue that we were possibly in a shady establishment – when they don't need to check our passports. We were on the second floor and shown to a surprisingly very nice, modern, light room. Two beds. Nice bath, with hair dryer. All righty!

We went downstairs to check for lunch and sat in the large bar. We ordered bocadillos and they were pretty good. Next up – nap. That was pretty good, too. We got up at 4:30 and showered, dressed, and felt better. We walked back to the monastery to hang out, though that's probably not the best term. We were thinking of attending Vespers at 7:30. We went into the gift shop again to look around. There was a group of people milling about outside. We learned they were waiting for the next tour to start. We asked inside and translated that there was a tour starting in about ten minutes. We decided to join them. We noticed they were all holding tickets, so we went back inside and asked about tickets. We were quickly given two, for three euros each.

We joined the tour and though I listened really hard, couldn't pick up too much. It was in Spanish. ("Guantanamera, da da da, Guantanamera...") A

A beer for the weary traveler upon his arrival.

Our credencials are filling respectably at this point.

Karen and Dave waiting for the tour of Samos to begin.

priest or monk or someone in a black robe was giving out all the info. Luckily, there were two women who also spoke some English and they translated a lot of what he said for Dave and me.

I took a lot of photos. There was a lot to see, most of it pretty interesting (if you like murals). There were murals painted all over the walls. These murals and paintings were done after a major fire had destroyed everything in the 1950s. The fire had started after an explosion in the distillery. We learned the painter painted real people he knew, though he imagined the angels, who were children. He also painted Alfred Hitchcock into one mural. That is a true fact – I did not mis-translate. He threw in a lot of tricks of the eye with other murals. In some, when you walk from one side to the next down the hallway, it seems the painted man's eye or arm would follow you. Very strange. He also painted other people from the town into some of the murals. He painted famous actresses into others. I didn't catch the name of the painter himself but apparently the whole town is painted on the walls.

We finished up by 6:30 or so but decided not to wait around and go to Vespers, too. We headed back to the hotel. Dinner was at 7:30 and cost 11 euros each. However, we were told we could eat at the bar area and not wait til 7:30, so that is what we did, though the menu of the day was limited if you were eating earlier. No matter, we just ordered what was available at the time. We both started with soup. I had a wonderful soup, again. It had shrimp and other seafood in it. Hopefully, no pulpo. Very good flavor, possibly due to the pulpo. Dave had the butternut squash or pumpkin soup. We then both had the meat for our second course. It came in a combined casserole and was pretty tasty. We finished with dessert - ice cream again.

As a special treat, I imagine, the bartender/server also brought us over a large platter of nuts - those big walnut/chestnuts we have been stepping on for weeks! A delicacy now – this dish was roasted or something because

A hand-lettered hymnal from the middle ages, in the Sacristy at Samos. It was saved from the fires that burned the monastery to the ground in 1558 and 1951.

These Benedictines have been tending to pilgrims for over 1000 years.

A marble of St Joseph at the Monastery. I especially like the shadow of the halo on the wall.

An excellent dinner in Samos.

A peregrino statue on the edge of Samos, heading to Santiago. I note he is not smiling, either. And he may or may not be clutching his chest from a heart attack. Allegedly.

they were hot. We peeled one back and tried nibbling on it. Kind of like sawdust. Dave had tried eating one off the ground (raw) a few days ago when we walked by the vineyards and I was having a good day – that day – but it wasn't any better cooked/hot now tonight. But, Dave ate a few. To be polite. Spain is sure full of these chestnuts on the ground. And poop. Lots and lots of poop.

We tried calling people from home again but ended up leaving messages for everyone. Matt was still in San Francisco with Robbie and David was out with Isaac.

We were in bed by 8:30. Other tidbits from today include learning that Eddie Miller is in hospice and not doing well. Dave's mom is visiting her sister, Mary Jo, in Kailua, Hawaii – lucky! I'm so jealous. They at least are walking on the beach and looking at the ocean. I don't remember any poop on the sand there, either. I also learned that Mark and Susan had finished their Camino and had left Spain (so I can stop looking for a woman with medium-length red hair). And, I'm still not having any profound thoughts. As you can tell, I am still focused on all the chickens, and the poop.

¡Sangria!

Monday, October 27
Samos to Barbadello
(23,935 steps/10.46 miles/76 floors)

Ohh, I'm still pretty achy. And itchy. I think there are some "Simpson's" characters named after me. My legs hurt again. My knee is hurting. My feet hurt.

This is getting old. Get up. Pack all your stupid belongings into your stupid backpack, that still falls over. Lug my bag down a bunch of stairs. Find enough euros and fill out the tag. Eat a dry croissant or burned toast. And walk. Don't stop. Walk some more. We left Samos in daylight after breakfast. We had our breakfast in the bar area again. At "our" table. Today, we were going through Sarria and onto Barbadelo. According to the alleged guidebooks, Sarria is where we should start seeing lots more pilgrims join the Camino. It's a little more than 100 km from Santiago and in order to get a Compostela, you have to walk at least the last 100 kms. We walked through a lot of beautiful countryside this morning. The vistas were breathtaking. Again. It was a bright, sunny, beautiful day. Beautiful colors, a wonderful day, and I was back to taking pictures of every flower I passed. My mood improved.

It was mostly downhill, so not a physically trying day. To start. Barbadelo was at a higher elevation but that was after lunch. I could think about that later. We were still ten km from Samos to Sarria, so it was a long morning. We finally reached Sarria and it was a big city. We had to pick our way through the outskirts of town, following the shells on the sidewalks. I've learned that I much prefer to walk in the country than through city streets. There was a detour but we eventually found our way through the town, across the bridge, along the river, and then we came to a flight of steps. A lot of steps. 63 steps. Up. We took them in stride and then at the top decided we should rest, right there, and we found the café at the top of the stairs to be perfect. I'll bet that café got a lot of business. We settled (settled, collapsed – pick your word) into a table outside. Dave went in and ordered us bocadillos and Coca Cola Lights, but immediately regretted his decision when the two Korean kids at the table next to us showed up with plates containing huge hamburgers and fries. You can get those here? At that point, we decided to

The road out of Samos.

Karen, the intrepid photographer, in fetching teal fleece. Again.

A flower I passed.

Those pesky hills keep reappearing.

We enjoyed the shorter day today. Karen is actually smiling in the afternoon.

have a glass of wine, too, you know, for the road.

Suddenly, there were indeed a lot more pilgrims everywhere. I don't know where they all came from. They milled about at the top of those stairs. A lot of them greeted each other with hugs like long-lost family members. I didn't recognize anyone. Of course, "our" people had way passed us and were long gone. These were newer, faster pilgrims. Younger. Much younger. Skinnier. Cleaner. We finished up our lunch and went on. I wanted to take a picture of a tall mosaic marker at an overlook of the city below us but a group of men were gathered around it taking picture after picture. We gave up and kept going down (up) the road. We passed a church and stopped to take a look. That same group of young guys passed us and then decided to check out the church, too. Then, with a quick look around them, they all darted to the parking lot, opened the trunk of a car, threw their backpacks in, jumped in the car, and took off. Hunh?

We walked on. It was not too bad. We had to climb one big hill. One giant hill. It was very hot and sweaty and difficult. We continued and walked through some fields, in the hot heat - the sun beating down. It was getting to be the time when I start to fail – my mood slips and I "allegedly" turn a little crabby. We walked some more. We finally reached the edge of Barbadelo and for once found our hostel on the near side of town and not the far side. It was right there. Casa Barbadelo – and, it looked nice! Moreover, it was nice! I hadn't been describing a lot of our hostels as "nice."

We arrived about 2:30 and walked up the drive and walkway. There was a nice covered patio with lots of tables and chairs in the sun. They were mostly vacant but in one of the chairs sat our old peculiar friend, Teri, from Seattle. We were frankly a little astonished that she was there before us. We greeted her and then went inside to check in. We had a nice private room in a strip

Dave in total shock at the steps.

The town crest of Sarria.

Our wing of Casa Barbadelo - a very nice albergue.

of rooms in a separate building, up near the pool. Yes, the pool. A real pool. It was very cold water, but it was in fact a swimming pool. We checked out our room, which included towels. There were three twin beds again, but that was as good as having an ironing board[15] – we set all our things up on the spare bed.

Priorities first, we went back to the patio to have a drink. And it suddenly hit us what we had been missing from our trip all these days – sangria! Here we were in Spain and we hadn't had any sangria yet. We had to rectify that and so Dave ordered us some sangria. Not just a glass but a pitcher full! It was delivered to our table and oh, my, it was delicious. The best drink I have ever had in my life! It tasted so, so good. It cost 15 euros or so, but worth every peseta. There was good music playing – American music – Hotel California was on at the moment, and it changed to Stairway to Heaven, and later the Hawaiian version of Somewhere Over the Rainbow, etc. This was a beautiful place and we were resting, feet up, drinking the best drink ever, and catching up on email. In the sun. Perfect.

But then we decided we should get our laundry done and set out to dry in the sun on the lines. So, we washed that up in the sink and hung it up. We sat by the pool for a little bit. I took a shower and sat out in the sun by the pool to get my hair to dry. A few other pilgrims walked up. One was a man who was giving advice to another man who had just checked in here. He said you didn't want to stay in the same place as the Korean man who was here – "He is a horrendous snorer" – "It's not funny!" "You will not sleep a wink!" "You have to stay somewhere else." He said they were all going to talk to the manager as a group to complain about this Korean and tell them he will

---

[15] The ironing board as knick-knack shelf is a great invention! It's wonderful for displaying all one's cosmetics, if one had any, or bits and pieces – not for actual ironing, of course.

Sangria! We eventually learn to order bigger pitchers.

have to sleep in another building or another room! Well, that information we overheard intrigued us and we decided to go back and check out what was going on. We also decided to have another pitcher of sangria – what the heck – and went back to the patio area.

Teri came over then and joined us. She doesn't drink wine but apparently has no revulsion to sangria, so she had a glass. We talked more about her situation and she clued us in about having to go to the doctor since she was so sick. She wasn't thrilled with Spain's healthcare system, but they saw her and then gave her some medicine so now she is feeling better. She kept coughing, though, and I kept leaning away. I really didn't want to catch anything. Teri had apparently had a different experience with the hospital and doctors than we talked about with David and Lynne at the Hotel Novo a few nights back.

We took note of the Korean man who was wandering around the compound here. Yeah, I'd avoid him, too. I don't know how that situation turned out but everyone stayed at this albergue tonight and I didn't hear any more about it. We did, however, run into this particular Korean man most days from here on out and we shied away - the pariah of the Camino! In fact, if I am not mistaken, I believe we first met the "Korean snorer" at our first stop – the Albergue de Jesus – and he was singing something about the Swanee River.

We left to get ready for dinner, which began at 7. They had a restaurant inside and we went over soon after 7. There were quite a few people staying here, obviously, as most of the tables were full. I didn't recognize anyone else. They were mostly older people and they seemed to speak English. We ordered from the menu of the day. I started with spaghetti carbonara, which was disappointing and not as good as Carlos or Luis's version. I finished with hake (fish) and that was not great. I asked for the homemade cheesecake for

Soaking my feet by the pool. This was more like it.

dessert which was promised to be great, but was not. Was our guidebook author in the kitchen? Shortly after we ordered, Teri wandered in and she came to sit down with us and eat. Again, I avoided contact and any coughing germs.

I wasn't feeling all that great or in such a good mood and we left soon after we finished. We went back to our room, collected our laundry from the lines and accounted for it all, and went to bed. Not to sleep exactly but I was in bed. We learned that Eddie Miller had died, so that was very sad news. Eddie was one of Dave's relatives - the "significant other" of his Uncle Bill, his dad's brother. Bill had died quite a few years ago and Eddie had moved to Johnson City, Tennessee, from where they had lived in Washington, D. C. Dave was close to him and Bill, and Eddie had been really good to our family. Dave had a chance to call him a few days earlier via Skype to say good-bye. He will be missed.

We Break the 100KM Milestone

Tuesday, October 28
Barbadelo to Portomarin
(30,187 steps/13.19 miles/98 floors)

We woke up and I had huge bites on my ankles. Three or four on each ankle were certainly bed bugs and they itched, but now I saw a bite on the inside of my left ankle that looked like a full-blown blister, full of icky stuff. It doesn't hurt or itch, though. I guess it's Spain's version of a brown recluse spider bite. Two years earlier I'd been bitten by one of these pests at home and was out of action for a good six weeks or so, and really suffered. I still have the scar as proof! So I didn't sleep well, but probably because I was being used as a chew toy for whatever lurked in this room.

We had breakfast in the dining room and set out on our walk. As we left the room, we saw Teri sitting there having breakfast. She hadn't joined us. We wished her a "buen camino" and checked out. The sun was rising and it was very clear and beautiful out. I had tummy problems today but I blamed it on the fish I had for dinner last night – should have known better. "No! Put the trowel away!" We saw more pilgrims this morning. Younger, faster, fresher.

We walked through a lot of wooded areas. There were riverbeds to climb over and fields to cross. We talked as we walked for a bit with a couple from Lethbridge, Alberta. It's only polite as someone is passing you to say "hola" or "buen camino" or start in on a short conversation. I mentioned I had gone to a rodeo in Lethbridge once, many years ago. They were excited to hear that. They talked about living near Glacier Park in Montana and I mentioned how I really liked the Waterton area up there on the border of Canada. They live close by on the Canadian side. The husband was having some bad problems with his leg and his hip. His whole leg was numb and he wasn't sure he was going to make it. They'd been walking since St. Jean and were going at a pretty fast pace. Well, for being at it for 60 days. They were about our age or a little older. They soon walked on ahead of us. However, we passed them a little farther down as they had stopped for "nature's call."

Sharing the Camino with our bovine friends. They don't use a trowel at all.

We stopped at a small café on the left side of the road where a lot of other pilgrims were resting. We ordered a café con leche and a powdered sugar-covered pastry. Very tasty. We sat on the side of the building and talked with a couple there. The girl was in her 20s and from Colorado. She was walking with a man she had met on the Camino from the Northeast U. S. They had obviously made a connection and, though they had started alone, were now a "couple." The bathroom at this stop was just an "outhouse" and not very pleasant, so I wasn't very happy. We continued on. Tummy still hurt.

We were on an uphill track today and on our way to a bigger city, Portomarin. It was probably about 18 km. I learned to use words like "probably" and "maybe" nowadays. I couldn't count on the alleged guidebook. We were feeling some excitement as we watched the stone markers steadily get closer to the 100 km distance. We were doing a lot of climbing and we finally reached the 100 km marker. We had another couple take our picture. There was an unofficial and an official stone and we took pictures of both. There was an exceedingly lot of graffiti on this marker - most markers had a lot of writing and colorful sayings drawn on them, but this one was special. It deserved lots of defacing. We also saw lots of little (or big) piles of stones, pebbles, rocks, miscellaneous items like shoes, on or around the markers.

100 km - it was like reaching an important goal. We were actually, truly, kind of, almost getting there! I was doing it.

We kept hiking upward though and passed through a lot of country. A

100 km left to go.

small herd of big brown cows was led on the road next to us by an old woman. We weren't trampled. The cows did not look too happy but neither did I. We then passed some sort of fenced-in nursery with rows and rows of beautiful flowers. Yes, I took a lot of pictures. We rounded a corner and then passed an ostrich. A live one. It was fenced in, too, and looked back at us like we were having a staring contest. I moved on. Not sure who won. Likely, it was me. And then more chickens, flowers, sheep, cows.

We finally seemed to reach the top of the incline and the path led to the left. Before turning back to the right, we stopped at the corner for lunch at a café there. We sat in the sun, panting. We had the usual – cheese bocadillo for me and jamon or chorizo bocadillo for Dave. With the usual Coca Cola Lights. Very tasty. They always come on a large baguette and you wondered how crusty it would be today. Pretty crusty today. The cheese was good. And that was the sandwich. Lunch break over.

We finished up and got back on our feet. Again, the guidebook and I disagreed on the perceived length. The afternoon went on forever. We walked our feet off. The one high point of the day was when we passed a farm with all the typical animals but there on the left side of the road, fenced in unfortunately, was a St. Bernard. With sad eyes. I crossed the road and took several pictures. It was awfully cute. I wasn't happy it was all cooped up but it seemed to accept the situation. I walked on.

We wandered through more fields and then seemed to be coming to the outskirts of Portomarin, according to the map and we saw a woman in the street. Dave pointed to the map and asked if we were really getting to Portomarin. She explained we were and it was "just ahead." I don't know her name, but she is on my list, too. She could have been a guidebook author, herself. Or aunt of one. A family relative for sure. We continued (no choice, really) and finally we reached a river and the sign there said "Portomarin" so

A very sad Saint Bernard.

I was hoping we were close. Even with pretty hard evidence staring you in the face, you couldn't be sure. We crossed the river walking on the long bridge and approached a set of cement stairs. Going up. Yes, the damn yellow arrow was pointing up, too.

My own arrow on my shirt was drooping. "After you," I gestured to Dave to start climbing the stairs. He made it and I followed. It was hot and I was very sweaty. We set off on the street to the right. Up a hill. Only three or four blocks up the hill and there on the corner on the left were our accommodations for the night. We went into the small alcove to check in at the desk. The girl put out her cigarette and I stood there dripping. My backpack had arrived – always suspenseful if it would – and she led us up a few flights of stairs and opened our door. We had the one room with a private bath but there were other rooms on the landing that shared a bath. The hostel was "completo" as in no more room at the inn. We were happy to have our own bathroom but later learned that the halls with the high ceilings in the stairwell echoed and we could hear everyone's bathroom activities. All through the night. And the morning. And people are pretty rude. Just an observation.

Dave went to sit at a table below on the small shaded patio right outside behind us and I threw him down (out of our window) some of our clothes so that he could air them out on the line there. We also washed a few more things and added them to the clothesline. We were now almost out of the liquid laundry soap I had brought with us. Dr. Bronner's peppermint-scented soap – I did like the smell of it. We'd have to look for more of it.

I took a shower and it felt great. Hot water, good water pressure. No hair dryer. But we did have towels provided. There were a lot of flies in here but I tried to ignore them. My feet were very itchy and Dave needed more Compeed, so we dressed and headed up the street to the pharmacy.

Crossing into Portomarin.

More darn steps.

Karen reaches the top of the steps. Her arrow is suddenly pointing up again!

Dave guards the laundry. And he might as well check his e-mail, as long as he is there.

Ice cream outside our albergue. Clean clothes and a shower: happy again.

We bought the stuff for his blisters and I got a "calamine" substitute lotion. We then found an ATM and retrieved some cash. Next up, a visit to the supermarket in the square. We purchased more almonds, a chocolate bar, and some ice cream, along with a bottle of wine that they opened for us. We took it all across from our hotel and sat on a bench in the park-like area overlooking the river and the mountains beyond that we had crossed. We sat and ate our ice cream cones and took a couple of "selfie" pictures with Dave's phone. We then moved back to the patio and sat by our laundry, eating the almonds and chocolate while sipping on wine with our little collapsible bathroom cups. The flies buzzed around us.

I put some of the new anti-itch lotion on my ankles – it was pink just like calamine lotion and it worked like a charm. It really stopped the itching and felt great. It was a great concoction. Better than calamine lotion. At 6:30 we went back up the street and up the stairs to check out the happenings on the plaza. There was an old church on one side of the square and a big space for crowds, bike-riding kids, or whatever, and then restaurants, bars, and shops surrounding the square. A nice area. The church service started at 7 and we were going to check it out. We sat down on a low wall to wait. The square had its own free Wifi, so you-know-who was ecstatic. Pretty decent, too. I wandered around a bit, looking in shop windows.

I looked back down the street and over the buildings. The sun was setting. The light was amazing. The colors and background were stunning. I took several photos. I loved it. Sometimes there are moments... I love when the sky

The varsity Portomarin peregrina-watching team. Waiting for a ten. (I was already behind them.)

Karen wanders through Portomarin.

Sunset in Portomarin.

lights up, either in the mornings with the sun rising, or the sun setting. The colors are so beautiful and the light is so interesting. It's different. Something is luminous and breathtaking. Like now. Those were the best times.

Shortly before 7 we went inside and took a seat in the church. There were maybe 50 people waiting and then Mass started and lasted about 20 minutes. Another pilgrim's blessing at the end. Nice touch.

We left and picked a restaurant for dinner, avoiding the pulperia. Dave was in the mood for pizza for a change and not the regular pilgrim menu, so we tried the "pizzeria." He got his pizza and I instead had spaghetti, which turned out to be very bland and uninteresting. We also had wine here and that always helps. We started at a table outside but I was too "frio" so we moved indoors. We ate and Dave took advantage of more free Wifi. I watched the TV at the end of the room. "Medicopter 117" was on - and what an exciting show that was. Kind of like "Baywatch" I'd guess but with helicopters. Not sure what the 117 meant. I did see lots of serious accidents. Blood. Like sharks. Maybe 117 accidents each episode.

We went back to the hotel, collected our nearly dry laundry and went up to bed. The room smelled very musty but we were tired and soon asleep. We collapsed by 8:35. We'd seen a lot of churches today, as well as a lot of cows. The smell of rural Spain was in the air. We also saw the Korean snorer at some point. Even though we were soon asleep, when various other pilgrims staying in the hostel returned to their rooms, they woke us up. It was very loud and the echoing was great, if you like that kind of thing.

Contemplating while waiting for Mass to begin.

"Medicopter 117" is more amusing with a nice Rioja!

Insanity Overtakes Us

Wednesday, October 29
Portomarin to Palas De Rei
(42.234 steps/16.63 miles/162 floors)

We planned to make up some time, so we scheduled a longer day for today – 26 km (15.2 miles). What a stupid idea. Whose idea was this? According to whose bad mileage "guesstimates?" Each night before having dinner and generally while drinking wine, we come up with our plan for the next day. Did we really drink that much wine yesterday? Dang it! Note to self - reread first page of this story ... Do NOT under ANY circumstances drink and plan. Geez! We have to decide where to send my backpack and find a hostel that is large enough to make sure there will be a room when we eventually show up. "Eventually." Key word, as you will see. Although we tried to get someone to make us a reservation, sometimes it didn't really get made, though we never had trouble getting a room. There were private rooms to be had. For a price. I'd pay.

And so, today we were off to Palas De Rei. We began with our usual "selfie" picture of us – two smiling happy faces out to conquer the world. Again. Another day. Deceptive. Most of the pictures we take are a little staged – it takes a minute to fix a smile on our faces. However, there are some pictures that are more candid – and truthful. I love the one (one!) of me grimacing at the camera. Now that's the truth. Didn't feel so smiley and happy then! Today we were starting at an elevation of 300 m and had to end at 560 m, though in the middle we had to climb to a peak of 720 m. The liar includes phrases such as "gentler climb" in his description of the day's activities in his so-called guidebook.

It's awful. We're back to "this sucks." We leave Portomarin after stopping for breakfast in a bar and then joining about a dozen other pilgrims leaving at the same time – we were soon in their dust. We walked down the street and across the river again. It was cloudy and cool. Rain was threatening a lot of the day, but it didn't ever rain. It was actually better than having the sun out. Eventually, there were not too many other pilgrims out that we saw. So, you know, we walk. It's uphill and cool but clammy this morning. Sweaty and damp, with flies. I'm decked out in calamine-substitute lotion, fly spray, and sweat. Ahh, the smell of rural Spain and it's me. What did I

Another sunrise.

More cows, leaving more cowpies.

"Gently climbing" over the hills.

step in? More uphill but this morning Dave starts singing. As he is wont to do. We're first on a "Wizard of Oz" kick and then it turns into other show tunes. At the moment, he has to go to the bathroom and he is singing about it. It really is terribly funny and we're laughing up a storm. The Korean snorer passes us and we scream with laughter. We are looking forward to reaching Gonzar – just a short 7.8 km from where we started in Portomarin - according to TGDB. Dave plans his bathroom assault for that lucky café in Gonzar.

We see the signs for Gonzar. We walk another two miles. We reach Gonzar. Not much in Gonzar. We pass Gonzar. No stopping. So, next up is Hospital and I do mean "up." It is not lost on me that nearly every day we walk by a town named "Hospital." Hunh. I was thinking a lot about certain people in my life. Family. A lot of friends. I spent a lot of time thinking of my sisters-in-law, Dianne and Allison. Praying, whatever that really meant. I hadn't actually been listening to music, much less the pray/play list I had asked for. I felt a little guilty about that except that I had listened to it several times at home while I was excitedly anticipating our Camino. Little details would pop into my head. Sometimes I spent most of the day thinking about certain issues or subjects. Dying, for one, which I hoped would be in the future and was not imminent. What I really felt about things – religion especially. I had long conversations with myself. I amused myself. I counted (as in 1,2,3... not that it meant something). I tried things to distract me from the misery and the motion of just putting one foot in front of the other and just keeping going.

So, when Dave started with his talent of making up the lyrics to familiar songs, it was a great relief and really, really amusing. I remember – in a past life it seems – when we were in Toulouse, France, and the restaurant was showing the movie "La Dolce Vita" on the wall – sans audio. Dave made up

Bury me on the Camino... if there is room...

the dialogue for hours. We laughed – it was so funny.

We laughed now. He had quite a repertoire going. I should have written a lot of it down – I wanted to remember. All I remember is that we were at that moment having "fun." I wasn't using the word "fun" to describe much of this adventure. We felt close and more bonded. Misery loves company, I guess.

We passed quite a few gravestones – not just Camino km markers along the way. I pointed out the place to Dave where he could put mine. A joke. I hope. A nice view at least would be important... a sense of humor is crucial. I was told later that any "transformation" – of life, character – not sure, had to involve struggle or be very difficult. Well, this was certainly very difficult – the most difficult thing I've done in my entire life for sure – but I'm not sure I was transformed. All this hardship for nothing? Well, except maybe who I am is who I am supposed to be. I don't need to be completely transformed. I was feeling a lot more gratitude. And being at the mercy of strangers. And of being in need and someone else providing what you need. More grateful. I know I already said that. Humble. And very, very, proud of myself. I was doing it. Maybe I needed fine-tuning, for sure, but it's okay to just be me as I am. And always help out someone else you see in need. It means a lot. Maybe that is the message. Oh well. Something to ponder another day.

Back to my thoughts on this day – arghhhhh! I am suddenly remembering an old show we used to watch and Dave really loved. So did Dave's good friend and Matthew's godfather, Rick Polo. "In Living Color." There was a sketch a couple guys (Damon Wayans and David Alan Grier) did on that show as two gay movie reviewers – "Men on Film." I can hear their voices now – "The Camino- haaated it!" No two swirls and a thumbs up.

I just wanted it to be over. It is really not fun. I am really not enjoying it. Yes, there are moments and the scenery is great and I'm getting a lot of

Now that is enticing the weary traveler to stop!

good exercise. But. Is that it?

Still no epiphanies. No profound thoughts. Difficulty in praying. I'm sick of talking to myself. I haven't made any great buddies out here. The food sucks. I'm tired. My body hurts. I itch now. I haven't assimilated any great changes about how the simple life is great and how wonderful it is to wake up and not have to decide what to wear. I want my things! I want choice! I want my wardrobe and I want to make a good dinner. I'm crabby and full of complaints.

But, yet. This really is kind of interesting. I am doing it. I am making it. I will do it. I'm doing it now for the pride. For the accomplishment. For the cows! If they can walk here, so can I! Even if they don't look so happy, either.

The bottom line that always comes back to me is that I would have regretted not doing this for the rest of my life if I never did it. I never would have known how difficult this is – how this feels – how terrific a challenge I've chosen. I've reached out of my comfort zone, tried something so not me, and have had an adventure I will always, always remember. So, that wins out over "this sucks." So there. Stop talking to yourself. Shut up. You shut up. Keep walking. I'm sure we're almost there.

We walk on. Up on the right we see an open restaurant with tables spread out over the lawn. Chickens mingling with the diners. A rooster or two. Our kind of place. We walk up the driveway and drop our backpacks. The Korean snorer is there. We go inside to order lunch. Ahhh, cheese bocadillo sounds enticing! Another pilgrim is there at the bar getting a drink. She explains it is called a "Clara." It's half lemonade and half beer. She says it is refreshing and very good. Sounds good enough to me. We order two. We take our drinks outside and wait for the sandwiches. I watch the chickens and other pilgrims walk by on the dirt road, not stopping. About a dozen cows are

There are hills in our near future.

herded down the street by an old man. Typical. I'm not thrilled with my "refreshing" drink. It sounded better than it tastes. The bocadillo is pretty good here. A nice mild cheese. Crusty bread. It'll do.

Sigh. We start the afternoon portion of the death march.

Again, at least the sun is not beating down on my head. That's an improvement and I appreciate it. Thank God. Reaching for straws, I know.

After our longest day, I think, at 42,234 steps and over 156 flights of stairs, we reach the outskirts of Palas De Rei. There's a big chart of hotels and restaurants on the map of the town. It looks like a very big city and we haven't reached "downtown" yet. We also don't see the name of our hostel on the list. A little alarming. We do, however, have the business card with the name and address of the place, so we just head off toward the main drag. We walk a whole lot more. We finally do reach the main part of town and when we reach the peak, there is the church. We stop, go inside, and get our credencials stamped. Now that we are down to 100 km, we are supposed to have our passport stamped at least twice a day. So, we are on the lookout for "sellos." A lot of times there is just an inkpad and stamp on a counter and you do it yourself. You are also supposed to get a pen and put the date right next to the stamp - no cheating! Sometimes, the people with the stamp pad want a small donation. Like at churches. Like here. And some have a priest or someone standing guard over the ink. So, we forked over a euro or two and stamped our arrival into Palas De Rei. And then the guy asked us to pray for him when we got to Santiago. Not too many people had asked us to pray for them, so this was a change. Sure. I put him on my list. Uh huh. At least, he was positive in that he thought we were going to make it to Santiago... He's right there after that bartender/saint who had my backpack and gave us a free beer...

Back outside we went down the stairs and followed the Camino shells a

Two Claras, please. With your Wifi code.

Who knew there were ostriches in Spain? He seems surprised to see us.

A very small bathroom.

little farther. The hotel should be on the path, at least. We headed downhill on one of the side streets, which may have been a shortcut to the main street. We found the right street and then stopped to ask if anyone had heard of the place we were staying. One man pointed just down the street and we headed off in that direction. One block away and we found it. For 38 euros we got a private room. Upstairs. Up a ton of stairs! 36 steps up. Narrow marble steps. No elevator. It was hard after such a long day to then walk up 36 stairs. We did it. Dumped our backpacks on the twin beds. This place was a dump. The girl from the night at our hostel before had insisted we stay here as there weren't any other places closer that were "nice enough." That was why we had to go the extra kilometers today. But this? This was "nice enough?" Ugh. There was a small, and I mean small, bathroom with a little enclosure I suppose you could refer to as a shower but this was a tiny room. It was depressing. I was tired.

So, what's a pilgrim to do in such a situation? Go find a nice glass of wine and unwind. So, back down the 36 steps and out onto the street. We had passed a lot of places on the way and we walked up to the corner and decided that that bar was just fine. We ordered a glass of wine and the woman asked what size and of course we got the "grande." We sat outside at a table and watched the world go by. My legs really hurt. But I was feeling very happy that we were done walking for the day. I was proud of myself and glad I was doing it. I was getting there. But, this was a hard, hard day. We did 26 km (15.2 miles). We did a full page in our guidebook – the full stage that it claims is 25 km. Impressive.

We did a little email checking and then I got up and went up the street to a store we had passed that I had noticed with some cute lingerie in the window. The first I'd seen! There were some nice-looking bras there in a pretty print. I wanted to investigate. I had only packed two bras, which at

Polka dots for the peregrina.

the time I thought would be fine, but I hadn't realized I would be so sweaty and soaked through, and two bras were really not sufficient. Uncomfortable. Plus, when we did our laundry the first time and Dave was wringing all the water out of everything, he didn't realize he had whacked the underwire way out of shape. It couldn't be bent back into a comfortable position, so it was poking at me and painful. The other bra was okay, but neither were merino wool and were not really suitable for a death march. So, I was interested in purchasing another option. The store appeared to be closed except the door was ajar a smidge (I pushed it) and I could see someone's feet in the back sitting in a chair – avoiding work I think. I decided to give it a few minutes and I walked back to where Dave was sitting on the corner.

We wanted to buy a few supplies and maybe some wine, and I wanted to go back and check on the bra store, so we split up and agreed to meet back here when we were done. I think. I wasn't really concentrating and processing that information. My mind was on bras. Dave came with me and pushed open the door and asked if the store was open. It apparently was, as the salesclerk girl reluctantly got up out of her chair in the back storeroom and stood behind the counter. I gestured at the window display and indicated I wanted to see the two bras I saw. She asked my size and I told her what it was in US sizes. She then got busy and up on a stepstool and brought down box after box of bras that she thought would fit. None of them were as nice or pretty as the ones in the window. Apparently, those were for small-chested girls and I wasn't there yet. I needed a few more weeks of death march before I lost enough weight to qualify for a smaller bra...

I did see one beige and white polka dot ensemble I liked and asked about it. It appeared like it would fit and it cost 21 euros. I decided to splurge and take a chance so I said "esta bien" and bought it. It came in a box with a pair of matching panties. I took my box and went back to the corner and

This is a man who knows how to pass the time while his wife shops for bras.

then decided to go sit across the street in the big covered plaza and wait for Dave. I had forgotten exactly where we were going to meet but this was right across from our hotel and almost in eyeshot of the corner bar, so I sat and decompressed. About half an hour passed and then I decided I should go looking for Dave since I hadn't seen him walk by. I was getting antsy. Needed a second glass of wine, to be truthful. I did find him back at the corner, just out of eyesight. He already had another glass of wine (jealous) and was doing his email, of course. I was annoyed. And tired.

Eventually, I stopped pouting and we went up to the room to clean up and take "showers." It was a slippery rounded shower and not very big. But, as usual, I felt much better after a change of clothes. My soap/shampoo little bar I had bought and brought with me on the trip totally disintegrated right here. I was disappointed in that but in the big scheme of things, I guess I'd consider that to be minor. First-world problem. I tried on the new bra (over my clothes) and it was going to work. Except, I didn't want to wear it and get it all sweatified and have to wash it here. So I stuffed in down in my backpack. I wanted to keep the cute pink box, but that was bulky and I couldn't handle the weight. So, the box stayed in the dump.

Dave showed me what he had found at the supermarket. His items included a box of wine made by Don Simon. After a bit of a laugh, we thought we would enjoy stopping to have a sip of wine on our walk tomorrow. Of course, he would have to carry the wine and the box was not all that light. Of course, of course, the wine didn't last long...

It was now time to investigate dinner possibilities. Dave had noticed a pizzeria up the street but I wasn't so sure I wanted pizza – Spanish pizza – as it always involved eggs or tuna. They didn't have a clue about pepperoni or plain cheese. Sausage? They have this thing with chorizo...

Ready for dinner!

We walked up a narrow street off the main street we were on right by the bra store. We saw a lot of familiar-looking pilgrims, though we had not had any real conversations with any of them. "Buen Camino" and a little chit chat was all, but we did recognize quite a few people. We saw the one German girl we'd been sort of trailing since Acebo. We saw a pair of guys we were on speaking terms with. We saw the couple from Australia on the trail today and the girl with the shaved head – they took our picture at one point. And we also saw a man, I think from South America, who kept talking to Dave as we walked on and off today. He was trying to instruct and correct Dave in his Spanish. I think that was what he was doing. He also asked if Dave was a "Boy Scout" after examining the neckerchief that Dave had made painstakingly hand-stamped. "No!" He was the man who told us about a "special" Compostela we could get when we got to Santiago – the San Francisco (St. Francis) certificate. This was the 800th anniversary from the time San Francisco walked the Camino. We had to go to a different church, but he wanted to make sure we understood that and would get the second one, too.

We watched him walk away and then chose the restaurant right on the corner. As did the other people I just mentioned. The two guys behind us recommended the beef for the first course as it was great – "melted in your mouth." I did order the macaroni with the beef and it was really good. The wine was great. As usual. And, as usual, they brought a whole bottle of local wine with the very small label at the bottom of the bottle. If you drank it all, they would just bring you another bottle – it's all included in the pilgrim's menu. Wine. Unlimited. Ice cream for dessert. Yummy.

We finished up and made our way back to the hotel. And up the 36 stairs. Groaning. We were in bed by 9 p.m. And then, squeakkkk. Squeakkk. Not what you think. The beds squeak. Any movement and you were making a

Dessert

racket. This was another slightly uncomfortable night – climate-wise. Nevertheless, we were soon asleep.

"Goodnight."

"Goodnight."

"Maybe I'll get my stick back tomorrow..."

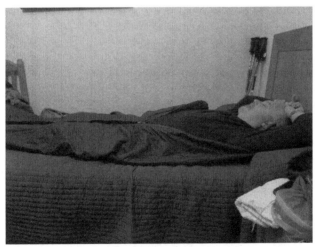

Dave dreaming of finding his walking pole again.

"If It Be Your Will"

Thursday, October 30
Palas De Rei to Portelas
(38,278 steps/16.72 miles/107 floors)

What the hell was that? Obviously, there was a dog kennel somewhere really close. Like on the next floor or in the building across the street. Good grief! We awoke early to a pack of very unhappy dogs – very loud and close by. The howling and crying were unbearable. Somebody feed those dogs! What is going on?

I laid there, stretching my legs. Ow. Ow. Ow. Woof, woof, woof. Owwwoooooo! (me or the dogs? Can't tell). I didn't need to get up – my legs already hurt and I was still lying down. But. I feel thin. I wonder if I've lost 20 pounds. Especially when I'm lying down. I feel skinny. I feel muscular. My pants are falling off me. My clothes are way too big now. At least I am losing weight. I'm sure my blood sugar numbers are really low, too. At least I am getting some benefit from this death march. Dave looks very skinny, too. You can tell we are losing weight like crazy. We are getting lots of comments on FB about our weight loss. At first they were annoying. Did we really look that bad before? And they just kept coming. This is not about weight loss! I am not doing it to lose weight! I feel very insulted. I am doing this for spiritual reasons! I am trying to pray! I want to be more in touch with my feelings! It is not about losing weight! Lay off!

Yes, I'm just a mess. I started out one way and see-sawed my way to different reasonings. The bottom line is – what the hell am I doing here – and why? I guess that will never change.

Enough lying here contemplating and listening to dogs howling in terrific pain or something awful and thinking too many thoughts. Time to actually move my legs and stand up. In planning the last few days of our Camino last night, we wanted to arrive in Santiago on Sunday – in the morning and in time to attend the Pilgrims' Mass in the Cathedral at noon. That meant we had to go a little farther today. Had to press it again. So, we planned to make it to Portelas tonight - about 23 km. It didn't look too physically trying – it was mostly downhill.

Except.

Statue dialogue. Female: "You said it was only this far!" Male: "The guidebook says it is just over this gentle slope!"

Except that that our "expert" guidebook says you have to cross "six river valleys" today but it's on pathways that are mostly through woodland. What I've learned in the past two weeks was that a river valley means you have to go downhill to get to the river and then you have to go uphill to get out of the river valley. So, we have to do that six times today? And woodland means damp, dank, flies, mud, rocks, and gravel, not to mention poop. So, on average we'd be on level ground, but there was a lot of up and down to accomplish that. Not looking forward to another long day. More chickens to see today – and more laundry drying on lines outside. I am constantly puzzled by the clothes. I get that there are not many dryers here in primitive Spain, but why are the clothes so dang ugly? Everything I see is really unfashionable – plain ugly. Maybe they save the "good" stuff and wash and dry it somewhere else? Maybe they do all the unmentionables inside? But no that can't be it either because we do see lots of underwear hanging outside – huge "granny" panties that are as ugly as sin. Of course, I shouldn't talk, what with my bra wires all akimbo and my stretched-out, stinky, awful "Camino" wardrobe, wool "sexy" panties, and all. Maybe today we'll see some nicer things...

We leave at 8:30 and there is nowhere to grab desayuno. Or anything. We stand at the corner, getting our bearings and figuring out where the damn shells start again. I'm already not in a great mood. Another pilgrim walks up to us and stops. "Buen Camino," we greet her. "Ugh! – a frickin' buen

Bev and Karen

camino to you, too" is the reply[16]. And so we meet my new best friend forever! Bev from Santa Monica. And she hates it, too! We bond instantly. I love her. We are laughing immediately and giggling and comparing notes. What in the hell are we doing? That guidebook! God this is awful. I can't wait to be done. We walk with Bev all morning and she is even slightly slower than us/me. We learn all about Bev's life.

And then. Dave and I look at each other and can read each other's mind. Where and how soon can we ditch her? Shallow or not, or even so, we had to make up some time.

But, it's not to be for an hour or two. We have our walking companion. We tell her we fly back home on November 6 and she says she is not leaving until November 10 and "God, I wish I could leave sooner." We hear about her family. She has some grandkids who are a joy and loves them so much. She goes on and on. Yeah, I get that. She gets to hear about Isaac, too. We learn that she used to be in prison and her husband, too – State prison. Drugs. Hashish problem. That was back in the '70s though. She's about 60. She's doing this Camino for her dad, who is loving hearing from Bev about it every day online. She is not walking very far every day and obviously has plenty of time to get to Santiago. She's had some health problems – a cold or flu and had to visit a doctor. She's not a fan, shall we say, of the Spanish health system. She did not have a good experience and it cost her a lot of money. Apparently, it didn't work so well for her as we have heard along the way with other pilgrims.

Bev reminds me of one of David's not-to-be mother-in-laws, an impressive woman who works with dogs, judging Labradors, selling equipment, and in her spare time, as in when she has time on her hands (ha ha), she commits to her business of being the number one exporter of chilled dog sperm in the

---

[16]She actually said something a bit stronger than "frickin." – Ed.

A very cool pilgrim shell mounted on the side of an albergue. Bev stopped for coffee, and we pressed on.

U.K. But, here Dave asks Bev who the most interesting person is that she has met out here. She goes into a lengthy explanation of meeting a German woman, just a day or two ago. The German lady used to work with Mother Teresa. She talked about what they used to do together. I then told her about Bruce, the maybe medic from London and how he told me that people can say whatever they want – no one knows if they are telling the truth. That shut Bev up. I didn't mean to say her friend with Mother Teresa was a lie but Bruce really got me thinking. I could have been giving people all kinds of fun versions of me. Instead, everyone is getting "complaining" me.

We're a little quieter and we approach a downhill patch on our descent to one of those six river beds – in the woodland. There are indeed a lot of rocks and large stones in the way. We have to pick our way over the path and it is tricky. Suddenly, Bev trips and falls, head first, and lands, rolling on her back. She's stuck there on her backpack, like a turtle. Can't move. We react and come over to help her up. She shrugs off her backpack and we pull her up. It was scary but she seems fine. Nothing broken or twisted. We rest for a minute. She thinks we are her angels that were placed there to help her when she fell. I kind of like the idea of being an angel. Someday.

We walk on, a little slower. She's holding us back. Dave can't get his rosary in this morning – every day Dave tells me he says a rosary as he walks – usually after our second stop for coffee. I know he is praying hard, for Dianne especially. I guess he'll have to do it this afternoon instead. I ask later if he'd done it – "of course" and ... if I had been able to keep up, I'd have heard him...

We finally reach a café about 10 a.m. and Bev decides to stop and rest, have something to eat. She's trying to do the Camino on 20 euros a day. Dave and I take advantage of the opportunity and say we are pressing on.

Two of the Korean girls, currently happy hikers.

We keep walking. Bev starts talking with a couple other pilgrims that she apparently knows and we move on. Never see her again.

I'm walking pretty well today. We've made good time so far this morning, even with Bev. I think we did 11 km in a couple of hours. Pretty impressive. We stop for a Coca Cola Light at a bar ahead on the left. There are a few other pilgrims there and we see a group we've seen before – five or six Korean kids – maybe 20 years old. Four or five girls and two boys. They were the boys who had been eating the hamburgers at the top of the stairs several days ago. I have a good memory. One of the girls was very chubby but she is a fast walker! I learn later that there are so many Koreans walking the Camino lately because a movie or documentary or maybe it was a book – something recently came out in Korea about this pilgrimage, so now there is a lot of interest there and many are coming to do the Camino.

We got up to put a few more kilometers behind us. We walked on and on and it was getting to be really warm. We are up and down all day. We take turns passing the Korean kids. They stop and rest and then they power past us. On a downhill path two of the girls come by us – walking very fast, in step, and holding hands – swinging their hands. Happy. Hunh. Where are the other ones?

It's true, we are in the woods most of the day but part of our walk is on streets in a commercial part of a town. We see various other pilgrims walk by us. Some of them are carrying unusual backpacks. I took a picture of one guy who walked by in very short shorts and he had a very large round pack. Really odd looking.

It's so hot. It is starting to affect me. Dave is pretty far ahead of me. I need to sit down. There's nowhere to rest. I stop in the sliver of shade from a skinny tree we are passing and give up. I throw my sticks to the ground. I'm miserable. Dave notices and walks back to me. He says he recognized

Dave is feeling tired, too, although he won't admit it.

the "international distress" sign – throwing your poles to the ground! Yes, Dave's pretty bright but swearing and crying were other clues. He makes me drink water and gives me a gingersnap cookie we had gotten days ago. After about five minutes, I'm ready to go on. Not happy, though!

From Facebook:

Camino Death March continues . . .

We finally come to the town, Melide, and are hungry for lunch. There is not much that we can see. That damn guidebook says to try the octopus in Melide. The "renowned octopus." I don't think so. Fricking Guidebook. Allegedly. New name. I don't care. I am picking up new swearing skills.

We have to cross a river, a bridge, and then there's a long uphill approach to the town and it is very hot. Still. I'm grumpy. Still. Hungry. Still. The day is only half over. At an intersection we spy a small bar a half block up to the left. That's it. We're stopping there. There is one little round table outside on the small patio. We sit there. We order our typical bocadillos and a beer. It tastes great but makes walking later much harder. The solo queso bocadillo is good – nice bread for a change. Small, but it lifts one's spirits.

Inside the little bar is one of the Korean girls. She is obviously upset. She is sort of crying and trying to order lunch. The owner does not understand and she doesn't get it. Dave tries to help. He translates the different kind of bocadillos and asks if she wants meat – chorizo – or just cheese. She looks at him blankly and really has no clue. We order her a jamon bocadillo. She

We didn't see any 'renowned octopus' in Melide. However, this porker greeted the peregrinos from the window of a butcher shop.

sits inside, crying, and we go outside. We can't communicate. The flies are terrible inside. They are less pesky outside but still annoying. We figure out that there must be drama with the Korean group and within the girls. We saw the other two Korean girls walking by, apparently so happy and in love – taunting the left-out girl. We figure that must be it. Deliberately cruel.

We finally finish up and decide to move on. Back on the path and it's a long afternoon. On the way out of town, we stop to look at the local church. We get a sello in our credencials. There's a plate of cookies outside for pilgrims. There's also a couple young kids right outside. Maybe 7 or 8 years old. They take all the cookies meant for the pilgrims. Sigh. We turn left and follow the shells. On the way out of town we pass a school at the top of a hill. There in the fenced field to the right were a couple of horses. One small horse was tied to its trailer. I looked over and saw the rope around the horse's neck was very short – it was tied tightly to the trailer. It wasn't able to move or do anything except stand there. I felt horrible. I looked around but didn't see anyone to complain to. There were no people around watching the horses or near the school. I had seen a lot of what I considered animal abuse or neglect over here in rural Spain, but this was hard to take. I couldn't do anything except walk on, sad, and praying that the horse would be let loose very soon. I hoped. It was upsetting and I thought about that for a long time. An animal in distress – and I'm thinking again about God and praying. Please God, let the owner come back to that horse soon and set

Happy kids eating the cookies left out for the peregrinos.

it free so it can move its head. Please. If it be your will, dang it.

So, as I trudged along in the afternoon, I thought about prayer. I had my list of my Facebook friends and there were a lot of them – about 200 or so – and most I knew pretty well. I had a list of other people, too, not on Facebook, family, friends, others who really refuse to get with the 20th century and maybe even the 21st century and get a dang Facebook account. Thought it was evil or it was going to steal their identity. Anyway, I thought about each one of them. It took a while. I remembered how we became friends, why I liked them, what we had in common. Good, fuzzy feelings. Laughter. That's the common thread. I also have several friends that I would like to "defriend" but keep them around to keep an eye out for what they say, what's up with them. Loose cannons. Quite a few actually, even though one of my life objectives is to avoid lunatics – they are only trouble and I have enough of my own... However, I am usually just sitting there, minding my own business... And I actually spent the most time praying for them. The ones I worried about. And, praying, well that is a loose term for me. But, I thought about them. A lot.

Then my thoughts turned as usual to how useless prayer was – well, actually how limited it is. Turns out I've been doing it wrong for most of my life. The secret is you can't pray for something specific, which I think is much more difficult and actually now it doesn't take long to "pray." "If it be Your will, God." "Do what You think is best, God." Well, if He isn't going to do that, then what use is praying? And, if it's up to Him, then it really doesn't matter what you want. Isn't God supposedly to be merciful? Be like a father figure – a nice father? Be approachable and nice to you? What if someone is sick and you want to pray for them? You can't pray, "Please God let them get better." I think you have to ask "Please God do what You think is best" and hopefully He'll think letting them get better is the right thing.

At prayer in Melide. Please, God, if it be Your will, let there be some cookies left outside...

For the longest time I would pray "please, please, please, God, please let Matthew pass English. A 'B' would be great. I'm not asking for an 'A' – just please get him through." I thought I was giving Him some wiggle room – not being too specific or demanding. Or, "please, please, let Jimmy stop drinking so much Diet Coke. And decide to go back to West Point." And David – I prayed hard for him, too – please! Please! Nothing so specific because there was so much there – just, please let him find a nice girl, settle down, and a good job would be great. And stop smoking. And realize it wasn't going to work out in the long run with the vegetarian belly-dancer. Even though she was very, very pretty and could knit. A dress. I mean, she was a really talented knitter. And we liked her, God. God are you listening? And then there was the really hard one – please, please, please let Veronica get better. PLEASE!

But, my will apparently did not matter. Doesn't work. That damn guidebook, er, God.

Much later I realized that, well, Veronica is better – she's just not here with us. Of course she's better. That's the whole point of religion, isn't it? That when you die you are free and now with God? In Heaven? Happy ending and all that. Father Bob says so. I've heard him preach that many times. "There is a 'happy ending.' " Direct quote. He promised. No worries. It's all gonna end just great. Sounds a little pagan there, right Dave? But priests don't lie, right? I mean, that would be the biggest lie of all. And up

Holy cards and mementoes in the Church gift shop.

there with The Camino being so great. And with Apple and their supporters saying how great their products are. Pick a gadget. Yeah, right. Dave switched over to a Mac. I know. I've heard the swearing. Or that a rice cooker is so great. You must buy one! Yeah, mine is now in the garage. And these new "Government-required" fluorescent light bulbs are just as good. Yeah – I'm squinting here, God! And, sure, Dave will get his trekking pole back. And the black fleece. And that I'm listening to that "Pray/Play" list that I requested and people sent to me. And that guidebook, the expert one. Yeah. Lies. Who's fooling who? There are a lot of lies out there. Apple, and the guidebook, and pick a brand of rice cooker (GE), and God. Yeah, they're all in cahoots.

And I thought too about how people turn to God when they are at the bottom – there is some crisis, health issues, facing death, problems. And is that fair? To seek religion then and not when things were going good? Yes, this was a long walk today and my mind was racing.

I've only been a Catholic for five or six years. I'm a little concerned that once I converted, the whole religion started going downhill. Nowadays it's not so cool to be saying you're Catholic. And now I've got friends who as I was growing up were Catholic and now I joined the club, they have gotten out – quit – not Catholic anymore. They've gotten some bad PR. And people don't want to be associated with "them" anymore. And not just Catholic, but religion in whole is not "politically correct." I'm really troubled that politics and religion are so out of hand. People don't think the same way they used to. The right way. Is religion supposed to change with the times? If some tenet is now politically incorrect, should you change it? Or just stick to your guns and be unpopular and have people label you as wrong?

One thing I liked about the religion was the ritual. The fact that every Sunday everybody in the world was hearing the same readings. So uniting I

Drinking with Don Simon

thought – all the same. I liked that idea. And, the black and white, the right and wrong of things. No gray matter. The history of the religion – geez, it went back to the very beginning. There was a lot I wasn't so sure about but that apparently didn't matter – you only had to agree with the big stuff. The dogmas. I could do that. And I wasn't so sure about the gimmicks – the go-to-church-on-nine-first-Fridays-in-a-row-and-you-get-to-heaven-faster kind of thing. Or visit the four cathedrals/basilicas in Rome and you get a prize. Something like that. Well, I've seen the four cathedrals in Rome so I'm anxious to see what I win. Later. Much later, I hoped. After I was done walking the Camino. Then what do I get?

I sure hope God has a sense of humor. Obviously, I think He must. This is a ridiculous walk. St. James? Bones? Field of stars? Really?

Faith. That's what it's all about. (Like "Beef. It's what's for dinner" and cue Copland song. Great ad campaign with good music.) (Yes, I used to work for an ad agency in Minneapolis.) But. You know, sometimes you do just have to take things on faith. And that is another epiphany for the list.

We were now back into the wooded areas, with just a few more river beds to cross... Later in the afternoon we decide it is time to see what Don Simon has to offer. We stop, wipe the sweat off our brows, and Dave breaks open the box. No corkscrew required! We get out our tiny leaky bathroom cups. Cheers! Not bad, Senor Simon!

Interlude over, we continue, and we walk until I am near madness. The Koreans pass us again. We see that apparently the girls have made up and now the other two are holding hands and swinging their arms as they march down the path. And, then there's a detour. An uphill detour. That never ends. Miles out of the way. Now we're walking alongside the highway. I'm really not happy. Dave keeps telling me the hostel is just ahead. It's so hot

Another day walking.

and I'm sweaty and exhausted. This has been the longest day. I hate you. I hate you. I hate you. I listen to more music on my iTouch and it helps a little as we trudge along the highway. I begin to dare the cars coming toward me to hit me. Go ahead! Try it! I don't care! We finally arrive at our albergue on the right side of the highway. It's about 5:30 p.m. and we've gone over 40,000 steps again. I'm mad. I'm hot. This sucks.

We check in and get a room with three beds again. It's not bad. Pretty spacious. I really don't care at this point. We are the only pilgrims here. It's rather modern and new. First things first, we finish the wine in the box. Note to Mr. Simon – I don't think that was a regulation-size box. It's pretty good but now it's gone. We do up some more laundry in the tiny bathroom sink and we take showers. Dinner isn't until 8 p.m. When we checked in, the girl asked us what we want, so we put in our order early. We tried to explain that we could eat earlier than 8 and then they could close it up but, no, dinner's at 8.

We sit outside and it is getting colder. The sun sets. Our laundry is nowhere near dry but we leave it there overnight. We try checking in with the kids and everyone. Jimmy now has his GI Bill money sorted out and his money has come in. I'm so relieved and happy that it is settled. He had to talk to people again because after they agreed he qualified, they said at first it would only be 90 percent of the GI Bill but now he has it fixed so he gets 100 percent, even though that is not nearly enough to cover Santa Clara's cost. But, at least he's getting everything he should. I'm happy about that.

Dave checks his email while we wait for dinner. Allegedly.

However, Eeyore, er, Jim, continues to be gloomy.

We're tired and so glad when it's 8 p.m. We watch the girl work on our dinner and the table from outside. There is a big glass window. She sets the table. She brings a basket of bread to the table. She spills the basket of bread all over the floor. She picks it up. She notices us watching. She brings the bread to the kitchen, out of sight. She brings a (the) basket of bread (back) to the table. Uh huh. We go in and she serves us the soup we had ordered earlier. It's fabulous. It was a thin, clear vegetable soup but the flavor was wonderful. Tiny chopped pieces of carrots and some other things. Very tasty. I loved it. I don't know the secret for how they make the soup over here that has so much flavor and is salty but yet it doesn't taste overly salty and you don't seem to be affected by the sodium. And the bread, too, was really good. Even from the floor. Maybe. Allegedly. Then, I had the steak, I believe, with French fries. It was a nice meal. Ice cream cake for dessert – my new favorite. And wine. Very good wine. Dave tells me the other room with the bar is hopping – lots of locals in there watching soccer or something. And drinking. Yes, this might be the hotspot of Northwestern Spain, or of Portelas, or of Bolivia[17], that's for dang sure.

My FB post for today:

> So today met some interesting folks. My new bff from Santa Monica wasn't having the best time and wished she could fly home earlier ... Learned she'd been in prison (small hashish problem) and met some lady yesterday who had worked with Mother Teresa. Dave bought a box of wine yesterday and carried it for our breaks today. Yep, gone now. Don Simon – not bad for less than 2 euros. Got the trifecta today too – shot of chickens, flowers, and

---

[17] *Butch Cassidy and the Sundance Kid*

Our bread at dinner. Fresh. Allegedly.

laundry drying on line ... Less than 40 km to go – should be in Sunday morning. Hate that lying guidebook. Today a very long day with detour thrown in (uphill of course). Waiting til 8 for dinner. More later.

Exhausted, we leave and collapse into our beds. We're soon asleep, for a while.

Our room in Portelas.

Boo!

Friday, October 31
Portelas to Salceda
(24,384 steps/10.65 miles/90 floors)

What the hell was that? It's 4 a.m. and there is a creature in the room with us, scratching. I hear a critter scurrying around near my bed! It sounds like it's near my bed. It's by the wall. Am I going to wake up early every damn morning to some weird noise? I nudge Dave. He's right next to me, sharing my fleece blanket. He turns on the light. The noise stops. He gets up and pokes around. Nothing appears. He turns off the light. The noise returns. Light on – noise stops – light off – noise is back. It seems like the critter is in the wall or the ceiling. We don't know why the light affects it but there really doesn't seem to be anything in the room with us. Sure. I can go back to sleep now. Right. Eventually, I do fall back asleep. I am not eaten (or bitten) during the night and nothing seems to be disturbed in the morning. My so-called Spanish Kleenex (toilet paper) and peppermints are all on the table where I emptied my pockets the day before.

It's Halloween. I wonder what Isaac is doing?

We get up and dress, kind of tired from being woken up early. My ankles still itch. I use my wonder-cream. It's 7:30 and we have to hang around for a bit because breakfast is not until 8:30. Dave checks his laundry on the line and sees he's going to have to pin the socks to the outside of his pack again today. It's another nice day but we have been told it is supposed to start raining soon - later today or tomorrow. Our luck has run out. We are going to Salceda today, not quite as far as the last two days – about 18 km, which seems just about right to me. It's also supposed to be relatively flat, overall, although we have a "gentle climb" into Arzua and there is a climb into Santa Irene. There are only three shallow river valleys. Maybe. The guidebook continues to allege, er, say that the Camino now becomes "ever more crowded as we near the fabled city of Santiago." ~~Just mark down everything it says as crap.~~ That statement continues to be false as we never see anything approaching a "crowd" on our entire walk. Even in Santiago, there is only a spattering of people in the huge courtyard in front of the Cathedral.

The man finally arrives and opens the main room for breakfast and we sit at our table. Still the only ones around. We order the café con leche and

A fitting morning sky for Halloween.

ask for pan. After a while he brings us our coffee. We then hear banging and such going on in the kitchen. He comes back to say either there is no pan or the toaster is broken. I'm not sure what he meant except the bottom line was there is no toast today. He still charged us. I went to the other room to see if we could buy any food but nothing looked too appealing in the store and I bought a chocolate bar but that was it. We left my backpack to be transported to Pousada de Salceda, collected our walking sticks, and were on our way. It is exciting to be getting so close – we love seeing the numbers on the shell markers get lower and lower.

We were slightly off the Camino path at this hostel and needed to rejoin it just up ahead a mile or two. We walked along the busy highway. Up ahead we saw a footbridge crossing the road. We then saw a few people on the footbridge with backpacks. Crossing the road. Uh oh. The Camino was up there. But we were down here. There was no way to get up to the bridge. Again, the guidebook had "allegedly" given us bad information. We couldn't get to the Camino from the highway.

So, following Dave, we crossed to the right side of the road and beat a path up the hill through the nettles and trees on the side of the road and climbed/clawed our way up to the bridge. We really did. Ouch. It worked. We cut a swath and pushed the weeds and limbs aside and kind of just reached out and fell into the path. Bam. No one was there, I'm glad to say, to see us pop out onto the trail. We just brushed ourselves off, adjusted our packs, and started off down the path. Dave fixed his sandals. He was getting pretty tired of digging little pebbles and rocks and dirt and now nettles, out of the toes and heels of his open-toed shoes. But – ta da! On the road again...

We walked our way through Ribadiso and then into Arzua. We stopped for coffee and a croissant at the bar right on the path. We sat on the sidewalk at a table conveniently placed there. There were a couple other pilgrims sitting

There are a lot of empties on display outside this Albergue. Karen's interest is piqued, professionally.

Up through the briars and brambles and back on the Camino.

We were used to cow dung everywhere by this point, but how does it get on the sign?

there and we saw a few pass us by. We stayed here for a while since it's been a long morning and my stomach is trying to catch up. I use their bathroom a few times. Every time I go in there and sit down, after 20 seconds the light goes out. I have to get up and run my hand over the switch again to activate it. I would just like five minutes in peace. It never comes.

We walk on and have about 12 more km to go. Dave is making up songs again. This Camino and our togetherness has ignited our passion (as in our ~~hate~~ dislike for our guidebook!). We are bonded – of one mind – in total agreement – ~~Kill~~ Edit the book!

Today, Dave starts in on his own Dr. Seuss story about the trip. Amusing. He is so good at rhymes. And making me laugh. I am reminded of years ago when we all lived at West Point and Dave was teaching there, we lived in a big three-story brick triplex. Those poor Heineys who lived in the middle and had to listen to us in the end unit. Playing games and laughing. Very noisy with three boys. The kids were very young; Matthew was in kindergarten at the time. We loved to play Charades and other games. I recall "The Oregon Trail" was especially popular in our household. "Battleship" and all versions of "Hide and Seek" and racing up and down the staircase to bed. I remember one marathon session of Charades late at night and Dave was acting during his turn, trying to get the kids to guess "Switzerland." Oh my. No one guessed. But we laughed. Nowadays those little kids have grown up and moved on to more exciting bouts of cribbage or Wii boxing or darts. Usually with a small glass of Scotch. Or two. Or three. They can play a long time – especially if Dave is providing the Scotch. But, oh, the power of laughter. It helped in lots of situations. It helped now. Too bad we didn't have any Scotch. Does Scotch come in a box? I wonder.

Rain is threatening but it seems to be holding off. Dave wants us to walk

Crossing an old Roman bridge into the outskirts of an even older village.

faster – as fast as we can today to avoid the rain. I say confidently that it's not going to rain. How could it rain on us? "And I am walking faster."

We stop for lunch and see lots of pilgrims at this spot along the road. I have a guess-what – cheese bocadillo. This time, they have used a different type of cheese – and probably two pounds of it. The bread is laden with a soft cheese. I can't eat that much of it. Luckily, we are joined by a friendly cat – he jumps up on the chair next to me. I feed him bites of cheese and he is happy to get it. I'm not sure but think it is a blind cat – its eyes are slits, though it does open his eyes a couple of times. Hopefully, I didn't kill it with all the cheese I fed it. Hey, it was hungry.

We walked on and then passed a wooded section. There was a long uphill looming in front of us and we encountered a girl – maybe 40ish in age running toward us. She was just running for the hell of it. Said she was just doing a km or so. Down the hill – and then back up the hill. A local lunatic I gathered. We panted our way to the top of the hill. It was hard. Very sweaty, damp feelings. More flies. We rounded a corner and then came upon the same lunatic, er, girl standing at a table that had been set up. She had carved a pumpkin for Halloween with an arrow, and had lots of different goodies on the table for passing pilgrims. She explained that she was just holding down the fort for her friend, who had just bought the "home" there. She pointed and we saw the collapsing ruins of a large country house. Oh my. Just a little work to do. She said the friend hoped to turn the place into an albergue. She then said her friend was driving a pilgrim who just came by to the hospital because she needed help. She was manning the table.

We declined the offerings but then she said she had Popsicles. "Popsicles?" Dave took her up on the offer and I continued to decline until I couldn't protest anymore. She said she had strawberry. So, I had a freezer pop thing she pulled from a cooler beneath the table. Very nice. It did taste good. In

"Hey! You, with the iPhone! Where did the nice lady with the cheese go?"

The jogger tears up the hill, greatly confounding Dave.

A Camino Jack-o-lantern. Very original!

fact, at that moment when I was so sweaty and hot and tired, it was the best Popsicle I ever had in my life!

We noticed a flurry of butterflies swarming the tree next to the table. I took a few pictures, and then we walked on.

The trudging took over. It was mid-afternoon and warm. My thoughts returned again, as usual, to how physically demanding and difficult this was. It was also emotionally challenging. Trying to figure out why you were doing this, thinking straight, keeping your mind mentally sharp. But, actually, you were freed up to think and now the thoughts were flowing. Emotionally challenging, yes, but not as difficult as standing up in court and declaring your two-year-old child to be "handicapped." Now, that was the hardest thing I ever did in my life. Admitting it. Telling the world, or at least Goshen, New York, where we had to visit the county seat. It had to be done in order for the State of New York to provide us with special-ed services for our son. Which they did. And lots of services. And which saved our son and put him on the road to success. And made us advocates of early childhood education and getting help at the first inkling your child needed it.

Yes, I'd faced some emotional challenges in my life. Like, hearing that your husband, in his early-30s, had mouth cancer and they had to operate the very next day and learning that luckily it was caught just in time (no thanks to the military dentist in Georgia who had misdiagnosed the roof of Dave's mouth and called it a "motor oil" problem).

Or, watching your dad die.

Or, standing by and watching your "sister-in-law" (we were very close and she was much more than a sister-in-law) in her 40s suddenly lapse into a coma and linger for years at home, unresponsive but obviously in distress a lot of the time, and then finally, have her die.

Or, watching your son at the hands of a manipulative, rather evil, vin-

"Hurra, Hurra, Hurra. Step right up and get your Popsicles. Fresh Camino Popsicles. Step right up!" Behind her is the "estate" her friend just bought.

dictive, lying, emotionally unstable wife, live together, rather estranged from us and refusing to listen to reason for years until he finally wised up and divorced her (yes, we are not fond of her).

Walk 200 miles across northern Spain? Day after day. Hill after hill. Yes. It qualifies as an emotional and physical drain that will mark your soul forever.

More trudging. More sweating. Brain engaged in the past.

We finally reached the town of Salceda and were unsure where our albergue was located. We followed a sign away from the Camino into the town itself. Good instincts, or maybe God was on our side or something but we did eventually walk right to the correct place. There were several buildings – it was a modern new establishment. My backpack was right there inside the front door. Yep, God.

The man manning the desk handed us a key and told us to go take a shower, rest up and then he would check us in later. My kind of man. His name was Santiago. We went up to the second floor and found our room at the end of the hall. The place was apparently full, and it was in fact completo, which we later discovered (by the noise in the rooms all around us). It was nice. It was sort of art-deco in style with strange lamps, orange-accent colors everywhere, one big bed. The bathroom was nice. We dropped our stuff and unpacked. Dave went to investigate about having a lot of laundry done and he came back saying the man told him his wife would do all of our laundry and return it. So, we gathered a lot of our stuff together and took it downstairs and left it. Whatever it cost was fine. I took a shower and cleaned up. It felt great. We went downstairs and over to the next building where the restaurant and bar were located. We ordered a couple glasses of red wine – pilgrim size,

Dave recuperating at the bar.

er, large size. We bought a bag of almonds to go with them. And potato chips. The salt tasted great. Well, so did the wine. I was feeling good again since the day of walking was over. Relief is a good feeling.

I was sleepy, though, and it was early enough to take a nap. So I did. Dave stayed downstairs doing iPhone stuff and talking with some other pilgrims. We didn't know it then, but our soon-to-be (tomorrow) new best friends, Lynne and Ray, were staying here, too. Pictures tomorrow...

I got up and went back downstairs for dinner, which was supposedly to start at 6:30. There were quite a few pilgrims assembled in the bar area, waiting for dinner. About 6:50 or so, they opened the doors and we took seats at tables. And then the rain started. And the hail started. Oh, we were so lucky to be inside. It came down in buckets for a while. I was so grateful and relieved to be here, dry and safe. And I was praying it would stop and not rain tomorrow! A couple new arrivals came into the room – drenched. I felt so sorry for them having to walk the last bit in the pouring rain and the darkness. But, they sat and had their dinner and hopefully dried off and felt happy they were at last inside.

I had the pasta or something for the first course and the chicken for the second. It was all mainly so-so. I picked at it and it was all right. The waiter came over to give us our choices for dessert – none of which included ice cream. "Ice cream?" I asked. No, he shook his head. "Ice cream?" I asked again. "Ice cream?" He relented and brought me ice cream. Persistence! It was just a lousy ice cream cone from the case they had in the bar, but it was better than that torte de Santiago everyone was offering. Where in the heck did they get all that Santiago torte?

We made sure all of our laundry was present and accounted for and went to bed. It rained hard again and the hail on the roof was fun to listen to – from the inside. We were asleep by 9. And awake by 9:30, and 10, etc. The

The weather outside was frightful, but the albergue was so delightful! This new albergue at Salceda was one of our favorites.

people in the room next to us near the head of our bed were a noisy bunch. There were two women and a man in there. They were tromping all around on the floor with their boots on. Very annoying! And then the people on the other side came in and were noisy, talking. Finally, most everyone settled down and we slept again. Until morning that is...

All Saints Day

Sunday, November 1
Salceda to Lavacallo
(28,514 steps/12.46 miles/111 floors)

It rained all night and early in the morning the people in the room next door were making noise. The clomping. The talking. The racket. Usually people are more considerate and I was surprised they weren't more quiet. And it went on for an hour before we even got up. I kept thinking they'd leave but they were hanging around. I don't know why or what they could possibly be doing. I looked out the window and it was all foggy and misty. Wet. Looked like miserable walking today. I had slept on and off all night because my legs were so sore. We finally got up about 7:30. When we were packing up this morning I had my first definite epiphany of the entire trip. Why, why was I even wearing the small daypack? I crammed most everything into my larger pack and then rolled up the green sack and clipped it on the back to be driven away to our next stop by Jacotrans! What a great idea. I stuffed everything I would need into the pockets of my yellow rain jacket. Camera, medicines, lipstick – all the essentials. I should have done this days ago!

Breakfast was downstairs in this building. As I went down the steps I glanced at the crib they had placed against the wall. Yesterday it was a porta-crib which I assumed they used for babies or toddlers that might be along with their parents but this morning it was the bed for a very big, furry black cat. It looked unhappy to be woken up as I looked at it. I know the feeling. It looked at home there.

We had breakfast served to us and it was very good. Café con leche with orange juice and lots of toast and other pastries. Very nice selection. Another couple sat at a table near us. They spoke English. We exchanged a few niceties and then got up to leave.

It had cleared a little and looked to be more pleasant. It was still chilly and I wore my headband but I was happier about the weather situation, and the totally freeing, no-backpack-at-all situation. We took off and the other English couple, Ray and Lynne – from Sydney or Melbourne, Australia – joined us. We introduced ourselves and felt a nice connection. We had a friendly conversation and they seemed to be about our speed, so we walked

The cat, resting like a baby.

Dave, Lynne, and Ray.

We are now on the last page of the guidebook – immensely exciting!

most of the morning together. We were walking buddies for hours. We learned that Ray had had a stroke and this walk was doing him wonders. His brain was rewiring and the air and exercise were a huge help. His short-term memory was affected and they explained all sorts of things that I don't remember but he was a nice guy and seemed to be doing well. They both talked a lot. I mean a lot. We talked about our experiences out here and Lynne agreed that she didn't quite "get it" either, like me. She wasn't in it for the religious reasons, though Ray was. He was Catholic and she was not. We learned about their family and kids and all about their trip plans. They'd visited the US twice and I heard all about it.

We stopped for coffee after a bit and to dry the sweat off our clothes. Well, Dave had a coffee – Lynne ordered a big plate of bacon and eggs. It was not raining and the sun was out. It was hot again. We continued to walk together. It was getting to be very exciting. We were getting closer and closer to Santiago and tomorrow we would arrive! I couldn't believe it. Today we had to get to the outskirts of the city and actually walk around the Santiago airport. We were staying in Lavacolla – only 11 km or so from Santiago, we thought. Lynne and Ray were going to go a little further today. Dave was still taking pictures of every km marker we reached and the numbers were decreasing and getting close to 0! What a great feeling!

We experienced a huge, emotional moment together in the late-morning. We finally reached O'Pedrouzo - the last page of our alleged guidebook! We were ecstatic! Ray in fact took a picture of us on the road there walking onto the last page of our book, so to speak. One page to go! Unless that kook had the maps wrong and Santiago actually was supposed to be on the next page – it is awfully near the top of the page. And certainly within the scope of the liar's abilities. Wrong again! What's another page of walking? I hoped not.

We left the café and continued walking for miles. We were going down a

It is a beautiful day in the woods, and we are so close to the end! Will the weather hold?

With Ray and Lynne, we try to make a 'horde.'

Even though we are getting close, it is still very rural.

hill and the guys were ahead of Lynne and me. Suddenly from behind us we heard a noise. A pack of bicyclists was approaching at a high rate of speed – very fast. There were six or seven of them. They were not peregrino bikers but local BMX racers, all wearing some team racing gear. Lynne and I were on the right side of the road, so we naturally started to walk farther to the right to the edge of the road to let them pass, when five of them veered to the left but one kept going to the right and started screaming at us, "no, no, no." We froze. He passed us on the right, nearly nicking me, sticking his arms and legs out. It was incredibly scary. We screamed. Lynne, I learned, was a very good screamer, and swearer! She yelled "idiots!" at them at the top of her lungs. We were both severely shaken up. We came very close to being in a terrible accident, and only ten miles from Mecca!

Dave and Ray stopped ahead and waited for us. They asked what had happened. They saw the bikers ride on ahead without stopping. We explained as we stood there shaking. What an ordeal.

We walked on, slower. That had happened in the past, having bikers approach, but they usually yelled out something and then passed you on the left. Pilgrim bikers , though, never went at that fast speed. I hated it when bikers came up on you because they were generally so quiet and you didn't hear them and then they were there. I'd read and heard about bike accidents. We were fortunate to avoid this one.

We stopped for a break and for lunch after coming out of a tunnel and up a slight incline. After we exited the tunnel, a pack of six or eight ATV riders raced through and up the hill. Man, what kind of town was this? On the left was a cafeteria with a large outdoor patio area. We dropped our backpacks (well – I didn't have to drop anything! What a great day!) and went inside to order. Bocadillos of course and Coca Cola Lights. Lynne had ordered a large salad to share with her husband. We saw a couple other pilgrims who were

Packing a Pekinese peregrino...

carrying their tiny Pekinese dog in a small carrier as they walked. Lucky dog, and cute! That's the way to do this pilgrimage – have someone else carry you.

We ate and then walked on, without our new best friends as they were going to be a while, eating that very big salad. As we were walking up and down some rocky, dirt pathways we looked behind us and there was that group of six bicyclists! Again! Must have been some bike club practicing, possibly for next July's Tour de France. They came pedaling down the hill toward us. We sucked in our breath and hugged the hill to get out of the way. I recognized the one guy in his red and white getup who had nearly done me in. I glared at him, one of my best skills. And about half an hour later, they came back at us from the other direction. Maybe there was some contest going on as to who can clip the most pilgrims. Fortunately, that was the last we saw of that group.

We reached the airport and had to walk around it. We heard a commotion down the road from us and saw about two dozen beagles there all excited with three of four men walking up and down and in and out of the rows of crops – hunters! I took pictures.

We couldn't just go straight across the airport – there were runways in the way and all – so we were directed down one long side and then across at the end of the runway, and then back to the center again. We did see several big planes take off – we were approaching civilization! The end of The Way! We left the part of the road near the airport and continued with our walk, which led up several hills. We seemed to walk a long time. We seemed to keep walking up hills, too. We were now out of any recollection of an airport. Back to the country it seemed. I wondered if we were circling Santiago. The city should be right here! But, it was not. And then we stopped seeing the Camino mile markers at 12.5 km.

Hunters on the Camino, just next to the Santiago Airport.

The last milestone marker we saw.

We finally reached the town of Lavacolla but our albergue was on the very far side of it. We finally saw a sign for San Paio and went down a hill and found the building. This was apparently the only local hotel. We checked in and went up to our room. Yes, my backpack(s) had arrived, too. The room was nice enough – it was a hotel after all. The downside: in rural Spain. The two twin beds were pushed together, which was a nice touch, and there against the wall was a small little "chair" (think airplane seat). It was very odd looking but of course the first thing we both thought was – Mimi's bed! We had a good laugh and I do wish she had come along on this trip – mostly because this is it! There's no second Camino in my future! Over the past several years, my sister had been my traveling companion. When Dave had to go somewhere interesting for work (interesting being the key word – for both of us), Mimi and I would tag along to socialize and keep Dave entertained when his meetings were over. A benefit, of course, for Dave – we were only thinking of his benefit, of course! Mimi, unfortunately sometimes got the short end of the stick, er, bed, as sometimes our accommodations accommodated two people quite nicely but a third was sometimes left in a corner. On a hide-a-bed. On a fold-out chair. A rollaway. Something that tended to collapse when sat on. An amusing aspect of travel on the government budget maybe. Always laughable. It added to the story. But we had some great trips. We saw London. We saw France. (We saw Dave washing his underpants ... another story of course). Toulouse. Lourdes. Paris. Rome. Capri. Sorrento. Amalfi Coast. Stateside there was Washington, DC, Hawaii, New York City. Great trips. Anyway, Mimi was not here, though I thought of her often and often was reminded she should have been right beside me, or ahead of me as she is more athletically inclined.

I had been wearing my waterproof shoes today because it was wet out and there was a chance of rain. So, now my feet hurt, and most especially my toes. I took the shoes off and put on the Jambu lightweight sandals. Heaven! Which made me think of "Jambu Heaven." During my sister's last visit, she really recommended the cute shoes she was wearing. The Jambu brand strappy sandals. I had my eyes out for some, and did see nearly the exact shoe at REI. They were fairly pricey but adorable. And so comfy! I bought them. Days later, while Mimi and I were browsing at the Barnyard in Carmel, I saw a sign for bargain shoes. You just had to go down the rickety staircase to the basement to the stacks and stacks of boxed shoes. And there they were - box after box of Jambu shoes! $36 with all sizes and colors. Yep, we were in Jambu Heaven!

I had been afraid the ball of my right foot would give me problems on our walk since it had been hurting for a month or two before we left Monterey. But, the sole of my foot never hurt. Just the toes.

We went back downstairs to the bar area. We were thirsty! And a little giddy. We were almost done. Really giddy! We asked if they had sangria. The young bartender guy said, well, he would have to make it. Ok, so what's the problem? We insisted. And then he asked how much and he showed us

Mimi's bed in Lavacolla.

various pitchers. No. No. No. That one! You know we picked the biggest one! He gathered all the ingredients, two bottles of wine, and such, and was mixing it when the old woman manager came over and in Spanish asked him why he was making so much – he just pointed to us! Sorry, thirsty pilgrims!

At last, he brought over the pitcher. He had covered it with a towel that looked like a handkerchief over the sangria's face. We laughed. Two huge glasses appeared. We poured and it was the best thing I ever drank in my life! And there was so much of it! We took pictures. We laughed. We drank. So, so giddy. I told Dave to hold the camera higher and higher – it's all in the camera angle you know – the higher it is, the thinner you look! See if you can make me disappear!

Well, the sangria was making me sleepy and I wanted a little nap-sy. Just like the good ol' days – in 1976. I went up to rest but Dave wanted to go back to the church on the hill – this was a Holy Day and he thought there should be a Mass at some point. When he returned to our room, he told me about not exactly going to Mass but there was a funeral there – a woman in her 90s had died from this town and the whole population had attended the service – which included Mass. They took her casket outside afterward and shoved her, well, nicer than that, placed her in a crypt in the wall in the church's graveyard with everyone watching. Dave found the whole process that afternoon fascinating. The women were all in the church attending the Mass while the men stood outside in the courtyard, but the whole town was there in attendance.

Sangria in Lavacolla. We "washed" it down.

Funeral in Lavacolla. The casket is being carried to interment in the open crypt. After the committal, workers sealed the crypt, and everyone adjourned to the wake.

Meanwhile, back on the Camino, I took a shower and got water all over the floor of the bathroom. We dressed and went down for dinner. Now that it was 7:30, we could enter the dining room. There were a couple other pilgrims eating here (I can't really use the word "dining"). We ordered from the menu of the day as usual. I asked for the cannelloni to start. I like cannelloni. Generally, usually, at home, if I make it. This was pretty disgusting. I'm not sure what was involved in the preparation, but this was kind of icky. I picked at it and the waiter was not pleased. He took it away. Lo siento! Second course – both Dave and I had picked the meat dish and they brought us a casserole dish to share. It wasn't too bad - like beef stroganoff with potatoes and some vegetables. And wine.

I made another list – a good one this time! These are the things I ate over the past three weeks that turned out to be the very best I've ever had:

1. One apple – Dave and I shared that apple on the trail after leaving our rocks at Cruz de Ferro; the apple that he cut into slices with his dull knife when we were so very hungry.

2. Limon drink in Rabanal when I felt like I was going to keel over and die.

3. The soups – The potato puree Carlos/Luis had made; the vegetable soup from Fonfria; the vegetable soup in Portelas, and the shrimp soup in Samos.

4. The strawberry Popsicle from the lunatic's Halloween stand when I was so hot and sweaty.

5. The pitcher of sangria in Barbadelo. And the second one, too, although the first one was the best!

6. The ice cream cake a lot of places serve as dessert.

7. Almonds; potato chips; Deer Farm mix – the salt served with drinks in most places.

8. Beer. And especially the gift of a beer from the bartender at the "non exist" Don Alvaro town.

9. The sangria in Lavacolla, when I was truly giddy.

10. Spaghetti carbonara at Carlos' place in Ruitelan, shared with 12 French citizens.

11. Ice cream bars at the Ultreia.

12. Queso bocadillos - most lunches were great, especially the first one.

13. Vino tinto (insert any date and time), even a box of wine that cost 2 euros (Camino version of Two Buck Chuck made by Don Simon).

As a last thought, I remembered something I had read about the town called Lavacolla. Apparently, this translates to "wash your butt." Many moons ago (ha ha), pilgrims reaching Santiago had to stop and take baths and clean up really good, which meant washing their asses (and I don't mean their donkeys), and they had to do this on the day before they arrived. I read that most pilgrims did not have a chance to bathe much on their pilgrimage and were quite dirty. So, the town of Lavacolla had places to wash and they were able to finally clean up. We did.

The happy couple with just one day left to go on the Camino.

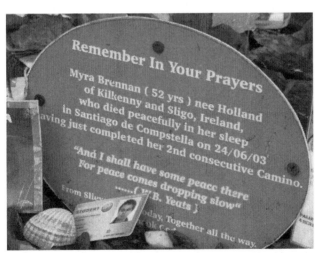
We say a prayer for Myra Brennan, as requested.

Hallelujah!

Sunday, November 2
Lavacallo to Santiago
(19,984 steps/8.79 miles/44 floors)
Karen Does the Camino. Or vice versa.
But, today, Karen Does the Camino.

    We're up early. Excited. We pack and drag my backpack downstairs to be picked up. For the last time! I send my smaller daypack on again today, too. It's so much better to not be loaded down. Dave considered just sending his backpack on again, but he was a true pilgrim and kept it with him. Anyway, from tonight on, I'd be responsible for carting my own pack(s) around. We filled out the tag and inserted three euros into the envelope – we were down to just a small amount of money to pay for the transport. "To: The Parador - Santiago!" A few days ago while scouring our alleged guidebook and deciding where we would stay, we elected The Parador to finish our pilgrimage. This one is known as the "Hostal dos Reis Catolicos," or the Hotel of the Catholic Kings, and is (allegedly) the oldest hotel in the world. It is on the same plaza as the Cathedral. Dave made reservations online and found a really good rate. The "over-55" rate. About 80 euros a night! This was better than the run-of-the-mill peregrino rate that was way over 100 euros a night – and on a weekend I think The Parador ran about $264.00. A night. I was looking forward to it. After all these seedy, run-down hostels, I was ready for an upgrade!

    We had breakfast downstairs in the bar area at 7:30. It was still very dark out. We took a deep breath and stepped outside. We walked around in circles for a bit, trying to find the Camino. We eventually located it up on the hill by the church. And, we're off! We hadn't seen any mileage markers in miles, and the last one we'd seen said 12.5 km. We knew we were close. Really close. We were on the lookout for the guidebook's "crowds." We hadn't seen any "hordes." Didn't see a darn other person the entire morning. No peregrinos at all. And the morning went on and on and on. Did they change the route from our guidebook? That book was so far off. We walked and walked while the sky grew darker and darker. Very ominous-looking clouds approached. The expert notes that we will walk through dense eucalyptus and then the "hordes" will take over. Sometimes, buses drop off loads of people to walk

The weather threatens us on the last day.

Where are the (alleged) hordes? We have the road to ourselves.

Dave makes the "long hike up to Monte do Gozo."

the last few miles into Santiago. Uh huh. Nuh uh. We walked and walked on streets in darkness and quiet. It was cold out and we put our heaviest jackets on, which meant we put our only jackets on. We had our hats on. My hands were cold but I didn't want to stop to fish around for my gloves. It actually felt good to be on the cold side instead of sweating and being uncomfortable.

The guidebook further says that the "long hike up to Monte do Gozo can be particularly tiring." I mentally prepared myself for a huge trek uphill. We eventually reached what we think was Monte do Gozo and there was a big metal monument up on the hill. Not much of a hill. I'm not sure exactly what that book was talking about but we never went up a big hill or were tired or felt any exertion. What? We thought we would see views of the Cathedral off in the distance but we didn't see anything like that. Somebody had planted a grove of trees in the distance and that blocked some of the view, but there was really nothing to see. Except dark clouds. Coming closer.

We marched on. From the top of the so-called mountain, we started on a steep descent. We then passed a sign that said the Cathedral was now 4.7 km away. What!!!? We were still that far away? And then it started to rain. We kept going downhill. The rain picked up. We were now in the city limits and walking on streets. There was traffic. Signal lights. Puddles. It was dark and miserable out. We ducked under cover and shrugged off our backpacks – well, Dave shrugged off his, and we got our rain pants out and put them on. I was wearing my waterproof shoes today and they were holding up for the moment but I knew I wasn't going to be able to avoid soaking-wet feet. Dave was still in his sandals but he was okay with going a few more miles in them, dripping wet and all. We were both so happy and elated that this trip was nearly over. We were almost there and then we could stop. Rest. Take it in and process what we'd just done over the past several weeks. Relish it all. We were so lucky with the weather the rest of our time here that we didn't

It's getting very wet out. Note the mud on Dave's feet and pants. We are starting to appreciate how lucky we have had it with the weather for the last two weeks.

begrudge a little, or a lot, of rain for a few hours. It was just fine.

We walked on, getting wetter and wetter. Click-clack, following the shells on the sidewalks and the yellow arrows painted on the walls of buildings and the streets. We were almost there. Right? We were coming to the older part of town. The buildings were ancient red brick and stone. The streets were cobblestone and narrow. There was no real traffic on these roads. There were people out in the streets – all with umbrellas. We still only saw a handful of pilgrims – you could tell them by the colorful ponchos they were wearing covering the large hump on their backs. The walking sticks. The determined look on faces. The misery. Crossing a street, I finally stepped in a puddle ankle-deep and my feet were completely soaked. Squish squish. Oh well, my waterproof shoes had done their job for as long as they could.

We finally reached the few final winding narrow streets that led to the Cathedral. We could see the spires. We turned a corner to the left and saw an old long building on our right. It was the Hospederia. It's not part of the Cathedral but we weren't sure what it was at that moment. We walked farther and went down some steps and through a tunnel. And there we were in the square in front of the big church. It was pouring rain. There were some people there but not many. The Cathedral is mostly covered in scaffolding. We took pictures and rejoiced. We made it! We really, really did it. Sigh. So, Cathedral. Check. Now, let's go find The Parador and see if we can check in

Karen takes a selfie on the outskirts of town. It is wet out.

Almost there.

Entering the main plaza through the passage way to Obradoiro square.

Made it! Now let's get out of the rain.

The Parador. Wow.

early. It's 10:45 and the Pilgrims' Mass begins at noon. We turned around and there on the square we saw the entrance to paradise, er The Parador. We enter, shake the water off our jackets and walk over to the reception area. We are allowed to check in and a man shows us the way. My backpack has not arrived yet. We go up to the second floor and are impressed with the hotel. It is built around two huge courtyards, in four squares. It is complicated but we are led to our room, which is a long way away. It is a lot to take in. The door is opened and we gasp. Wow.

There are two big twin beds pushed together with a small canopy on top. There are two chairs and a table by the window and an alcove. The bathroom is out of this world – full of granite, marble, porcelain. There are lots of amenities and products to try. Two shower heads in the enormous tub. Heat. I'm thrilled. We shake out of our wet things and hang them up to dry. We sit for a minute to catch our breath and then plan to get back out there. From Facebook:

> *Ta Dum. Made it. Can't believe it. Checked into the most amazing "room" in the Parador. Only three hours of walking this morning but the last two in steady downpour. Feel lucky it held off that long. Drenched but don't care a bit. Only saw two or three other pilgrims this am – thought we missed the memo that the pilgrimage was canceled... Waiting for noon mass at Cathedral (all under scaffolding) and then I'm putting my feet up.*

We head over to the Cathedral and it takes a bit to find the right door to enter. We go inside and the place is jammed full. Where were all these people before? We choose a pew toward the back where we can get a clear view of the altar. We see the botafumerio hanging there from the ceiling. With a lot of rope. Just like in the movie. We don't think they are going to swing it at

It is really raining as we check in.

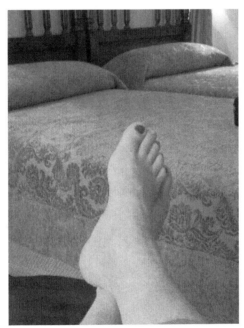

I'm putting up my feet! In style!

The facade of the Cathedral is being repaired.

this Mass, though, because we had heard they only do it on Fridays. We had heard they already did it last Friday and on Saturday because it was a Holy Day – All Souls' Day.

We sat and watched. We recognized a few other pilgrims. There were thousands of people inside. Most were not pilgrims. Mass started and we followed along. This was not to be your typical 15-minute weekday Mass that we'd encountered over here. This was the full-blown, hour-long Mass. With songs. Hymns. Readings. Homily. Collection. One of the songs they did was "I am the Bread of Life." I do like that song and I know it is one of Dave's favorites. I know we sang that at Granny's funeral. One of the distracting things, though, was as Mass was going on, at the far end of the church behind the main altar we could see people walking in single file, going up some stairs, passing by a statue, and then going down the stairs. We wondered what in the world was going on down there. Why weren't they stopped? Mass was going on. It was terribly rude and it bothered me. Most of all – it was a mystery – what was back there? Where were they going? I knew I was going to investigate later but you'd think they shouldn't be tromping up and around during the sacred ceremony! And then some woman put her arms around the big statue down there at the top of the stairs. What in the world?

We went to Communion. And then the priest gave a Pilgrims' Blessing – in Spanish of course but I caught a little of the gist of it. He congratulated everyone for making it and was very proud and happy. He said when we went back to our homes in our own parts of the world to take what we'd seen and experienced here in Spain with us. And, blah, blah, blah. And then, when Mass was just about over, they did it. Several of the monks gathered at the front and they got the big silver botafumeiro swinging. Incense was burned but because we were back pretty far and the place was full, we didn't smell

The botafumeiro swinging at the end of the Pilgrims' Mass. Aaah. So satisfying. You can see our video at http://youtu.be/rtPz8KDL-k0

the intensity of it. Today was All Souls' Day so that was the special occasion. This was cool. Very Cool with a capital C. Now this – this – was just like the movie. Wow – what an ending! "Gotcha, suckers!"[18]

Afterward, we took a lot of photos – a whole lot of photos. We walked around but so did everyone else and it was crowded, so we decided to come back later. It was now time to make this official. We left to find the Pilgrims' Office and get our Compostelas.

It was still raining but we ventured down the street. We were walking down some stairs when we heard our names being called. It was Ray and Lynne from the top of the steps. Hey! Congratulations! They had arrived the night before and were at the Pilgrims' Mass, too. They were just sitting down to lunch at the restaurant right up there. They had taken our advice and were also staying at The Parador. At the online rate. They had tried to check in at the desk with just the "Peregrino Rate" but the place wanted a bundle of money, so they left, went around the corner, booked a room on the Internet as we had suggested, and came back and claimed their now affordable room. We said we'd catch up with them later.

We stopped first at a small gift shop to buy a round cardboard tube to protect our certificates once we received them. One euro. Next we went to the Pilgrims' Office. We were here at a lucky time – I've read that in

---

[18] From the movie, *Bowfinger*. The triumphant ending part of the movie!

The tomb of St. James. The point of the trip, allegedly.

the summers and at other times, the line can stretch for blocks outside and they can process up to 1,500 certificates a day! We just walked right up to the person behind the desk. We handed over our stamped credencials. We verified that we did the Camino for spiritual or religious reasons. Yep. We did. I was moved. They skimmed them. Yes, we walked the whole way. Well, from Leon. You gotta problem with that? They did not. They then filled out the Compostelas – in Latin – and gave them to us. Very Cool! Proof! Of course, they changed my name, and Dave's name, translating into Latin maybe, but I know it's me. "Call Me Catharinam." Maybe. We rolled them up and stashed them in the tube and then in a plastic bag and then inside my raincoat. Safe.

We now ventured back up the stairs and saw Lynne and Ray sitting at a table just inside the window and they were waving. We went in to join them. This was a paella restaurant run by a group of Palestinians who had decorated it in early pro-Hamas, but they said it was very good. We ordered a vegetable paella to share and got two glasses of wine. We are happy and jubilant and best friends forever! We're in great spirits. It's very noisy in the small bar and after we finish our lunch we leave Ray and Lynne.

On our way back to the hotel, we stop back inside the Cathedral. We take many pictures. There is no line now in the nave to see the bust of Saint James. We climb the stairs behind the altar, pause a moment at the top, and touch the back of the bejeweled and enameled sculpture. I take a picture (a venial "no-no" but luckily I don't get caught and no one is here to scold me like in other various European cities where they don't take kindly to one snapping pictures of their beloved cathedrals and basilicas.... geez!) and then we walk down the other side of the steps. I check that off my mental list and bucket list.

We go back to our lovely room and decompress. My backpack is still not

It's official: we made it.

A close-up of the botafumeiro.

The scapular view of the statue of St James that faces out over the altar.

here. We rest for a little bit and then go out again to find a supermarket with some necessities – a bottle of wine, some chocolate, nuts to munch on. Success and we bring everything back again. We find my backpack has been delivered and is sitting on the floor by the bed. Dave takes a bath to soak his poor blistered feet. I later take a shower. It feels heavenly. I use the hair dryer. I put on clean clothes. Amen.

We don't have all the money in the world, so decide not to eat at the restaurant here in the hotel. We go out in the rain to wander the streets and find a decent place to eat dinner. We walk for a long time but don't see much in the way of open restaurants. We do a little window-shopping but there really isn't much to ogle. Well, there is a lot to see, but it is pretty much awful. Clothing that you wouldn't want to be caught dead in. Knitted items. Heavy ornate jewelry. "Frozen" t-shirts. Ugh. We finally come back down the street toward our hotel and go in a restaurant that is open and fairly busy. They have a pilgrim's menu and we order. Dave gets a pizza and I ask for the soup to start, which looks and tastes very familiar like Lipton's Cup O' Noodle soup, and then the pork chop with French fries. The waitress is not in the best mood, at least at our table, and she doesn't cave to my "ice cream?" pleadings. Not available on the pilgrim menu. "Esta bien." I had wine and Dave had a glass of sangria – neither remarkable. We leave and go back to the room.

To my dismay, we learn The Parador does "turn-down" service. They have been in our room, turning back the sheets. Unfortunately, I had left my underwear and other items on the floor, here and there, not really caring about the state of the room when we left. Oh dear.

The beds are wonderful. The sheets – amazing. I wonder what the thread count is. We're back in the real world. Well, at least the real world for people with a lot of money.

Our lovely room

Off to dinner. So very happy!

I checked my email and looked for responses to my Facebook postings. I see that someone's loved one has died. Another friend posted something about the loss of someone. Other people were commenting about Dianne and her struggle with cancer. I was reminded of a posting my high school friend, Sue, had put up a few months ago when she lost her dad. She said someone had posted it on her mom's site and hoped it was comforting. When I first read it I thought – hunh? But I keep coming back to it and thinking about it. I decided I wanted to put it out there to hopefully make others feel a little better. Or give them something to think about.

So, since I am working on my ancient iTouch that doesn't give you any support, I found the poem I was looking for and then copied it down, word for word, in my notebook. Then, I typed it out, one little tiny letter at a time. It took a long time. I was satisfied. Dave was fast asleep[19] by the time I had finished.

The next morning I had a lot of comments saying they appreciated it and thanks for posting it. Dave mentioned it was "very pagan." So, I guess I'm a pagan. I really like the comforting words. I wonder why it is pagan to feel hopeful about death and seeing the people again who have left you. I am always conflicted between feeling like you have to fear God and be afraid, and with a God who is good and merciful and is a father figure. You should not have to fear him. You should not have to fear death. Right? I understand the purpose of religion is not to "feel good" but but but – it helps.

---

[19] Fast asleep? Or slow asleep, as Isaac might chime in, a la "Casey Jones."

This is the poem[20]:

Death is nothing at all.
It does not count.
I have only slipped away into the next room.
Nothing has happened.

Everything remains exactly as it was.
I am I, and you are you, and the old life that we lived
So fondly together is untouched, unchanged.
Whatever we were to each other, that we are still.

Call me by the old familiar name.
Speak of me in the easy way which you always used.
Put no difference into your tone.
Wear no forced air of solemnity or sorrow.

Laugh as we always laughed at the little jokes that we enjoyed together.
Play, smile, think of me, pray for me.
Let my name be ever the household word that it always was.
Let it be spoken without effort, without the ghost of a shadow upon it.

Life means all that it ever meant.
It is the same as it ever was.
There is absolute and unbroken continuity.
What is this death but a negligible accident?

Why should I be out of mind because I am out of sight?
I am but waiting for you, for an interval, somewhere very near, just round the corner.

All is well.
Nothing is hurt; nothing is lost.
One brief moment and all will be as it was before, only better!
How we shall laugh at the trouble of parting when we meet again.
Infinitely happier and forever we will all be one together in Christ.

By Henry Scott Holland

---

[20] In the public Domain

Around and About Santiago

Monday, November 3
About Santiago
(8,817 steps/3.85 miles/21 floors)

Today is a big day! We had lots of celebrating to continue doing, and by celebrating I meant sitting around. Vino tinto was still on the agenda – walking was not.

"Today Is The Day!"

"Today Is The Day The Lord Hath Made?" I asked.

"No! – Today Is The Day I Get My Pole Back!" Dave declared that he planned to stand in the middle of the square outside the Cathedral all day long and wait for the Japanese girl to arrive with his trekking pole! This was the last chance! We were leaving tomorrow for Madrid.

So, he didn't actually do that all day but he talked about it...

I slept okay. That's the best I can say. My legs ached. The bed was comfortable – it was so nice to sleep under the sheets for once. We did not unroll our sleeping sacks! I did not unfold the fleece blanket! I did not wear socks to bed! I did, of course, wear my usual sexiest nightie, er, black wool leggings with black wool long-sleeved top. But, my body was still sore and tight and very achy. It's pouring rain out – still. We dressed and planned to go out to find some breakfast. When we checked in, they were excited to offer us the "desayuno special" if we bought it then - it is usually 30 euros but we could get it for 18 euros right then. That's each, as in per person. We passed. We could probably buy a flock of chickens for that and have fresh eggs for life. But I don't live in Prunedale...

First, we stopped at the Concierge desk to work on arrangements for Tuesday – tomorrow. We had no idea how we were getting to Madrid, where we were staying, or what we wanted to do there for a couple of days. We pantomimed with the concierge man about train tickets to Madrid, now that we knew that "Renfe" did not mean bus. He called his assistant over to help us. They printed off the train schedule and pointed out the best train for us. It left at 9:05 tomorrow morning and would take about five hours to get to

Madrid. We asked about getting a taxi in the morning to the train station and they said "no problemo." The girl was not very helpful coming up with hotel ideas for us in Madrid at a reasonable rate, so we said we'd look into that later on the computer ourselves in the hotel's computer room.

We turned around and there were our BFFs! Lynne and Ray were on their way to find breakfast, too, so we headed out the door together. I had my umbrella that I was using for the first time and I shared it with Lynne. Dave and Ray walked on ahead - quickly. We walked through the square, darting around deep puddles, and down a few streets before ducking into an open restaurant. We saw a dry opening – and took it. We found a table and sat down. Lynne, apparently a good eater, ordered the large plate of bacon and eggs. She was always ordering bacon and eggs. She said she'd lost about 20 kilos on their walk (they'd started in St. Jean). I was impressed, though I don't actually know what 20 kilos translates to in pounds. Sounds like a lot. Dave and I had a café con leche and a croissant and/or toast. Ray ate off his wife's plate. We had noticed that in the two days since arriving here and not walking so much, Ray's speech was not as clear as it had been when he was pumping all that oxygen into his brain while walking. I think that's a lesson that translates to walking is good for a person. Epiphany? I think so! I will add it to the list.

After breakfast, we were off to the San Francisco Church to get our second Compostela, for the 800th anniversary of Saint Francis completing the Camino. It was still raining cats and dogs but we fought our way down the side street to the right church. Yes, they gave us the super-secret, super-special certificate called a *Conventus Compostelae*. A man filled out Dave's and a woman filled out mine. The woman who did mine had very bad handwriting and she scribbled my name. Dave's name is perfectly scribed by the man. Grrrr. I wanted to ask for another one, but the woman did not look amenable, so I accepted it. My name wasn't even in Latin. Geez. Dave went off to buy another tube to put them in to protect them from the rain and then he returned and we stored them safely.

The artwork at the San Francisco church was amazing. The statue of the Death of Saint Joseph was touching. There was an excellent bas-relief painting of souls in purgatory appealing to the Virgin Mary and St. Francis for their prayers. Dave told me later that this was his favorite piece of art he saw on our entire trip. I liked the sculpture/statue of the Death of St. Joseph best. Funny, we both had our favorite pieces in this last church we visited – San Francisco!

We wandered around the church. We talked to a few people and the question inevitably came up – "where are you staying?" At first we were reluctant to actually say "The Parador." But after admitting to it a few times, we actually got a few responses from people saying, "we're staying there, too." And then Dave came in for the killer – "and it's especially great with the online rate..." and seeing the sick look on most other people's faces... "Online rate? We're paying about $264.00 a night... what are you

Obtaining our second Compostela. Note the woman on end must have flunked kindergarten handwriting lessons.

The Death of St. Joseph.

Souls in Purgatory appealing to the Blessed Virgin Mary and to St. Francis. St. Francis, in turn, appeals to the Crucified Christ, above, on their behalf.

paying?" Dave got to mention our great rate to quite a few people while we were there. Not quite pilgrim spirit-like, but kind of satisfying. And we did think back to our first night in Leon – we probably should have checked the online over-55 rate instead of just paying the pilgrim rate, which we assumed would be the best out there.

We headed back to The Parador since it was kind of miserable wandering around in the pouring rain. Cold, too. We sat in the lobby and then went into the restaurant/bar area and had a coffee. It was nice to just sit and rest, knowing we didn't have to walk anywhere today. Still flying high... Dave went to the computer room in the hotel to look into where we could stay the next two nights in Madrid. He got to mention our online rate to a few people there, too. He came back to our room excited he had come up with a plan – and it made sense. We now had reservations to stay at a big hotel near the airport and then we would figure out how to take the Metro or a bus into the city each day to visit. The important thing was being close to the airport since we flew out early on Thursday morning.

And now what else to do? Go find lunch. By now, it had cleared a little and it was not raining. We walked to the center of the square in front of the scaffolding, still amazed. And suddenly, there in front of us stood Joe – the 22-year-old from Rome we had met and eaten dinner with on our second or third night of the journey! We were so happy to see each other! We hugged and took a picture. Of course, he had arrived in Santiago over a week ago and had been to Finisterre and back, but still, we managed to cross paths again and see that we had each made it. A great accomplishment! We wished each other good luck and walked away and now we'll never see him again. It's a sad feeling. You meet someone and they make a tremendous impact on you – and probably for a lifetime. And they never know exactly how much they meant

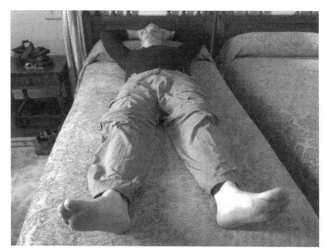
Dave soaks up some of that over-55 Parador discount rate!

to you at that time, in the future, or that they did make a difference. What's this? Another epiphany bubbling up? Know that you make a difference in someone's life. It can be in a positive or a negative way. But, try to help. Be kind. Be a pilgrim: grateful, and helpful to all you meet.

We walked up another cobblestone street and picked a place to eat. We opened the door into a large, long room that was pretty busy. It reminds us of a French kind of pub, if that makes sense. A place in New York City maybe? There are comfy chairs and tables near the windows. It's rainy and the panes are steamy. The umbrella stand at the front entrance is full. There are lots of tables lining the sides of the room. Wood floors. Interesting pictures hanging on the walls. Is that Rachel and Monica over there in the corner on the couch? At the end of the room mounted high near the ceiling is a large screen and they are showing a loop of Camino slides. Familiar places. Fun to watch.

We sit at a table and the waiter brings us the menu. I order the risotto with seafood and Dave orders a pizza. And wine. We see that near the window at a table sit our fellow pilgrims from Lethbridge, Alberta. His name is Doug but I can't remember her name. Apparently, he made it with his numb leg and all. He later walks over and we talk for five minutes. It's fun to see all the other people who struggled to get here, get here. They'd been here for a few days, too - since Thursday, I think. We mentioned The Parador – the online over-55 rate and all... They weren't staying there.

Our lunch is very good. My risotto is really tasty. We have another glass of wine. It's good to sit. (I am saying that a lot, I know. It is true.) And then in walk two more pilgrims we had bonded with days ago – David and Lynne from Australia. Hotel Novo time! Me, locked in the bathroom and so angry! Ages ago it seems. She was the one who couldn't walk down the hills – bad knees. It was fun to see them. We talked for a minute... staying at

Karen and Joe in the square.

Posing at the cafe as if Mimi was with us.

David and Lynne with their ice cream.

The Parador – online over-55 rate and all... and then they grabbed a table with some other people in the back. They had arrived several days earlier, too. As we were leaving, we went over to their table to say goodbye and take a couple photos. They had eaten by now and were having dessert delivered – they had huge ice cream sundaes that looked amazing! Three big scoops of ice cream, chocolate sauce, and whipped cream. I wish I'd ordered dessert now! Deprived, I've been thinking about that huge serving of ice cream for days now. I'm still thinking about it.

We walked up and down more streets – it was time to buy some small souvenirs. Most shops sold the same variety of junk. I found a few mementos; mostly refrigerator magnets to remember our pilgrimage. It was time now to do some more celebrating – I wanted to go take a nap. Dave wanted to do the tour of the Cathedral in the basement. So, we split up and did our own thing for an hour. The shops were closing now and wouldn't open until 4:30. I did want to go back to visit the "official" pilgrim store next to the official Pilgrim Office. We also planned to go to the Renfe office, conveniently located right next to the pilgrim store, and buy our tickets with assigned seats for the next day.

I didn't sleep but I rested. "Just closing my eyes," as my dad would say. I'd thought about him a lot during our walk. He's been gone for 20 years now, but small things always remind me and, crazy or not, I believe he is still sending me little messages and presents in my daily life. But, that's another story... Dave came back to the room and then we went back out. The Renfe office was now open and we bought our tickets on the 9:05 speedy train to Madrid from the man sitting there. Seventy euros each, I think. Fast. Efficient. Coach 8. Then we went on to finish up our bit of shopping. I found quite a few little things I wanted at the official shop and bought the sweatshirt I had contemplated earlier. I should have investigated that purchase a little

Someone is so happy!

harder because when I got home and opened the package, even though it said XL, it was indeed for a kid. If it wasn't pink, I'd think Isaac could soon wear it. Sigh.

While buying my selection of mementos at the counter Dave pointed out two little yellow rubber duckies sitting right there – peregrino ducks! Cutest thing ever. I had to have one and I gave it to the woman to add to my purchases. Seven euros but, my, it meant something what with all the Cottey College[21] paraphernalia I had accumulated over the years. Ducks have a special meaning at Cottey. Turns out all my must-have souvenirs totaled a bigger amount than I had expected, but, heck, I hadn't been shopping in weeks! Plus, Dave reminded me that when we leave Spain at the airport we can file to get our VAT back and they refund ten percent of the sales tax we non-residents paid! That makes it sound much better! Glad I got the duck! I should have bought two!

We wandered for a bit more and then ran into more acquaintances from the Camino – this time it was the couple who were now a "couple" – the young girl from Colorado and the older guy from the Northeast. We were very glad to see each other and happy we had made it safely! And over there, skulking around the corner! Walking down the street was the Korean snorer in his blue jacket! He had not been murdered by his fellow bunkmates! Good for him.

---

[21] Cottey is the college I attended in Nevada, Missouri. It is a two-year girls school, and boy, is that another story...

The Peregrino duck.

Karen with the Camino Couple.

Dave, Ray, and Lynne.

Again, and for the final time, we saw our friends, Lynne and Ray, and they were headed over to the Hospederia to visit a friend staying there. We said our last goodbyes, as indeed we don't ever see them again. We have exchanged email with this couple, though, so possibly... Dave had taken video of the Botafumeria ceremony and posted it on YouTube and Lynne wanted a copy, so he was able to get it to her via her email.

We bought another bottle of wine from a merchant who was happy to learn we were from Monterey - there is a Monterrey in Spain, too, besides Monterrey, Mexico, and they apparently make a lot of wine there. But, we bought a bottle of wine from Monterey County - USA, and headed back to our room. Approaching The Parador we could see down the quaint street in front of us and the red tile roofs of buildings down the hill. The rain had stopped. It was about quarter to six and the sun was sinking. But, the light! Oh the light! It was a beautiful sight. I took several pictures but I've learned that a camera just can't catch some things. You had to be there.

Inside, I unpacked some of my purchases and then I noticed that the girl had not put the duck in the bag! Tragedy! I was very upset. The receipt definitely showed we had bought it. I was unhappy because just about every place we bought something, meals included, Dave would catch some error or other where the place was overcharging us. He pointed it out and every time they adjusted the total, but it made me wonder... Now, I wondered if the girl meant to gyp me out of my duck! Dave said he'd go back and retrieve it. He was back in about 15 minutes – "quack, quack" – someone was at the door. I let him in. Squeak, squeak. I was very happy to have my peregrino duck. Well, until I got home and Isaac seemed to think it was his duck. "Thanks, Grandma!" And then he left it on the counter and Misty seemed to think it was her duck. "Squeak, squeak." I reclaimed it and stashed it up high – until the kid with his memory like a steel trap remembered it.

Karen is enchanted by the evening light.

Meanwhile... back on the Camino, about 7:30 or so, we ventured out again to look for dinner – our last meal in Santiago. We headed down a different direction this time and then turned right onto a side street. It was pretty dark out and didn't look encouraging. There were a few places open and we scoured the menus posted outside the door. We decided on one restaurant on the right side of the street. We think it's the one our friends from Lethbridge had recommended. It's small, very warm inside, and we are the only ones there. Well, personal service, right? We ordered off the menu del dia. We read on signs posted all over the walls that they are going to be closed on Wednesdays. Not that that's an important detail here, but in my attempts to be detailed and truthful, don't try to get a meal here on a Wednesday / miercoles.

The wine we get is excellent. The bread is excellent. About half an hour later, we finally get our first course and it is excellent. I have ordered the soup and it's flavorful and just great. Another half an hour, and we get our second courses. We have both chosen the chicken and it is excellent. It's tender, roasted, flavorful, and just delicious. With French fries, of course. All in all, an excellent meal. One of the best we've had in Spain. The one odd thing about this place, though, was the atmosphere. As in, creepy. The waiter stood over Dave's shoulder by the bar the entire time. Staring straight ahead. He'd come over to check on us every once in a while, and his wife was doing the cooking in the back behind the curtain, but then the man would just stand there and be right in my field of vision. Odd. Heroin problem?

Dave overseen by his waiter.

We'd heard there was a big problem here.

And then the peculiar waiter came and asked about dessert and we said we'd have ice cream. Well, not like that – "helado, por favor." But, he just returned to his post, lurking near Dave's shoulder. We waited for half an hour. We were still finishing up the excellent wine, so I thought maybe he was waiting til we finished that first. Another group entered the restaurant and he waited on them. We continued to wait. If we weren't having ice cream, you'd think he'd be bringing us the bill then. But, no. Finally, we motioned him over and asked, "Ice cream?" Oh, you want ice cream? He then went over to his cart and brought out two ice cream cones and that was dessert. So, not a great ending but an interesting dinner. Let's say memorable, which is a good thing. Adds to the story, er, experience.

We had planned to go back to the Cathedral one last time. I wanted to check out the pole – the one you aren't allowed to touch anymore – it's really a statue of St. James and is in "the movie." "The Way" with Martin Sheen (#2 on my list). Dave had seen it (the pole) earlier today and I now remembered it and wanted to see it. I'm sure I could touch it. I was confident. Just need a distraction, right? So, we went off to the square and it was a little past 9 p.m. There had been a Mass at 8 p.m. But by the time we got there, all the huge wooden doors were locked up tight. I was disappointed. I blamed it on the ice cream – that dang delay getting our dessert and out of the restaurant! Or that heroin-crazed waiter who was too stoned to remember "Helado, por favor." Rats! I thought we could maybe come over first thing in

The "Pole." Also known as the "Tree of Jesse" on the mullion in the entrance to the Portico of Glory. Dave saw it. He did not touch it, as it was off-limits.

the morning and check it out, but alas we didn't have the time and I ended up not touching, er, seeing, the pole, er, statue.

We got back to the room, packed, and redistributed everything. From here on, I would carry my own backpack again. I surely would have liked to stuff a couple of those gigantic white fluffy luxurious bath towels with the big embroidered "P" into my pack, but they wouldn't fit – that's one excuse. We left to go wander the halls for a little bit, check email downstairs one last time, and let the staff do their turn-down service for the night. I had picked up my underwear from the floor and everything was neat and tidy tonight. I wanted to leave a good impression.

We returned, set the alarm for sixish, and were soon asleep.

Happy Parador Peregrina!

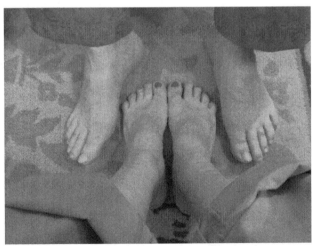

So nice not to walk. Our feet have held up pretty well.

Adios, Santiago

Tuesday, November 4
Santiago to Madrid
(10,400 steps/4.54 miles/12 floors)

It was a short night – my legs ached and I woke often. My mind had started again – thinking, planning, worrying. I had set my alarm (twice) and Dave had two or three alarms set. Not sure why – we hadn't used alarms since we'd been in Spain. But we did want to make sure we were out of here around 7 and downstairs to find a taxi. Uncertainty – we didn't know how long it would take to round up a taxi and how long the taxi would take to get us to the train station. The concierge had told us we could walk to the station. After we stopped laughing, we asked how long it took a taxi to get there. Five or ten minutes.

We packed up and I had the brilliant idea to just wear my backpack from here on and not bother with stuffing it in the luggage bag that made the whole thing so ungainly. And heavier. I'm sure of it. So, we were up at 6:30, shut off the extra alarms, dressed, and took a last loving glance around the five-star hotel of the kings or Gods or whatever Catholic royalty this place was named after. We trudged down the hall, around the courtyard, up the stairs, through the center atrium, down the other hallway, up the other stairs, to the short hallway with the elevator. Downstairs and we checked out quickly. A taxi was summoned. It was raining lightly but not cats and dogs like the other day. I had given up on the idea of heading back to the Cathedral to see the "pole" of St. James.

We tossed our backpacks in the trunk and I had a vague fleeting memory pass through my mind of watching five or six bellmen in Barcelona try to load our five or six huge suitcases into the back of a taxi – years ago. We jumped in. He took off and we sped down the dark, wet streets of Santiago. This was a large city now that we could actually see through our glasses. The taxi went so fast. We hadn't been in a car for ages, my short quarter-of-a-mile jaunt days ago a distant, and alleged, memory. We went around corners, stopped at lights, turned this way and that. It was certainly not a five or ten minute ride. Possibly 20 minutes later and we arrived at the train station. We were there in plenty of time. We already had our tickets and now just had to wait to find out what platform we needed to run to.

It was dark and wet as we arrived at the train station in Santiago.

We went into the cafeteria and set our backpacks down in the corner. Dave went up and bought us cafés and croissants. It wasn't yet 8, so we had lots of time to kill. We ate and watched the TV in the corner. Apparently, that Spanish nurse was cured of Ebola. Great news. Too bad for her dog, though. The place was starting to fill up with other pilgrims getting out of Dodge, er, town. It started raining quite hard and we were glad to be inside. The tracks were covered, so we wouldn't get wet but it was awfully gloomy outside. Other trains came and went. We started paying closer attention and finally it was about 9. Our train was going to be late. They announced it would be here about 9:15 and they gave us the platform number. We went to stand in the correct place and waited.

After a few betting opportunities (which direction the train would come in from, how late would it be, etc; etc.), and it arrived behind me. I won. Wasn't late enough, but whatever. 9:14[22]. We took our seats and the train soon left the station.

Not much to report here except sitting, riding, and watching the speeds approach 240 km. We bet on that, too. Over or under 240. The weather was improving. There were monitors throughout the train car showing movies. I didn't plug in my headphones but watched some of the first movie starring Julieann Hough, whom I recognized from her dancing days, not the judging days because this was obviously pre-boob job, but she was cute enough. She might have killed someone or else was escaping a crazed boyfriend, moved to a beach community, liked to ride an old green bike, got involved with an attractive young man with a young daughter, then there was a lot of disaster, some fires, beach times, pictures being taken, and then the lunatic

---

[22] Over the years, Dave and I often amuse ourselves with these little "games." He should know better by now, of course, as I'm a good guesser. And I have a good memory. December 12, a day that will go down in infamy....

Leaving the Santiago train station

On the train to Madrid.

Arriving in Chamartin.

old boyfriend or husband showed up and tried to kill her. It all ended well. I think. Next up, a Greg Kinnear movie and again I did not listen to the dialogue. Something about him, an ex-wife, their teenage son having growing pains through puberty, a possible girlfriend, and I think Greg and his ex-wife ended back up together. Maybe.

Anyway, we got into Chamartin at 2:45 and it was not a bad ride. We had bought a couple of croissant sandwiches at the station café before we left and some potato chips, so that was lunch. Can't live without my daily staple of potato chips. Now, we just had to remember how to do this commuting stuff in reverse from when we arrived on October 15. We wandered around Chamartin for a bit but it was easier wearing the backpack. Our commuter ticket on the local train was included in the price of the ticket from Santiago to Chamartin. But, we had to find the right ticket counter to get the ticket exchanged. We stood in line and eventually we had our local tickets in hand. We waited again by the big board to see what platform the train would arrive on. Panic was setting in because we only had two or three minutes now before we were supposed to leave on the train to the Bajaras Airport. Dave ran back to the ticket agent and asked and she wasn't sure either, but said to try 10 or 11. We gambled and went over to 11, which was down the hallway, escalator, tunnel, hallway, and stairway up again. They finally announced the local train and we were in the right place. We jumped on and it didn't wait around long. We rode the ten minutes to the terminal at the airport.

In reverse, we got off, rode up the escalator, and wandered back and forth for a bit until we figured out the best way to get to our next hotel, which was supposedly "close" to the airport. We were booked at the Hotel Auditorium, which has 869 rooms – this place was huge, huge, huge. They had an airport shuttle van. But first we had to take the regular airport shuttle from this

The room in the Hotel Auditorium was nice enough, and a relative bargain. Relative. It cost more than the Parador in Santiago, though.

terminal, T4, to the regular terminals, 1, 2 and 3. Half an hour later, we stood outside again in the designated area for hotel shuttles. Soon the hotel shuttle arrived. Fairly easy. We got on and the driver was friendly and gave us some suggestions that we tried to understand in his "sure I speak English" voice. The ride to the hotel took about 25 minutes. It was close to the airport but not really that close. He said this was the only hotel near the airport. Sort of. We saw some others. He gave us recommendations for dinner tonight as we told him we'd be going downtown into central Madrid after we checked in and then figured out the Metro system.

So, in not too long a time, we had swooped into Madrid, figured out their entire transportation system (in a foreign language), and were able to get around and into Madrid and back to the airport and the hotel. Not bad.

We entered the huge lobby at the hotel and checked in. We were in Cell D. Not kidding. This place was arranged in four giant cells. Big squares built around atriums. We were in the farthest cell away. Of course. We walked and walked down the gigantic first floor and found Cell D and then the elevator up to the first floor, which was really the third floor because in Spain they don't count all of their floors. Room 1406 – down a looooong hallway. The room was not bad. One pretty big bed. Spacious. Bathroom. Hair Dryer! We unpacked and did a little laundry. And then it was time to venture out again. We were pretty hungry. Now we had to do almost the same thing in reverse. Again.

We went back down to wait for the hotel shuttle, which left every half hour. It would take us back to the airport. There, we got off at Terminal 2 or 3 and wandered til we found the entrance for the Metro station. We talked to the agent there and bought the two-day package and got our Metro ticket. Then, just like in London, Washington DC, or NYC, we entered the

There was an interesting car display in the lobby of the Hotel.

turnstiles, went up and down tall escalators, avoided crowds, and studied maps of all the stops with strange names. We found the right Metro line and got on the right train. We had to change three times to get to the center of Madrid. We were going to Plaza Mayor.

We finally left the Metro station and went up to street level. The place above-ground was hopping. Lots of people out milling around. It reminded me a lot of London. Lots of shops. Everything was lit up and open. People all over. Police there, too. Loud. Not pilgrim-like. We started looking around for some of the street names and restaurants our shuttle driver had recommended. We couldn't find any of that. We walked on. We passed El Corte Ingles! My favorite Spanish department store that I remembered, especially in Barcelona with Matthew.[23] I planned to check the store out later. But, we were on a mission now to find Plaza Mayor that I remembered from my high school days – peel your own shrimp, rip those heads and legs off, rum and coke and sangria, flamenco days. We passed lots and lots of drunk young guys – singing, drinking, carousing. Really making a disturbance. The police were all over, watching. So many young men and singing drunken songs, weaving all over the streets and sidewalks. What was going on?

We finally wandered our way into the right plaza. Wow! We couldn't believe our eyes. The place was trashed! Never have I seen such a disaster, not even with some of the people who have lived with us in our house[24]! Bottles, glass, paper, junk everywhere! All over the plaza! All over the restaurants and bars and outdoor cafes bordering the plaza. It was a huge mess. What in the world? Then we learned from other people that there

---

[23] In April, 2009, Dave had a consulting gig in Barcelona, and Matt and I came along to keep him company. And to see Spain. And then afterward take a 14-day Mediterranean cruise, while we were there. What the heck. But that, too, is another story: *Huevos Dias*.

[24] Yes, another story.

Liverpool soccer hooligan mobs out on the streets of Madrid.

A very trashed Plaza Mayor.

We did not eat here.

was a soccer game and the Liverpool people were in town to play the Madrid team. A huge deal! Wow! I wondered who had won and who lost. It turned out that they hadn't even played yet!!! This was pre-game celebration, or destruction. I really couldn't believe my eyes. The bar managers and waiters had big brushes to clean it up and they were trying to sweep it all away. They looked resigned but not mad. This must happen all the time!

We walked and walked in circles. The place was a madhouse. The soccer game was to take place at 8:30 tonight. Right now it was 7 p.m. We were trying to find a "nice enough" place for dinner. There were no pilgrim menus or "menu of the day" here. The prices were outrageous. We studied menus posted outside the restaurants. Nothing appealed. Didn't want to pay that much anyway. No wine included with the dinner? Outrageous! Yuck. Ick. No way. Eboli. Yes, we passed that restaurant. Keep walking...

Down one side street, through another plaza, another square. More people. Lights, open bars. Laughter. Noise. Music. Drunken people. We even saw Mickie and Minnie Mouse, Disneyland style. Crazy. We finally decided on a corner place – nice looking. Busy but not too busy. It was a "traditional" paella restaurant. They had the TV on at the end of the restaurant and other screens mounted in places around the ceiling. They were showing soccer games, apparently warm-up games. We ordered the special – paella with seafood. And sangria. A big pitcher. It was really good sangria. It didn't taste as good as we'd had back on the Camino, though. Maybe we weren't thirsty enough. Or among pilgrims. Or something. The paella was the traditional Spanish dish, served in a huge black cast-iron skillet. It was fine, good, adequate, for saffron-flavored rice with big prawns, clams, mussels, shrimp, etc. You had to peel the seafood but it was okay, for the little bits of seafood you could pry off. And then your fingers were a mess. But, we were grateful to be there. For many things. Amen.

We have a little Sangria before dinner.

Dinner was good, but something was missing. I think it was the feeling of exhaustion...

The piano man serenades the soccer crowd back at the Hotel Auditorium.

Annnnd. Reverse. Metro. Metro. Metro. Airport shuttle. Hotel. Ahh, we entered the lobby and there was that dang soccer game on the TV in the lobby bar, which was enormous. Lots of tables, lots of people watching. We sat and had a glass of wine to watch for a minute and check email. At the same time, there was a man playing the piano up near the TV by the wall. It was slightly distracting with the nice, classical pieces and the soccer match, all at the same time. He'd leave for a break and the woman next to the TV would turn up the sound. He'd come back to play and turn it down. Interesting dance. I preferred the piano, but then, soccer's not my thing.

We had enough and went off to bed. It was 10:30 PM– so late!

Happy Anniversary!

Wednesday, November 5
About Madrid
(15,885 steps/6.94 miles/15 floors)

"Happy anniversary, baby, got you on my miiiiinnnddd." Little River Band. I like that song.

31 years! It was going to be a good day. And a good year. I have a positive attitude.

I slept well.

Oh, it was great. Got up at 9:30. AM! Starting to act like a Spaniard. Stay up late, get up late. We dressed and started our usual day. No breakfast here. We hopped on the hotel shuttle and rode to the airport. Found the Metro and took our three trains to central Madrid. We were headed back to Plaza Mayor to see if they managed to clean up the disaster area from the night before. I wonder who won the soccer match? We headed off in the general direction and then noticed another crowd – good grief... a huge crowd. All standing outside the gigantic white palace. We joined them. It was now about 12:15 p.m. I remembered this from 1976 – changing of the guard? Was that it? We stood and waited for something to happen. I was hungry. Kind of had to go to the bathroom, too. Impatient. Darn – the trowel was back in the hotel room– LOL!

About 12:30 the action began. We saw some horses prancing about, approaching. Guards, a band. The Army? A big procession, that was for sure. This appeared to be a huge deal. We watched, everyone's arms stretched out, cameras and iPhones held high and protruding; blocking my view, sort of. I was actually up fairly close to the action in the second or third row. The whole she-bang marched into the courtyard right smack dab in front of us and did some drill movements. The band played, marched, paraded, and exited stage left. The crowd followed. We followed, too, as the crowd dispersed, heading off to the left. Everyone seemed to turn right at the corner of the building, and filed into the tunnel and gates to the center of the palace. We went inside, too. Everything was assembling there. Horses, band, cannons, Army. More crowds and lots of stands set up. More ceremony.

We watched for another half an hour as the parading continued. We finally had enough and backed out and left. We went to find something to

Parade begins at the palace in Madrid.

More from the parade.

More horses!

eat. We walked up one of the center streets and entered a small plaza. We had a clear view of the palace courtyard and it was all still going on. But, we ordered. Anniversary – so, wine, right? Yep. And we pointed to the menu at something that seemed equal to a "cheese bocadillo" – which turned out to be bagel-like sandwiches with ham and cheese. Very tasty indeed. And the plate of potato chips that accompanies every foodstuff anyone ever orders in Spain, and the French fries that accompany every entree for dinner. . .

It was a nice day. The sun was shining. It was cool and breezy but with the sun beating down, if you were in the direct rays, you were fine. We sat outside at a patio table and turned our faces up to the sun. Heaven. Grateful. Nice wine. The waiter was kind of rude to us, but, whatever. We sat and enjoyed it for about 40 minutes. The crowd broke up and we watched people mill about. Dave "Googled" what this was all about and we learned that once a month they have a grand event like this and the whole town turns out. The first Wednesday of every month. Well, we certainly timed that out – I do like somehow meandering into where you're supposed to be. Providence. Again.

Unfortunately, Dave did not feel so good today and wasn't in a great mood to do a lot of exploring. He wanted to get his hair cut, so we finally left our place in the sun and walked off. We passed a couple of "hairdressers" but they weren't open, and then we came upon that El Corte Ingles store I was looking forward to seeing. They had a barber on one of the floors, so he went off to see about a haircut while I found the cosmetics floor and the Givenchy counter. So many weeks without makeup. And now – Givenchy! I loved my Givenchy lipstick in fuchsia that I had bought in Hawaii – the only place to find it in a store, I thought. I may have been misinformed. So, I was thrilled when I saw they had the brand there, and they had the lipsticks in the little leather containers I wanted. The saleswoman was thrilled, too.

The peregrina shopper with her camera and bag of Givenchy products.

I picked a couple. Hell, I picked out six. My rationalization – at least I'd get the value-added tax back at the airport when we flew out. And, a couple of these lipsticks were "special-edition" colors. Yes, I was doing some binge lipsticking.

The rest of the store sucked. Well, there were floors and floors you went up on the escalator, sort of like the old Dayton's in downtown Minneapolis, but there was nothing of interest. I tried. I was quite satisfied with the lipstick selection. Grateful. Well. To be truthful, I did go back to the Givenchy counter ten minutes later on a whim to see if they sold my favorite scent, my "signature" perfume by Givenchy – Eau de Givenchy. I asked a different saleswoman there as apparently the one I'd seen ten minutes before left on early retirement, but she asked another woman and they had to go to the back of the cabinet and did in fact pull out a bottle of what I wanted. "Old." "Si," I nodded. "Esta Bien!" When I'd been in Spain in 1976 and staying with my family in Seville, the girl, Conchetta, took me to the department store and said the Eau de Givenchy scent was her favorite. I liked it, too. I bought some. And ever since, I think of it as my perfume and it reminds me of that time in my life, Spain, youth, and Julio Iglesias. He was popular back then, too. "El Amor" – I bought that LP and brought it home in my luggage. That's a vinyl record, to explain to my kids who may only know iTunes or CDs. Glorious. All that. And, Eau de Givenchy is hard to find now. I think only Harrods in London sells it. Plus – I'd get my VAT returned at the airport – about ten percent of the price back!

Anniversary macarons! With gelato! And a happy bride! Still in her teal fleece!

Dave got his haircut but wasn't very happy with the results. I thought it looked great. He was meeting with the provost the day after we got back, Friday, and wanted to look good and he needed his hair cut after all these days. It was nice. Looked good. He grunted. We left.

We walked on and found Plaza Mayor and it was indeed cleaned up. We wandered around and decided to just stay in this area and not try to take a Metro train to Retiro Park, another area I remembered from my high-school trip. Vaguely. Ah, sangria-inspired memories. I kept sending postcards home to my mom and dad telling them how great this drink sangria was, but that I kept feeling so dizzy. I didn't know what was wrong with me. I kept drinking the sangria, though.

Then, after that flash-back and while aimlessly roaming, we came across a shop with macarons in the window. Well, it being Anniversary Day and everything, we went inside and bought a couple, along with three scoops of gelato that just happened to be right next to them. We sat and enjoyed the sugar. Then we found Madrid's version of Cottage Sweets, Carmel's local candy store. Walking down a side street off Plaza Mayor, we (Dave) noticed the display of tempting colorful licorice ropes decorating the window. He went in and I wandered a little bit more looking in souvenir shops. Geez, it was taking him forever to buy a piece of licorice. Finally, about 15 minutes later, he comes out and he's carrying this large bag. "They had a sale!" He ended up with ten long ropes of licorice for 10 euros. The downside was they

The licorice.

would only let him buy one piece of the black licorice. It's a very colorful assortment. Isaac should love all that. "But I kept the receipt to get the VAT back!"

Next up, Dave thought we should try to find a church he'd read about – something modern and interesting that Pope John Paul II had been to. We walked forever trying to find it, even though it was supposedly right next to the Palace. We found another church, locked, but that wasn't the right one. We checked the map and again set off. We finally reached it – the Almudena. Yes, it was impressive. I took lots of pictures. I was impressed. Kind of reminded me of La Sagrada Familia in Barcelona – Gaudi style but modern. At least no one stole my wallet out of my purse here – another long story.

It was a nice day. Sunny and pleasant. However, we were getting tired with all this aimless walking and we were happy with what we'd seen. We wanted to just go back to our hotel, rest, have dinner there and, frankly, collapse. Enough was enough. But first, we stopped in a supermarket on the corner to prepare. We bought wine, a couple bottles, some snacks, etc. One bottle was Cava and the other was a Rioja. And so, to the hotel. We found the Metros, and waited at the airport for the hotel shuttle. However, tonight we were not so lucky, timing-wise. It was 6 p.m. but it took over an hour for it to arrive. Tonight on the shuttle we met another man – probably late-30s. We chatted a bit. I think I remember he was from the U.S. but his dad lived in Madrid and he was here visiting. We got around to talking about us walking The Camino. He mentioned that it was so great that "at our age" we could do this kind of thing and he hopes to do some walking someday. Then he asks we're "what – early-late 50s?" So, should we be offended? I sort of understood him but it was a bit jarring. Possibly Dave should be thrilled but I was annoyed. Grateful? Hmmmm.

We got back to the Auditorium and passed the buffet room – Dave un-

A side altar honoring the Blessed Virgin Mary.

derstood that the dinner was to start at 8 p.m. I understood that it ended at 8 p.m. Place your bets... (Please consider my "A" in Spanish and all that.)

At 8:10 we walked down to see about dinner. The buffet was closed... So we went past the bar and checked on the restaurant. Only option. We were seated and we ordered. We had already drunk most of the Rioja we had bought in our room and it was so good. Here, we ordered more wine and dinner. I had chicken with some risotto kind of rice – rather tasty. We also had dessert, anniversary celebration and all. The place was not very busy but it filled up with about four or five other tables.

We took a few pictures with Dave holding the camera progressively higher and higher and I look quite silly. Doesn't everyone know that the higher the angle, the thinner you look? I should be disappearing by now! Yes, at least we lost a lot of weight... We spent the evening reminiscing over the past several weeks. The highlights. The lowlights. I can't believe all those people who said they'd do this again! That couple Dave knows from work who walked for ten days with a tour company and they said they'd do it again! Amazing. And that other guy that Dave knows – he said he'd do it again, too. And so many of the people we met were doing this for a second or third time. What got into them? I can't imagine doing this again. And that one pilgrim who told me that if you didn't feel anything now, the "magic" starts when you get home. Magic? The only magic I wanted was clicking my heels three times and getting back home. We'd been gone long enough. I was exhausted and even when we were resting and not walking, my body ached. I wondered how

Anniversary dinner.

long before I felt back to normal. No sore legs. When would that spider bite disappear from my ankle, or was that going to be a permanent reminder of Spain, like my other spider bite just a little higher up on my calf?

We discussed what we shouldn't have packed. The people we met. The places we stayed. Couldn't wait to get home to weigh ourselves on the scale. No, we didn't need the trowel. We wondered where Dave's trekking pole ended up. And the black shirt. We wondered if our guidebook author was still alive. I wondered if he had a sense of humor. ~~Or a lawyer.~~

We talked about how we were so lucky neither of us got sick – no coughing, sneezing, vomiting. My shoes held out. I didn't get any blisters. The weather was terrific – in fact, probably so terrific that we missed out on more of the traditional pilgrim "experience" – walking through tough weather. We debated what the impact would have been if we had been able to walk all 500 miles – we would have acclimated and felt different about the walk after we'd been doing it for three weeks, instead of being done and going home. Maybe we never reached that "moment."

But. We were still riding high and giddy from our accomplishment of walking over 200 miles. We walked up and over four mountain ranges! We remembered the scenery – we were on top of the world some days! Just like The Sound of Music! I could have danced around in those giant fields up there, except I was wandering around trying to go to the bathroom instead, and avoiding cow shit. And rocks. And other pilgrims. A lot of the time walking in the sun was actually pretty nice. I was getting a nice tan. I was developing nice muscles on my arms from depending on my two walking sticks – I didn't take a step the whole time without the two poles. They helped balance me, helped me up mountains, and helped my knees and legs going down those mountains. I never fell. I never injured anything. I learned that going down the hills was harder than going up.

The anniversary girl. Note the downward camera angle and the "I-made-it!" smile.

Our anniversary wine.

We came to the realization that my first comment was really true – if all you had to do was walk... Well, not that it couldn't be that hard, but that it freed you up to think, to look around you and take in all of that scenery, Mother Nature, the flowers, the animals, the culture, the other pilgrims. You weren't straddled with work and emails and so many other chores and daily constraints, and you could actually live. That's right – live!

It wasn't hard to let go. That was the easy part. If we could only "live" like this all the time!

We finally got up from the table and walked all the way back to our room in Cell Block D. We had another early morning and we needed to finish packing.

I also wanted to post one last thing on FB:

> *While I have a moment... I want to thank everyone who offered support, thoughts, prayers, and humor to me when I needed it so much. Thank you. And, yes, I thought and prayed for everyone of my FB friends (well, and others) who either asked, responded, or didn't. I figure it can't hurt and hope some of you are not offended that I did. I hope everybody can somehow tell and it makes a difference. And I do mean everyone. I thought about how we are friends in the first place... our experiences together, fun, laughter, friendship, family, etc. etc. Everybody on my list – check! What a trip. Got to see the big silver bottumuchi thing with incense swing, mass in Spanish, paella lunch with our new bff couple from Australia, and now to rest up, eat some chocolate and almonds and drink some wine. Got the Compostela official doc signed too. Rain stopped for now. Lots and lots of pics to come...*

Home

Thursday, November 6
Madrid to Monterey
(6,508 steps/2.84 miles/0 floors)

    This is it. Done with Spain. We're up at 6 AM. We dressed and fine-tuned our packing. At the last minute, I remembered the Cava, still in the little refrigerator. We opened it and poured two glasses to toast our departure. Ugh! Yuck! I'm glad we didn't end on that note yesterday! We had the best Rioja instead! We left the Cava for the maid to dispose, and a tip.
    We lugged our stuff down the hallway, down the elevator, and across the long long hotel. We waited outside for the shuttle. We had missed it by apparently five minutes. We could see the freeway right there and it was a parking lot. There were also apparently a lot(!) of other people waiting for a shuttle to the airport. The sun was rising and it was beautiful – so orange! So great! And then I could see the mountains in the distance and they appeared to be covered in snow – white stuff! We were leaving just in time! It was all so beautiful. I took several pictures. We stood there in the cold and waited. And waited. I wasn't panicked yet because our plane didn't leave for hours but if traffic on the roads was that bad...
    Finally, the shuttle van pulled up. Dave was in the back with our bags and I jumped up and grabbed two seats in front. The little bus filled up. Completely. To overflowing. "Un problema!!!" The bus couldn't take off because there were two too many people. Two people had to get off. Now! Leave! No one gave up their seats. Two people standing in the aisle refused to leave, too. We sat there. The minutes ticked by. The driver came on and shouted two people had to leave. It wasn't our problem that the hotel didn't have another shuttle and this one was late and there was not enough room! A man behind me started yelling at me in Spanish and wagging his finger at me. I got his gist – he thought we hadn't been waiting as long as everyone else! Wrong! We had. We were just on the other side of the door. I wagged my finger back at him. I glared. I glared very hard! No! It turned out that he and someone else had to get off. Oh well.
    We left and it did take a while to get to the airport. We arrived about 8:30 and found our check-in line. United SPECIAL PERSON FOR LIFE! That's me. Dave with all his traveling at work had flown so many miles that United

Our final sunrise.

had pronounced him a 1K or Premier something or other – for life! And he got to choose one person to be at that rank with him. That's me. I have the documentation. The security line was next. Apparently, they don't have an international special-person-for-life security line. But, no problems. Well. One problem. A tiny problem. You may recall I bought six lipsticks. In little boxes. So neat. So nice. So beautiful. So bullet-looking. Well, going through the scanner, apparently six little boxes of lipstick may look like a security risk (nice little bullets all lined up?) because I got pulled aside and the nice man pointed at his screen. I didn't know exactly what he meant at first but then I thought well maybe I was over the legal lipstick limit or something, and then I remembered that the cosmetics clerk had also thrown in quite a few samples in my bag, too. Lots and lots of little packets of wrinkle remover and cellulite reducer, that kind of stuff. Stuff appropriate for a woman "my age." You know those makeup counter girls are so critical – especially in Europe. And me being from the U. S., too. Yes, let's blame it on the U. S. I rambled to the security man, "Uh – lipstick? I went shopping???" I apologized. Pointed to my body, my face – "wrinkle cream???" He shrugged. Me, too. He let me pass.

Because we were flying overseas as United special-people-for-life, we got the use of the nice lounge area. We headed off to the right area. First we passed more shopping opportunities. Ohhhh – that looks interesting. I saw a tiny shop on the right and there was a shawl in yellow and black yarn that looked like "Spain" to me. I must have it! I checked the price. About 17 euros. That didn't sound like much to me in my head, trying to translate euros into dollars. One other woman was at the register. Of course, she was trying to purchase about two dozen necklaces. And, apparently, the register was broken. Really badly broken. The saleslady was writing each purchase down on paper and trying to add it all up, all those numbers. Dave, who

Modeling the 17 Euro scarf.

had been waiting outside and trying to check his email, ha ha, came over. He sighed. Actually, he didn't sigh – he seethed. If you know Dave, he hadn't gotten that much more patient after walking across Spain. We tried to interrupt and ask if we could come get the scarf in 20 minutes. The woman agreed. We thought.

We did have one other stop to make, though. The VAT office. It was time to get our value-added tax refunded to us. We were gonna get a bundle back. A big refund as we'd tediously folded and squeezed every receipt from the past 26 days into a little ziplock bag and then caressed it into Dave's money belt with the broken zipper he wore around his waist. He swore every time trying to get stuff in and out of that fanny pack. Dave gathered our stack of receipts and headed over to the right window.

I looked in a few more shops – last chance to buy "duty-free" goods. What is this Fly Emirates? I bought Isaac a shirt with that saying – something to do with soccer. I think. I hope. Hopefully, he doesn't get kicked out of daycare because it's not a kid-friendly saying. Lo Siento! I also bought him a "Bad Toro" shirt. It had a picture of a cute bull on it. Again, that may have gone over my head, but what a nice little Spanish kid's picture on the t-shirt. Next, I tried to find some pistachio-flavored liqueur. No luck. I wanted to surprise Becky with some since she had bought a bottle in France that ended up being stolen out of her suitcase by the baggage people and I felt bad for her. I know how upsetting that might be losing a fantastic new beverage. However, I guess it wouldn't be wise for us to buy liquor anyway because we were going to have to go through security again once we got to Newark and cleared customs before we could get our flight to Los Angeles.

I saw Dave coming back – that was fast! Grmmmph – apparently you needed to get a form from each department store or wherever you bought your stuff. Hotel receipts don't count. Food doesn't count. Bullet train tickets don't count. Taxis don't count. Drugs don't count. Compeed doesn't count. Wine doesn't count. Entrance fees to churches don't count. Donations don't count. Sello fees don't count. Man, that was a lot of receipts he was carrying around – I wonder how much all those weighed? Only souvenir stuff would have counted. And Dave's waterproof hat that cost 60 euros in Astorga, which we didn't keep the receipt for. That was purchased before we remembered to hold on to our receipts. I had neglected to get any forms filled out by El Corte Ingles – and they certainly didn't offer to give me the right form. I was not correctly informed. Sigh. But I still had six gorgeous colors of lipsticks. And perfume. And a peregrino duck. And a kids' size sweatshirt. And a Camino Santiago Buff! And I was about to take advantage of the free lounge area with their ample selection of booze for international travelers.

So, we headed up to the lounge and ate doughnuts and vodka. No, sorry. Giddy here. Doughnuts, though, and coffee. And a plate of potato chips. Well, that part is true. Can't live without the potato chips. Had a couple plates full. And a couple of chocolate-covered doughnuts. The manufactured kind. Entemann's? But still pretty tasty. I ignored the giant bowl of Deer Farm corn/nut mix.

Time to leave now and we went back to the shop to see about the shawl I wanted. We had counted out the cost in exact change. 17 euros in coins. We were trying to use up all our loose change and euros. We were close but still brought home about ten to 15 euros. For next time. Uh huh. Right. LOL. The register was still not working and the girl had put the scarf back on the rack, but I grabbed it and Dave dropped the coins on the counter and we walked away.

We found our gate at 10:30 AM. There was the usual stress over the middle seat. Ten minutes before we were to leave no one was scheduled to sit between Dave and me. Unfortunately, the few minutes before we were to take off, someone took the middle seat. Sort of. A couple got on and the wife was to have the middle seat but her husband who was supposed to be seated in the opposite side of the row (in that middle seat) asked if we would change seats so she could have the aisle and we would take the middle seat. Uh? What? No. He asked the person in his row on the aisle seat if she'd change with him. She was wearing a mask over her nose and mouth and I kind of wished she would have agreed to be farther away from us. But, no, she glared at him, too, like he was crazy asking her to give up the seat she specifically purchased at the last minute. He complained and despite being a late-add, the attendant found them other seats in the back of the plane. It was nearly full but we ended up having the row to ourselves. So nice. Even though the person right there on the other aisle was either sick or trying to

Snow in the mountains. We timed our trip perfectly, weather-wise.

avoid being sick by wearing a surgical mask. On second thought, she did get up to use the bathroom a ton of times, so she was probably sick. Not that it matters. I am a pilgrim. I am at peace. Kumbaya. Or however you spell that.

I am at peace, except for the taking-off part of the journey. That will apparently never change. We took off about 11:20 a.m. or so. Not too much shaking or screaming or crying. By me. No scene this time. Man, look at all the snow on those mountains we were flying over – my mountains. Boy, we timed this great!

It was pretty smooth today. We were en route to Bangor, Maine. The pilot, or copilot, who knows who gives those announcements? well, someone had informed us that the headwinds were so severe, we would need to make an unscheduled stop to refuel. "Sorry." We were back to English now. I didn't catch a "Lo Siento." I do remember when I returned from Madrid in 1976 we also had to stop in Bangor. Sounds familiar. It was going to take about eight hours to get to Maine. I settled in. I played a lot of Bridge Baron on my iTouch and listened to music. My play list. "It's a Small World?" – well screw that. "I Lived" – what a great song! Dave again got his 'special" meal and made another mental note to change his United profile as soon as we landed. (Dave: "Should I write that down? No, I'll remember." 10 years from now he'll still be eating soy chips and cous cous on his flights.) Vegan. We bought a big bottle of United wine (for me) and it was pretty good. We/I was celebrating. We had tried to upgrade to First Class but there were no seats left. Oh well – a whole row was just as good! Grateful.

We flew west. It was a long flight. A lot of hours til Bangor. And then on to Newark. There was a lot to think about. To digest. To drink. To ponder. To process. Hmmm, a glass of sangria would sure taste good now. I slept.

I thought, what a horrible trip. What a lot of work. How difficult it was.

The Camino calls us to next time.

This was not in any way "fun." The hardest thing I've ever done in my life. The pain. The exhaustion. The heat. The madness. The annoyances. The itchiness. The sickness. The achiness. The panic. The rain. I should have paid more attention to the fact that this walk used to be a prison sentence for convicts.

And, the questions:
How high can it be?
How much farther can it be?
How hot can it be?
How wet can it be?
How much can it cost?
How long can it take?
How many more people can pass us?
How much more cow shit can there be?
How many more flies?
Can people who write guidebooks even count to ten? {I'm sure they can. – Ed.}

And yet.

Still.

What would I do differently? What will I pack?

Next time!

Epilogue

Last Thoughts

It took a while, but a few **epiphanies** came. Nothing earth-shattering, some reinforcement, most self-evident:

1 : There's No Place Like Home.

2 : Why am I carrying a backpack at all?

3 : If bad decisions make good stories, this one is gonna be a doozie.

4 : Walking is good for keeping one's mind sharp.

5 : Take everything you hear (or read) with a grain of salt.

6 : Always look on the bright side of life (and dancing is fun!)

7 : If you can help someone out in some way, do it.

8 : I need a "theme" song and that "I Lived" will do just fine – "It's A Small World" is a nice thought, but good grief!

9 : Sometimes you do have to just take things on faith.

10 : I did it!

11 : Muscle weighs more than fat (sadly).

As for my Pre-Camino concerns, here are the afterthoughts:

1. **Bathrooms** Turned out to not be an issue. Plus, I'm a quick learner. Did not use the trowel. The woods were perfectly fine as a bathroom opportunity, if needed, and I noticed lots of pilgrims taking advantage of the free service. Plus, all of the cafes/bars we stopped at had facilities, some more adequate than others, but at least available and welcome for pilgrim-usage. Most did not include paper towels for drying hands, some considered toilet paper to be optional, and I believe all had lighting on a timer, set to go off and leave you in darkness after 30 seconds, an added incentive to quickly get out of the bano and back on the trail. There were a few days I had tummy issues but you know that every

afternoon there would be the chance for medicinal therapy in the form of alcohol – vino tinto! And there was always Imodium – my drug of choice!

2. **Feeling sick** Yes, at first I was feeling sick to my stomach. I ended up chewing a lot of that pink chalky Pepto Bismol and was worried I would run out. We tried to get some at a pharmacy but they sold me anti-acid stuff instead. But by that time, I had figured out that the Advil I was taking regularly was upsetting my stomach, and once I stopped taking it, my nausea disappeared. I did feel very sick a few times but never actually threw up. Usually, I would eat a few bites of something and that helped, too. Wine helped.

3. **Spanish food** As I remembered. Not so great. At least, what we ate most days. Some days were pretty good – others just passable. The queso bocadillos I ate for lunch most days were really good for basic bread and cheese, nothing else included. The tapas we munched on for snacks in the evening or at bars were not too bad. Mostly because I wasn't so sure what we were eating. Luckily, we didn't contract any food poisoning along the way and we survived just fine. Most of the books I've read had a chapter devoted to the author suffering from food poisoning and I was grateful I didn't have to write about that.

4. **I hear this experience "changes" people** Transformed is probably the right word. I'm still processing it all. Writing it all down helps work through our experience.

5. **Walking in the rain and mud. Weather.** We lucked out with the weather. Well, except for the very first day and the last day. The weather added to the lasting impressions – that first day of walking, being in shock, wondering what we were doing and why God was punishing us. And, the last day, making our entrance into the Cathedral square. Soaking wet but as happy as I can remember. So giddy. In-between, we were grateful to not have to be changing in and out of rain gear and walking in our heavy shoes. The scenery was spectacular in the sun with the blue skies. Lovely.

6. **Hot flashes** No problems.

7. **Can I actually do it?** Yep. This was the hardest thing I've ever done in my life, but here I am. Sitting at home writing a memoir of my travails, er, travels. Sitting at home complaining about it. Yes, I did it.

8. **Getting lost** Didn't happen. Those yellow arrows are everywhere. We strayed several blocks on a couple occasions but quickly backtracked and found the trail. It was pitch-black when we started out most mornings, so the signs were hard to locate. Dave had his flashlight out most mornings and it proved to be useful.

9. **It won't be like our favorite movie** Nope. It wasn't. And Martin Sheen is on "my list." Didn't rain in their movie. They seemed to be having a grand old time. Laughing. Lots of fun. No show of hills, mountains, rocks, or anything past Leon – the next scene and they were in Santiago. I did recognize one scene – it was at O'Cebreiro and just as we reached the top of the mountain and were seeing the town. We were walking along a low stone wall. They had filmed it backwards, looking back, and not forward like when you come off the trail into the town. Our pilgrimage was, however, similar to the next Camino movie we saw – "Six Ways to Santiago," which is a more realistic picture of The Way. I could relate to many of these actual pilgrims shown in the movie. I hope it wins "Best Documentary" for 2014!

10. **Can I get up that early every morning?** Easy. It wasn't actually all that early – usually around 7 a.m. It was so dark, you couldn't safely get going til at least 8 AM. Also, we went to bed fairly early most nights —- by 9 at the latest, so we did get lots of sleep. Or rest. We woke up many times during the night with aches and pains, and difficulty sleeping because we were so sore. And the beds collapsing. Well, Dave's.

11. **Blisters. Really?** I lucked out in the blister department. Poor Dave. His feet suffered the most. My toes hurt but his heels were bad.

12. **Getting annoyed with Dave** Within the first hour of walking? He wasn't satisfied with my rate of speed. I was much slower than I even thought I'd be. Steady, but quite slow. So, let's say, Dave getting annoyed with Karen? Yes. No other issues or problems came up.

13. **Really get hurt** Didn't happen.

14. **Training** I actually don't think training would have helped too much. Yes, it would have helped condition me. I should have found time to train more and wear a backpack around, go up some hills, sweat a little. But, this was rough terrain and mountains. The weather, the heat, the flies, the sweat, the sun beating down, the rocks, going downhill, going uphill. All hard. I was better and stronger at the end, but not by much. I don't know that training would have helped with me walking faster. My legs probably wouldn't have been as sore and achy and I would be in better shape, but not sure about getting any faster than I ever was. I am surprised that in most books this trail is rated as being mostly on level, flat ground and is supposedly not terribly difficult. Most also say that you don't need trekking poles 75 percent of the time. I find those comments laughable. Really not my experience!

15. **Bedbugs** Yes. We saw people who had serious bites all over. They are out there. I did get bitten three or four times on my ankles. You can tell by the two or three little bite marks clustered together (their fangs

I guess). They did itch. And I did get bitten by maybe a spider or something that really swelled up, though it didn't hurt. It's left a scar, though. In Camino books I've read and also on the Camino Forum, there are members who are adamant that there aren't any bed bugs or they aren't a problem, but I beg to differ. I saw them myself. They are out there and some girls we saw were miserable with bites all over. One person had 85 bites. It all depended on how lucky you were and with the place you slept.

16. **Break a tooth, break glasses, break a bone, an ankle, etc.** No. We lucked out. No need to worry about something that didn't happen.

17. **Something happens at home while we're gone** The kids were resilient and managed to keep themselves alive without me. Of course, they are in their 20s and really ought to be able to survive on basic living skills. Matt even drove to the Oakland Airport and then to San Francisco for the weekend. I would have worried terribly if I were home with him doing that. Jim managed to get his GI stuff under control. David said he and Isaac had a great time and did fine with just them.

18. **Being over-prepared/under-prepared** That takes balance. It was not like I expected.

19. **What to pack** I wore or used everything I packed. Well actually I didn't use the earplugs, but they didn't weigh much. Happy with the selections, with a few exceptions. Would have taken a regular sleeping bag (lightweight down) and then maybe no fleece blanket. Also would have taken one or two more merino wool t-shirts. Only had two and I sweated through those quickly. The only thing worth wearing was 100 percent merino wool. Also would have done more in choosing a better bra and packed three or four. People say not to pack medicines and extra stuff because you can buy everything you need over there, if you need it. I would still not rely on that strategy. We couldn't find the exact items we needed, or else they were sold in huge quantities, like laundry soap. I couldn't find more Pepto Bismol. I didn't try their version of Imodium, either. Next time I would include a corkscrew. And little cups that didn't leak. And I may take advantage of mailing a package to myself in Santiago with clean, better clothes, for when you arrive. A lot of our fellow pilgrims had done that.

20. **What not to pack** The trowel.

21. **What is your reason for walking The Camino?** I am still working that one out. However, I have no regrets whatsoever for walking – I would have regretted not doing the Camino. I did realize, once home, that all of my thoughts and the (limited) hard thinking I did was about the past. I concentrated on history – my life, the kids, the bad stuff, the good stuff – all that happened before. I didn't spend any time working

out future plans, problems, goals. Next on the bucket list? Nope. I think I've made a huge mistake. I did it wrong. Maybe I should have been looking forward, planning, making strategies for change, thinking out ideas, wondering what to do with the rest of my life. Geez. Now it comes to me. I'm gonna have to go back and do another 500 miles to think about other stuff.

22. **How much is this going to cost?** I am still wondering about that, too.

And what I packed:

1 50-litre Osprey backpack
1 pr waterproof rain pants (black)
1 waterproof/breathable Omni Shield rain jacket (yellow)
1 pack cover
1 sturdy backpack container bag to check for airport baggage
1 pr waterproof gloves
1 waterproof hat (black)
1 sun hat (beige)
1 pr leggings (to wear under waterproof pants if necessary and to sleep in)
1 pr lightweight Jambu shoes
1 pr low-profile Merrill walking tennis shoes
1 pr waterproof Ahnu hiking shoes
1 lightweight sleeping sack
1 fleece blanket (2.5 pounds) – questionable
1 light scarf (beige with salmon trim to match jacket)
1 warm lightweight jacket – packable/very light (salmon colored)
1 travel-size umbrella
3 pr merino wool socks (plus one pair I will wear)
1 pr liner socks
1 pr gray socks for tennis shoes
1 gray down vest (packable/very light)
1 lightweight merino wool long-sleeved black top to wear for sleeping
1 bra (plus 1 bra I will wear)
4 pr merino wool underwear (plus one pair I will wear)
1 pr gray pants (to wear)
1 pr beige pants (spare)
1 UA compression black top – long-sleeved
1 fleece (teal)
1 bright pink compression zip top
2 merino wool short-sleeve t-shirts (light weight – black, and green striped)
4 lipsticks (just kidding –seeing if you are still reading)
1 bag of toiletries; minimum makeup; sunscreen
1 bag medicines

1 bag gadgets, etc. (notebook, camera, card, charging stuff, extra battery, pens)
Sunglasses and spare glasses in cases
Small vial laundry detergent
Itouch and earphones
Fitbit and charger
2 rocks
1 empty water bottle – deflatable
1 lightweight daypack (lime green)
2 trekking poles
Money belt for passport, credential and credit card/money

Bottom Line:

What a trip! But, I've gotten it out of my system for a while.

Dave, though, has just been encouraged to walk more. He is talking eagerly of starting in Paris and walking a pilgrimage. Or walking to Rome. From England. Or another route. He just needs to get time off from work. In the meantime, to satisfy his walking bug, Dave has now taken it upon himself to help attract attention to a "new" pilgrimage route here in California – the Mission Trail. Father Junipero Serra, soon to be named a Saint by Pope Francis, started all 21 missions on the west coast here, starting in San Diego and heading north to Sonoma. All about a day or two apart, walking-wise. Of course, there is no real infrastructure in place here, and not many people have done this – less than 20– and Dave wants to be included during the start-up. So, he's been doing short day walks in our locale. It's 800 miles to do the whole length and he hopes to accomplish that. Me – I'm just support for now – driving and packing lunches, helping find stuff for him. But...

I think my arm could be twisted to go back and start from the right place this time, St. Jean Pied de Port in France and trudge myself back to Santiago. Of course, I say that easily now because that walk is far off in the future. My ticket's not booked yet. No time off from work for now, either. And, next time, I'm insisting my sister walk, too. She needs this kind of experience in her life, right?

Seriously, I do encourage everyone to consider walking (or biking) this pilgrimage. It's not something one will ever forget and the experience just might transform you, too!

A Note of Gratitude

First of all, thanks to Father Tom Hall, who urged us to walk and to Walk Now! Walk Now I Say! That was good guidance. It's what I'd like to say to anyone considering this pilgrimage. Do it now. You won't regret it.

Thanks also to my supervisor at work, Andrew, who approved my leave of absence, and for my coworkers who picked up my slack – Virginia, Jean, Teri, Penny, Percy, Rosie, Lindsey, Kendall, Samantha, Annicette. I work for a great company and I am proud to be associated with CIG.

Thanks to David, Jim, and Matthew. Great sons. Wouldn't trade you for the world. Thanks for holding down the fort, for surviving without mom, for not burning the fort down. For giving me so much "material." But, you know, that's another story. Or two. God, David, you can really pick 'em. I am extremely proud of the three of you, despite the volumes I could write. And, no matter what, at least I've got good-looking kids!

Thanks, of course, to my mother, Donna Hosler, of Brooklyn Park, Minnesota fame, for caring and for always telling me how she loves reading about what I've done – after I've done it. For the newspaper articles she sends on various subjects, for the gingerbreadmen cookies, for the fun visits we have when she comes to Monterey, for the memories... and for Mary Ellen, aka Mimi, my younger sister, who is a great traveling companion and confidante. For encouraging me to go on this journey, even if she chose not to come this time. Holding out for Paris. I know. For the laughs most of all.

Thanks, too, to that guy, I don't know his name, who invented Facebook, who allowed me to reconnect with so many "older" friends. What a great idea. It's wonderful to be able to pick up with a lot of friends just like when we were younger and experiencing college or earlier jobs together. Or extended family or friends of friends, or others we have connected with in the past.

Thanks and tons of gratitude to the bartender working at the hotel next door to the "non-exist!" albergue who found us lodging, gave us a free beer, invited us for dinner even though his hotel was booked, and for caring enough to take the time to do all that.

But, thanks most of all to Dave, for slogging away with the typesetting, inserting pictures, offering suggestions, and doing my hard-to-read handwritten corrections, making this whole manuscript sound perfect, while I sit in the other room knitting and drinking wine. Oh, and for walking and being there. For your strength, understanding, inspiration, humor, vocal talents, giving me the left-over wine in the bottle, for carrying my pack, for offering great suggestions like sending my pack ahead, for ordering exactly what I would want, for making me smile, laugh, and helping me stop throw a tantrum. For holding my hand, for saying I look "great," for showing up with a box of Don Simon wine, for ordering extra black olives on pizzas, for all those back rubs and rubbing the exact right spot, even though it hurts and your hands are too strong, for always knowing what I mean even if it's not what I said, for kindness and thoughtfulness that no one else seems to show, for just the right thing to say, for motivational speeches, for knowing me exactly, for

Dave and Karen.

holding the camera at a higher angle (finally learning that), for swearing at Brierley with me, for ordering the "pilgrim" size glasses of vino tinto, for the laughter, the morale boosting, the aisle seat, and the lifestyle to which I have become accustomed. I appreciate it and I appreciate you. You aren't taken for granted. 31 years. More to come...

Made in the USA
Middletown, DE
27 May 2015